THE
WOLVES OF
HELMAND

A VIEW FROM INSIDE THE DEN OF MODERN WAR

FRANK "GUS" BIGGIO

FOREWORD BY GENERAL STANLEY A. McCHRYSTAL (RETIRED)

Forefront
BOOKS

For Caroline and Elizabeth Cahir,
and those like you

There is but one world and everything that is imaginable is necessary to it. For this world also which seems to us a thing of stone and flower and blood is not a thing at all but is a tale . . . We can never be done with the telling. Of the telling there is no end . . . Rightly heard all tales are one.

—CORMAC MCCARTHY, *The Crossing*

CONTENTS

★ ★ ★

AUTHOR'S NOTE

I SERVED IN THE UNITED STATES MARINE CORPS FROM MAY 1993 until December 1997. After leaving active duty, I went to law school and then worked as a lawyer, first in New York City and then in Washington, D.C. Following a chance meeting with a now-retired Marine general and several discussions with a recruiter, and then receiving the selfless (but slightly conditional) support of my wife, I rejoined the Marine Corps as a member of a reserve unit called the Civil Affairs Group. That was in October 2007, nearly ten years after I had first left the service. My country was at war, and the same itch that drove me to volunteer in the 1990s nagged at me to serve again.

In early 2009, my unit was activated. I was part of a team of six Marines and one U.S. Navy corpsman assigned to support the First Battalion of the Fifth Marine Regiment—"one-five" or "1/5" as it's referred to in Marine lingo. My team joined 1/5 as it trained for its upcoming deployment to southern Afghanistan's Helmand Province, the heart of the insurgency wreaking havoc on the country. The battalion took part in Operation Khanjar (meaning "Strike of the Sword" in the Pashto language) that began with the largest helicopter-borne military offensive since the Vietnam War. We remained on the ground for seven months to stabilize a district in Helmand called Nawa.

Nawa was a violent and lawless place when Marines arrived there during the scorching summer of 2009. By December, when 1/5 handed over its duties to the next battalion churning through the deployment cycle, schools had reopened, clinics were functioning, a district governor had a staff of Afghans to manage and solve Afghan problems, commerce was vibrant, and locals greeted Marines on patrol with handshakes and cheerful salutations. In short, Nawa was a success story for a country that badly needed one, and I was privileged to have played a role in that success.

By sharing my story, I have tried to capture the essence of what the Marines in 1/5 experienced. It was a team effort, and I hope I am honoring the team's service in a way that pays respect to their selfless nature and highlights the magnitude of their legacy. Although this book is about our time at war, readers should not expect a nail-biting, shoot-'em-up thriller. I don't claim to be the most battle-hardened warrior, though I experienced enough combat to conclude that I don't particularly enjoy being shot at. Many of the stories in this book describe other war zone experiences, which often consist of anything but taking part in intense combat.

It's important to note, too, that our success would not have been possible without the team of interpreters who marched by our side, endured the same hardships, and forged the same camaraderie as the Marines with whom they served. Without them, our words, and those of the Afghan nationals we befriended and fought alongside (and sometimes, those we fought against), would have been just noise. Unless specifically noted that an Afghan was speaking English, the conversations with Afghans described in this book were conducted through our interpreters. All quotes in this book are based on my memory or hastily scribbled notes, but I believe the spirit and intent of everybody quoted is accurate, even if I did not capture their exact words at the time they were spoken.

FOREWORD
by General Stanley McChrystal and Ellen Chapin[†]

IN A WAR ZONE, IT BECOMES HARDER TO BREATHE. NOT SIMPLY because of the heaviness in your lungs and the burden that you shoulder; on a day-to-day basis, I witnessed soldiers regularly holding their breath, living their lives seemingly without oxygen. No matter how much combat I saw, I shared the same hope as these young individuals—that a small act of control would keep the world intact.

This was especially important in 2009, when the world seemed to be falling apart. After spending several years as the leader of the Joint Special Operations Command, where we worked to dismantle al-Qaeda in Iraq (a fast-moving and versatile terrorist network), I had been promoted and directed to turn my focus to Afghanistan. Eight years into the American Global War on Terror, there was no end in sight. The invasion of Afghanistan, initially designed as a short-term light footprint to capture senior leaders in al-Qaeda, had turned into a new and ever-shifting combination of combat and nation-building.

Worrisomely, though, I saw that both soldiers on the ground and senior leaders had developed a level of apathy about the success of the mission, including how to address the changing nature of the mission itself. Our forces had not captured Osama bin Laden,

---

[†] General Stanley McChrystal retired from the U.S. Army after thirty-four years of service, having led the Joint Special Operations Command and the International Security Assistance Force in Afghanistan. He is the founder of the McChrystal Group, a leadership consultancy firm based in Virginia. Ellen Chapin, a counterterrorism expert and PhD candidate with Stanford University, who was General McChrystal's speechwriter, contributed significantly to this foreword.

grappled with the political consequences of the Taliban, or made major inroads with our Afghan partners. We weren't losing, but we absolutely were not winning. Without a major shift in our investment or our attitude, I did not believe we would have any chance at success.

The new administration appeared to agree with me. President Obama, in February of that same year, had approved an increase in American forces in Afghanistan. To some, this signaled a renewed energy for U.S. operations in this region. To me, it was an essential injection of life into an otherwise unmoving coalition. Without more troops on the ground, we certainly couldn't begin to understand how to strike the balance of security and stability in the region, let alone begin to attempt to win the war. When I assumed command of NATO operations and troops that summer, I knew all too well that the future of Afghanistan would depend largely on the accomplishments of these additional boots on the ground.

One of the first impacts of President Obama's surge landed just as I was arriving in Afghanistan. In June, we launched Operation Khanjar in Helmand Province, a strategic area that was in desperate need of assistance and is the setting of Gus's forthcoming story. Our International Security Assistance Force (ISAF) had struggled to defeat Taliban insurgents within a province widely known to be their stronghold and a center of opium production. By 2009, both British forces and U.S. Marines had struggled to maintain a stalemate—hence, the importance of Gus and his comrades in the First Battalion of the Fifth Marine Regiment. They represented some of the eleven thousand additional reinforcements that were deployed specifically to push the Taliban out of Afghanistan's southern region at a crucial moment in the country's history.

It is challenging to overstate the importance of Operation Khanjar in the broader war. Helmand was an important tactical area—the U.S. had invested heavily in irrigation systems there to reinforce the province's agricultural capabilities. But with the Taliban takeover, the whole community became unrecognizable: schools closed, homes and farms were abandoned, and the vibrant shops that lined the streets were quickly boarded up. Any victory in Afghanistan would require bringing Helmand back to life.

Most important, though, were the August 2009 Afghan presidential elections. Commonly cited as evidence of how the U.S. presence could be viewed as positive for long-term change, the elections were viewed by some as losing credibility before voting had even begun. With Taliban militants controlling so much of southern Afghanistan, free and fair voting seemed (rightfully) impossible to the global community.

What you are about to read is Gus's account of his life in the trenches in Helmand, as one of America's heroes who helped to turn the tide of the war at a pivotal moment in combat and in leadership. While our country has always relied on the courage and ingenuity of its young people, Afghanistan (and Operation Khanjar, in particular) marked a new standard for what we asked of those Americans who choose to serve. Rather than simply fighting for military victory, those service members acted as far more than combatants. They embodied an important hybrid in our government today: the diplomat-soldier, acting at any given moment as both measured and bold, equally driven by thoughtfulness and instinct.

By 2009, so many individuals who had served in Afghanistan, Iraq, or the broader Middle East had returned to their homes, careers, and families. However, I have come to learn that the importance of service is embedded in the DNA of some of the most honorable people I have ever met. When I deployed to Afghanistan, I did not do so alone. I had asked my most trusted and talented colleagues to come with me, to leave behind (in many cases) the family to whom they had just returned. It is a testament to their love for their country and dedication to the mission that they all said yes.

Many of the 1/5 Marines, like Gus, were not first-time soldiers. They recognized that the story of Afghanistan remained fundamentally unwritten, and they wanted to take ownership of its future. Having already seen the changing nature of warfare, they recognized the ways in which small teams of soldiers could make the biggest impact. But most presciently, they recognized that any effort to win a war in Afghanistan required a deeper investment in the culture, the people, and the country. Counterinsurgency cannot succeed without local political infrastructure—the two are inextricably tied. Because of this commitment, leadership, and valor, the 1/5 Marines were a remarkable example for both U.S. and Afghan brothers- and sisters-in-arms. The relationships they cultivated with the local population, in addition to their established linkages with USAID and PRTs (Provincial Reconstruction Teams), were critical in ridding Helmand of its infection of terrorism.

To see the impact of the 1/5 Marines, we can simply look to the ways in which the region has changed since the U.S. began to withdraw its troops. No matter their success in standing Helmand back up, America's hastiness to leave Afghanistan left the embattled area vulnerable to the Taliban all over again. In 2017, the U.S. deployed hundreds of Marines to Helmand in an effort to turn back time and resecure the area, no doubt with a sense of despondent déjà vu. Contemporary foreign policy is, devastatingly, a series of mistakes that we make until we learn our lesson.

History's cyclical nature also confirms, though, that we have much to learn from the unvarnished life of a soldier. That's why I tell young men and women never to hold their breath in a war zone. They should breathe in the country and breathe their heart back out into it. What you are about to read is Gus's effort to keep breathing deeply, before, during, and after the summer of 2009. Read carefully; he has much to teach us. Feel the texture of the details; envision the landscape that he paints. Every battlefield and its surroundings are terribly beautiful worlds unto their own. Knowing that across the world and ten years later, the village of Nawa may not look tremendously different than when Gus and I arrived, I hope that you will visit this one with care. You'll want to be as present in reading this book as he was in telling his story—and breathing alongside him in his journey to Helmand and home.

CHAPTER 1
HIT THE GROUND RUNNING

War is hell, but that's not the half of it, because war is also mystery and terror and adventure and courage and discovery and holiness and pity and despair and longing and love.
—TIM O'BRIEN, *The Things They Carried*

JUNE 4, 2009

WE COULD ONLY FLY IN AT NIGHT. A DAYTIME FLIGHT IN A CH-53 Sea Stallion was too risky, particularly during its relatively slow hover into a landing zone (LZ), when the semi truck-sized helicopter made an enticing target for an insurgent with a rocket-propelled grenade (RPG) or a machine gun. From the relative safety of the airfield at Camp Bastion, the British-run military base in the desert of southern Afghanistan's Helmand Province, we lumbered onto the "bird" at around 10:00 p.m. I was part of a small advance team headed into the Afghan hinterlands to help prepare for our major operation, which would begin in early July.

The moon rising in a cloudless, starry night provided enough illumination to guide our way onto the helo's back ramp. Our packs were stuffed with the gear we would need for the next six or seven months. We dumped them on the helicopter's metal deck, strapped them down with a canvas cargo net, and then buckled ourselves into the fold-down aluminum-frame seats and waited for liftoff. The helicopter's two pilots and three crew members moved with impatient intensity as they made their final preflight inspection of the cargo and Marines on board. Seeing my rank insignia, the crew chief handed me a helmet with a headset so I could hear and, if required, speak to the pilots and crew. I clipped the chinstrap of my Kevlar helmet to a carabiner on my flak jacket, put on the radio-equipped helmet, did a quick sound check, and flashed the crew chief a thumbs-up to confirm that it was working.

"We're flying over some hot spots, Captain, so don't make too much chitchat unless you really need to," he said.

A few minutes after getting on board, we were airborne, on our way to Patrol Base Jaker, a small post in the heart of the Taliban-led insurgency in Helmand Province. Our flight path would take us due east, then south to the Helmand River that, clearly visible in the moonlight, would guide us to our destination.

The rhythmic thump of the helicopter's rotors put me in a comfortable but sleepless trance as I stared out its open back ramp, taking in the scenery through the night vision goggles (NVGs) I held up to my eyes and which turned everything I saw into various shades of phosphorescent green.

Thirty minutes into our flight, my reverie was suddenly broken as the helicopter lurched upward and banked to the left, spewing a dozen chaff flares—pyrotechnic countermeasures designed to distract heat-seeking surface-to-air missiles. The flares burst apart like fireworks, leaving a brilliant display of explosive light in our wake. The Marine manning the .50-caliber machine gun on the port side of the bird fired a dozen rounds at muzzle flashes he spotted on the ground, then a dozen more, and a dozen more after those. His aim was guided by streaks from the .50 caliber's tracer rounds that reminded me of laser bolts slicing through the night sky.

I gripped my seat and anchored my feet on the deck, wondering if the belt strapping me in place would hold, briefly musing that the contract for its design and installation had probably gone to the lowest bidder. The cargo strapped down in the middle of the deck shifted heavily into the legs of the Marines sitting on the port side, then lurched back to starboard with a solid thump, volleying back and forth a few more times as the helo evasively weaved its way through the sky. Through my NVGs I saw the bright, wide-open eyes of the other Marines on board as they hurriedly craned and pivoted their heads to catch sight of and make sense of what was happening around them. The tail gunner echoed the door gunner's fire with three rapid bursts, the cracking of the rounds leaving a ringing echo in our heads louder than the constant high-pitched whine coming from the helo's whirling engines.

Then, as quickly as the chaos had started, it stopped. We leveled off and continued flying toward our objective. The whole episode had probably lasted only ten or twelve seconds.

"You cool, sir?" came the crew chief's steady voice over my headset.

"Yep, just another day in the sandbox, right?" I said, trying my best to avoid sounding as if I'd just been scared shitless.

"Yes indeed, sir. We're touching down in five. Let your boys know."

I held up a hand with all fingers extended, shouting, "Five minutes!" to my fellow passengers, who all gave me a thumbs-up to acknowledge the message. They began shifting in their seats, checking the straps on their gear, charging their rifles to Condition 1—a round in the chamber ready to fire—and putting their hands on their seat belt clips so they could pounce out of the helo once they felt it bump the ground.

Through my radio headset, I could hear a forward air controller (FAC) on the ground talking the pilots into our LZ. The crew began unhooking the straps on the cargo net. We would have about a minute to get our equipment and ourselves off the bird once it touched down. The pilots and crew didn't want much idle time after landing. The longer the helo was stationary, the more time someone in the tree line near our LZ would have to get into a good firing position. While slowly lifting off the ground and silhouetted by the moon's rays against the bluish black sky, a helicopter would be an enticing target for an insurgent with an AK-47 or an RPG wanting to make a name for himself.

The descent into the LZ was quick and steep. We hit the ground with a solid thud, and the crew wasted no time shouting us out of the helicopter as we formed a daisy chain to heave our bags and other cargo out the rear. I put my Kevlar helmet back on and took one last look through the bird to make sure we didn't leave anything behind. The crew chief's pat on the shoulder was more like a shove out the back ramp than a friendly goodbye. He and his crew were eager to get back in the air, out of range of small arms and rocket fire.

As soon as I stepped out of the helicopter and was on solid footing, the FAC vigorously waved both arms, yelling at me to "Get the fuck down!" The helo started its ascent and the Marines who had just rushed off it hugged the earth in the wake of its rotor wash. As the bird's blades revved up, dirt and small gravel pelted our exposed skin, covering us in a fine layer of sand and dust that clung to our sweaty uniforms. I squeezed my eyes shut, plugged my ears, and thought how this was like a baptism of sorts, but rather than the purifying waters used in a religious ceremony, we were being anointed with the soil and grime of a war zone.

When the helicopter that dropped us off was safely airborne, we stood up in the suddenly quiet LZ and were greeted by a few of our hosts, soldiers from the British Army and a squad from the Afghan

National Army, who had been defending the patrol base for the past several months.

"Gents, welcome to Patrol Base Jaker. Let's get your kit inside, and then we'll show you around your new home," one of the British sergeants said.

There was a spooky, almost mystical ambience about the patrol base, like something out of the movie *Apocalypse Now*. The main building was a two-story unfinished brick structure about forty by sixty feet. If it had ever seen better days, they were long ago. Its brickwork was exposed, inside and out, and all the walls that faced likely enemy firing points were supported by stacks of sandbags piled on top of old ammunition cans filled with dirt. It had never had a roof, so a makeshift web of two-by-fours supporting corrugated tin sheets with two layers of sandbags on top provided some basic overhead cover. More sandbags served as window frames, and strips of brown and black burlap hung from the glassless openings to obscure the views into the building from curious eyes outside the wire. The floor was made of uneven concrete slabs, chipped and crumbling in many places. Machine guns were posted at each window, their fields of fire drawn on range cards placed next to each gun position. From the second floor, we could see over the wall of large dirt-filled barriers that surrounded the patrol base and its LZ.

There were no outside lights. They would have emitted a glow that insurgents could home in on at night. On the ground floor, some of our British hosts wore red-light headlamps and sat around tables crudely constructed from discarded pallets and other pieces of lumber they had scavenged. Pasted on the surface of the tables were photos of topless ladies clipped from magazines called *Nuts* and *Zoo*— roughly the U.K. equivalent of *Maxim* but with more flesh exposed. Staples and duct tape held down a sheet of clear plastic that had been rolled over the pictures. A few small candles placed around the table gave off just enough light to read or play a game of cards. We spoke in subdued murmurs, always with an ear primed to hear the short conversations interrupting the static hiss and beeps coming from the tactical radios propped against a wall.

Nawa was far from an electrical grid, so the radios and other equipment were powered by half a dozen diesel generators that hummed at all hours. A bug zapper, plugged into a power strip connected to one of those generators, hung in a corner. Its dull blue light sparkled occasionally whenever a fly or mosquito was lured to its crispy death. Several Afghan Army soldiers milled around, some making efforts to communicate with their British counterparts using their limited English or with the help of one of our interpreters, while others sat quietly at a table, staring dreamily at the images of the naked beauties under plastic wrap, perhaps imagining their smiles were meant just for them.

Everyone carried a weapon with a casual sense of confidence. It was either a rifle slung over the shoulder or a pistol holstered at the hip. One of the interpreters, who insisted on being called "John" but whose real name was Mohamed, liked to wear a belt of machine-gun ammunition crisscrossed over his chest, even inside the relative security of the patrol base. He added to his swashbuckler appearance by combing his black hair straight back and constantly molding his beard into a point at the chin.

Two other Marines and I climbed a makeshift wooden ladder and stood behind a machine gun emplacement to look past the patrol base's outer walls. A sense of fear and marvel swept through me as I contemplated what lay among and beyond the shapes and shadows visible in the scant moonlight. Adjacent to the patrol base's west side was a large wheat field that had been recently cut, its stalks drying on the ground waiting to be harvested by a family of farmers. One hundred meters beyond that was the first of several rows of trees that straddled the small irrigation ditches adjacent to the fields.

"That's where we always get hit from," said one of our British Army hosts who was in the guard post with us, pointing to the tree lines. "Don't stand around in the open up here during the day, Yanks. You'll likely catch one in the beaner before you know it."

We found a niche to place our gear for the night before settling down for a few hours of sleep. My radio operator, Bobby Darhele, on leave from college to serve on this deployment, gazed around with impressed curiosity, then turned to me and said, "Damn, this war's for real!"

He's right, I thought, smiling to myself as I reflected on the long path that had led me to this point.

CHAPTER 2
COMING HOME (PART 1)

Home is the place where, when you have to go there, they have to take you in.
—ROBERT FROST

DECEMBER 1, 1997

"OK, SIR, SIGN MY COPY RIGHT HERE . . . THANK YOU . . . AND HERE'S your copy. Make sure you don't lose that. It's been real good knowing you, sir. Good luck in the First Civ Div."

The Marine in charge of my battalion's administrative office presented me with my formal discharge papers, shook my hand, and then marched off to attend to other matters. With a few pen strokes, I was officially released from active duty in the United States Marine Corps.

A little over an hour later, I saw Camp Pendleton disappear in my rearview mirror. I had a meandering road trip ahead of me, but I knew my final destination. I was going home.

Driving up the California coast, I reflected on the Marines I'd served with and the experiences we'd shared. I joined right after college, so I missed Operation Desert Storm, the big war of my time, by just over a year. But the post–Cold War world needed an expeditionary force of Marines more than ever, and I stood ready to play my part when called. I had the privilege of spending my entire active duty service in the infantry, much of it overseas. I had felt the sweltering burn of deserts, been soaked to the bone in jungles, and trekked around the Horn of Africa while in uniform. It was time well spent.

In the small Ohio town where I grew up, many of my friends' fathers and nearly all the business and civic leaders I knew had served in the military at some point. As my father's occasional Rotary Club lunch guest, I always noticed the lapel pins worn by some of its members designating their unit or a personal award from their time in World War II, Korea, or Vietnam. The idea was never pushed on me, but joining the military seemed to be a logical and expected part of growing up and becoming a well-rounded adult.

Before joining the Marines, I had been in the Boy Scouts, played on sports teams, and joined a fraternity, but it was the Corps that ingrained in me a sense of collective duty and responsibility. Marines across generations have endured common hardships, shared core values, and defended a noble heritage. They are unapologetically patriotic, equal parts profane and polite, and have an air of confidence bordering on arrogance that sets them apart from other services and the population at large. It's a special tribe, and I was proud to be a member.

By the late summer of 1998, with my active duty service behind me, getting my law degree had become my main objective. As I settled into an apartment on Cleveland's east side in early August, a little-known terrorist group called al-Qaeda took credit for bombing two U.S. embassies in eastern Africa that killed about three hundred people and seriously wounded thousands more. Though the embassy bombings were directed against the U.S., Americans paid them little heed as the summer ended and the country turned its attention to the prurient details of President Clinton's dalliance with Monica Lewinsky.

As I cracked open my books, I reflected on the things I missed about the Marine Corps. The camaraderie and sense of purpose I shared with my fellow Marines was notably absent in law school. Late nights were spent deciphering the nuances of appellate decisions rather than huddling over a map with a red-lens flashlight. My backpack was filled with textbooks rather than field rations, spare socks, a radio, and boxes of machine-gun ammo. The background noises in the law school library were more like quiet murmurs, rustling pages, and whirring printers—a stark contrast to the orders barked by noncommissioned officers (NCOs), the thumping of helicopter rotors, or the crackling machine gun fire that had been so familiar to me before this. The Marine Corps had become part of my DNA, from the way I carried myself to the outlook I had on the world, and I knew I would always think of myself as a Marine before I'd ever think of myself as a lawyer.

As I continued to wrestle with the details of civil procedure, constitutional law, and torts, the U.S. military stayed busy, but mostly in low-intensity conflicts such as assisting with peace-keeping efforts in the Balkans and providing humanitarian assistance in places like Turkey and Southeast Asia. I had been out of the service for two years when, on December 31, 1999, a tearful (and probably drunk) Boris Yeltsin resigned from the Russian presidency, handing over the role to a former KGB officer named Vladimir Putin.

Ten months later, on October 12, 2000, an explosive-laden speedboat rammed into the USS *Cole*, a Navy destroyer anchored in Aden, Yemen, killing seventeen sailors. Al-Qaeda claimed responsibility for that, too, just as it did for the U.S. embassy bombings in Africa two years earlier. The group had emerged as an example of "asymmetrical warfare" enemies, which are more likely to be terrorists, insurgents, and rogue militias in lawless, ungoverned regions than traditional nation states. The urge for justice after this attack—or at least, vengeance—ebbed, and our country's attention turned elsewhere once again.

As the bitter Cleveland winter melted into the spring of 2001, I kept my nose in my books. While managing a heavy course load, I was also planning for post-law school life. A young doctor I had met a few years earlier, and who was now living in New York City, kept my focus on opportunities on the East Coast. She was smart, pretty, laughed at my jokes, and tolerated my stories, many of which began with the phrase, "That reminds me of this one time when I was in the Marines," so I knew she was the one.

Two weeks into my final semester in the fall of 2001, I was organizing notes for my Tuesday morning class when a friend casually mentioned that a plane had flown into one of the Twin Towers in New York City. I gave it little thought, assuming that a rookie pilot in a small aircraft had made a grave error. Minutes later, the sobering reality of what had happened became clear as the other tower was hit by a commercial passenger plane on live TV. Further reports of the Pentagon being similarly attacked blazed across televisions in the student lounge that my classmates crowded around.

I knew the U.S. military response would be fierce and swift. In the weeks after the 9/11 attacks, I proudly pointed out to anybody who would listen that some of the first U.S. forces to hit the ground in Afghanistan in October 2001 were from my former unit, led by a one-star Marine general named James Mattis.

As I prepared for my last round of finals, the demise of Enron Corporation was sharing front pages with stories describing gunfights in places such as Kandahar, Kabul, and Tora Bora, locations that people would now recognize on a map rather than mistake as places in a *Star Wars* movie. At the same time, my Marine friends began deploying in support of what was being called the Global War on Terror, or GWOT. While I looked for corporate law jobs, I envied their work more than ever and found myself wondering whether leaving the military had been the right decision. I faced a future of pinstripe suits and wingtip shoes, reviewing financial statements, and drafting lengthy contracts. Theirs entailed wearing combat fatigues, leading Marines, and serving at the forefront of the United States' military efforts abroad.

President George W. Bush included Iraq as a member of the "Axis of Evil" in his January 2002 State of the Union speech, leading many to wonder where the GWOT would reach and whether he intended to complete the war some felt his father had not properly finished a decade earlier. The fighting in Afghanistan continued to be fairly low key, largely conducted by special ops forces, and often with a cautious backward glance at earlier military failures in what has been called the "Graveyard of Empires," where Alexander the Great, the British, and the Russians had all suffered crushing defeats at the hands of the rugged Afghans.[1]

In August 2002, I went to work for an Ohio Congresswoman in Washington, D.C., while saber-rattling between the U.S. and Iraq was beginning. Marine friends were deploying to bases around the Middle East or aboard Navy ships patrolling the Arabian Gulf in anticipation of military operations against Iraq. Throughout that time, I had been traveling to and from New York City most weekends to visit the doctor I was still courting. After almost four years of dating, I decided to make things official. On an otherwise cold, wet, and miserable New Year's Day of 2003, under a bridge in Central Park, she agreed to my marriage proposal before hustling back to her apartment to put on her scrubs and start a twenty-four-hour on-call shift.

In February 2003, Secretary of State Colin Powell made a speech to the United Nations, providing details of Iraq's weapons of mass destruction (WMD) program, laying the groundwork for the justification of an invasion of Iraq. Congress debated the merits of invading Iraq while millions of people thronged the streets in major cities around the globe to protest the seemingly imminent war. At work for the U.S. Congress, I frequently visited a Marine captain working in the Marine Corps' Office of Legislative Affairs. We shared news of mutual friends and lamented that we'd be watching the war on TV rather than serving with and leading Marines in battle. We were certain the shock and awe campaign expected in Iraq would bring an unequivocal victory.[†] In the corner of that office sat a quiet and stern-looking Marine major named Bill McCollough.

The U.S.-led coalition launched Operation Iraqi Freedom on March 20, 2003. Forty days later, President Bush stood on the deck of the USS *Abraham Lincoln* in front of a banner that proclaimed "MISSION ACCOMPLISHED" to announce that major combat operations in Iraq were over. Fighting in Afghanistan continued to be discreet and largely unreported, while military resources and personnel were diverted to a budding insurgency in Iraq.

As fighting in Iraq intensified, I attended the dedication of the World War II memorial on the National Mall in Washington, D.C. Standing among those aptly called "the Greatest Generation," I thought about the Marines and members of the other services currently putting themselves in harm's way and knew they were the greatest of *my* generation. I had nothing to be ashamed of in my service, yet I felt a guilty emptiness for not being with them and sometimes daydreamed about the possibility of serving again. However, summer wedding plans and a pending move to New York City took priority, so I put those thoughts aside.

By late 2005, U.S. forces were fighting on multiple fronts other than Afghanistan, and operations in Iraq remained their focus. At the same time, a new professional opportunity persuaded me to trade a prestigious, but short-lived, job on Wall Street for one on

---

† That captain eventually got his chance to fight in Iraq and Afghanistan (several times, in fact) and was awarded the Bronze Star for his service.

Pennsylvania Avenue, and I moved back to Washington, D.C., with my wife.

In my new office, just a few blocks from the White House, I labored over the finer points of complex contracts. It was work that, in theory, seemed interesting and worthwhile but in practice was often dreary and repetitive, with little opportunity for creative thinking. As I kept my wing tips shined, my Marine friends were getting promoted and embarking on their second or third deployments since the GWOT began. While my career was steadily advancing along a law firm partnership track, my former peers were quickly becoming battle hardened and worldly. We remained close, but I felt a void growing between us, as I no longer felt the common purpose and shared history of brothers-in-arms enduring hardships together. Keeping up on my billable hours requirement played a bigger role in my life than many other things, including maintaining a fitness regimen. What's more, the lawyer lunches I enjoyed softened me up and filled me out more than I cared to admit.

My heart would drop whenever my ringing cell phone displayed an area code from Southern California or North Carolina, where Marine friends were stationed while they were stateside. I choked back tears upon receiving calls with the news that Rick Gannon, Ken Hunt, and Ray Mendoza, friends from my active duty days, were killed in Iraq. I thought about the Marine Reserve unit I briefly served with in Ohio; they lost eleven members in an IED explosion so powerful it flipped their thirty-ton armored vehicle onto its top. I wondered what I was doing to honor their sacrifice. By this time, interest in the wars in Iraq and Afghanistan seemed to largely fade from the public's attention, much like the yellow "I Support the Troops" magnets people had put on their cars when the war began.

In late 2006, I ran into a Marine general I knew at a lecture hosted by a D.C. think tank. We talked about mutual friends and common interests, sharing laughs at things only Marines would find humorous. I admitted that I missed the Corps and told the general I occasionally mused about getting back in uniform to serve one more time. He pondered my comment for a moment, took a card out of his pocket, and wrote a name and number on it. "Call this Marine. Tell him your story and see if there's a fit at the CAG for you," he said. I thanked him, pocketed the card, and made my way around the reception.

A few days later, I was tucked into my desk at 8:00 p.m. when my cell phone rang, showing a number with the Southern California 949 area code. I answered reluctantly, worried I might hear bad news about another Marine I knew. Instead, it was a friend telling me about some promotions and awards several other friends were receiving and letting me know he was deploying—*again*. We chatted about nothing in particular until I glimpsed the general's card on my desk and asked my friend what the CAG was.

He told me, "It stands for Civil Affairs Group—a pretty small unit, mostly reservists. They do good stuff. Why?"

"I had this crazy idea about coming back in to do one more tour," I said. "Someone suggested I check out that unit, so I wanted to hear what you thought. But I doubt anything will come of it since I've been out so long."

In his typical blunt manner, he told me, "You can get a waiver for just about anything. If your fat ass can pass a PFT and you can put up with the admin shit to come back in, they'll find a spot for you."

The next morning, I decided to gauge my fitness level, so I jogged from my house to work along the National Mall, a distance just a bit longer than the run requirement for the Marine Corps physical fitness test (PFT). Then I got on the pull-up bar at the gym I rarely visited. I was in shape—but it was more like a pear shape. I had a lot of work to do if I were seriously going to consider getting back into the Marine Corps. When I got to my office, I called the number the general gave me, told the major who answered the phone what I was interested in, and set up a meeting where I could fill out some paperwork and take an "inventory" PFT.

Before we hung up, he asked, "Are you married?" I said I was, and he followed with, "Is your wife cool with this?"

"I'll find out," I told him.

There's someone for everyone, and I could not have found a better or more understanding partner than my wife. What I was asking her to consider was astonishing. I had a great job, good pay, and a comfortable life in a world-class city. Yet I wanted to trade that comfort and prestige for the hardship of a combat zone. The wars my country were fighting evoked the same sense of duty and adventure that led me into the Marine Corps in the first place. I felt like another stint in the Corps would reforge the bonds I had with my friends who were still serving. It would also allow me to play a role in what they were achieving rather than just envying them from afar.

My wife knew I had loved my time in the Marine Corps and cherished the friendships I developed there. She understood my desire to be part of something bigger—something that mattered— even if I were to have just a small role in that effort. And she knew I would never find that sense of achievement as a corporate lawyer. To a degree, the Marine Corps had become part of *her* life as well. She patiently endured my repeated stories, became close with my Marine friends' wives, and often listened sympathetically as they described the anxiety they felt when their husbands embarked on yet *another* deployment. So it wasn't much of a surprise when she said yes, but with a caveat:

"This will count as your midlife crisis, so no fancy sports cars or motorcycles, got it?"

I never had much of a thing for sports cars. But I like motor-cycles, so I tried to appeal to her concern for the environment by pointing out that they're more fuel-efficient than most cars. I even explained that motorcycles are safer than cars because they have fewer distractions, like radios and climate control systems, to take the driver's eyes off the road. My persuasive skills weren't at their best as I asked for clarification as to whether I was required to foreswear *both* items, or if I could pick just one. Considering that I was asking her permission to once again put myself in harm's way in service to my country, I was not bargaining from a position of relative strength. She firmly reiterated her conditions, to which I humbly agreed.

The Marine Corps is one of the world's most advanced and lethal fighting organizations, but it's still a government entity with plenty of bureaucracy. When I began my re-entry process in late 2006, I naively assumed that after passing a PFT and signing a few forms, I would buy a new uniform, get a smart haircut, and jump right back in the action.

I was wrong.

My file had to make its way through the several offices whose approval was required, and I received an age waiver, separation from service waiver, and command endorsement from the CAG to join the unit once my application was finally approved. I underwent several physical exams and raised my fitness level to the point where I could easily get a high first-class PFT score. This process took close to a year to complete.

In early October 2007, the Marine who had been shepherding my paperwork through the reappointment process called to tell me my application had been approved. I was eager to get back in uniform and we set a time for the following day for me to come to his office to be recommissioned.

At 8:00 a.m. on a brisk October morning, I faced a Marine major and once again swore to "support and defend the Constitution of the United States against all enemies, foreign and domestic."

When I finished the oath, he shook my hand and beamed, "Welcome back, Captain Biggio."

I was a Marine again. I was home.

CHAPTER 3
PRAY FOR PEACE, BUT PREPARE FOR WAR

I love the infantry . . . They are the mud-rain-frost-and-wind boys. They
have no comforts, and they learn to live without the necessities. And
in the end, they are the guys that wars can't be won without.
—ERNIE PYLE, writing from Northern Tunisia, May 2, 1943

OCTOBER 2007

IN THE TEN YEARS BETWEEN MY LEAVING THE SERVICE IN LATE 1997
and rejoining in October 2007, some things about the Marine Corps
had changed. Brown suede boots had replaced the black leather
boots I'd spent hours polishing in the 1990s. The new camouflage
utility uniforms with a trademarked design didn't require ironing
to maintain crisp lines. Personnel records were kept online, and
Marines were able to access and update their record books through
a web-based portal.

Also, in the post-9/11 world, reservists were no longer just
"weekend warriors" whose obligations were limited to training for
one weekend a month and a two-week session per year. Reservists

were being called to—and volunteering for—active duty for lengthy tours to support the GWOT on a regular basis. And that's exactly what I had in mind when I signed back up.

In other ways, things were exactly as I remembered. Chief among those was the character of the Marines. Marines have an innate intellectual curiosity that belies their rugged image, and those in my new unit were no exception. They were just as inclined to read *The Economist* and *The Wall Street Journal* as *Guns & Ammo* or *Sports Illustrated*. Junior Marines from the CAG confidently led impromptu discussions on the useful cultural insights in books such as Greg Mortenson's *Three Cups of Tea* or Sarah Chayes's *The Punishment of Virtue* to audiences of Marines several ranks higher. The unit's roster included a senior attorney with the Department of Justice, a NASA scientist, congressional staff members, policemen, firefighters, graduate students, a journalist, a CIA analyst, and private-sector business executives. Many in the CAG had served multiple deployments to Iraq, Kosovo, northeast Africa, or other distant places where small elements of U.S. forces were serving in support of the GWOT. They could speak insightfully on a wide range of subjects, from Heisman Trophy winner Tim Tebow's NFL prospects and the tactical employment of light machine guns, to the implications of U.S.-Pakistani relations on operations in Afghanistan.

But while I was glad to be back among Marines, in late 2007 there was something else on my mind. During the second weekend in December, I was shaken awake by a heavy pat on the chest, and my wife's words: "It's time to go." We rushed to the hospital, and after a long day, we welcomed a baby boy into the world. I put on a blue tie, cradled my son, and stood next to my wife in her hospital bed for our first family portrait.

As any parent can attest—and as any prospective parent should be warned—a new baby is a wonderful but bewildering experience. In some ways, it was another layer of training for the unpredictability of living in a combat zone—you're never fully in control in either situation. Events such as feedings and diaper changes consume your schedule; you sleep whenever you can (but never for more than two or three hours at a time); and even when things seem calm, you're always on edge because you know they won't be that way for long. With the help of family members and close friends, we managed to take our changed circumstances in stride, often literally. My son became part of my fitness regimen; I would strap him in a baby carrier and hike with him around our Washington neighborhood. After cutting through the park near my house at the end of a long walk one day, an African American woman I recognized as a newcomer in the neighborhood stopped me to, in her words, "Check out this little prince!" (She meant my son, not me.) We exchanged pleasantries, and she advised me, "Spoil him, but not too much." Then she wished me well, and as she shook my hand, she said, "My name's Michelle."

While 2008 began on a high note for my family, other global events promised a bleak year ahead. Global stock indices were plunging, leading to speculation of a looming recession, while frustration with the progress and direction of the GWOT weighed heavily on many people's minds.

By the time General David Petraeus and Ambassador Ryan Crocker urged Congress to halt withdrawals of the more than 160,000 U.S. troops from Iraq in April 2008, the war in Afghanistan—where the GWOT began—seemed to be an inconvenient side story for policy makers, with just over 33,000 "boots on the ground."[2] How to execute the "long war"—as the GWOT was now called in some circles—was a hot topic in the presidential primary debates, and some commentators and candidates even tried to distinguish between the "good war" (as if there really were such a thing) in Afghanistan and the "bad war" in Iraq.

A few months after joining the CAG, it was clear that a lengthy deployment for the unit was almost certain, but *where* remained less so. Absent a known destination, we focused on fundamentals such as patrolling, marksmanship, and communications skills that we would need no matter where we were sent.

As autumn approached, demand for CAG Marines to augment units deployed in Iraq and Afghanistan intensified and mission objectives became more defined. I turned down a few offers to be a staff officer because I knew that a midlevel captain on a general's staff would be relegated to making coffee runs and PowerPoint slideshows. I had rejoined the Corps to lead Marines and wanted my time back in uniform to be filled with long patrols rather than long shifts in front of a computer in a brigade command center. I wanted to make sure my rifle and tactical radio were clean and functional rather than worrying about whether an attachment emailed to subordinate units fit file size standards. I wanted to get dirt under my fingernails and eat MREs, or whatever else I could scrounge in the field, rather than rushing to the base chow hall to get three squares a day.

In a few months, I would get my wish.

By the early evening of November 4, 2008, it was clear that my neighbor Michelle, who had patted my son's cheeks and had given me friendly parental advice that day in the park, would be moving to the White House with her husband, Barack Obama, newly elected as my next commander in chief. Outgoing President George W. Bush went on a farewell tour in Iraq and artfully dodged a shoe thrown at him by an angry Baghdadi reporter. The global economy had spiraled out of control and was headed toward a long recession. As I watched the clock strike midnight on New Year's Eve, I knew 2009 would be the year I would go to war.

In early 2009, with protracted wars being waged on two fronts, the fighting in Afghanistan had entered its eighth year. The evolving nature of the conflict saw the U.S. military mission there morph from engaging in direct combat operations, to advising Afghan military and police units, to ultimately launching and executing counterinsurgency (COIN) operations. Military budgets, personnel, and equipment were strained as policy makers considered how to replicate in Afghanistan the recent successes we'd had in Iraq. Some commentators rejected any continued presence in what they felt was a "quagmire" and a "fool's errand."[3]

The Taliban—deposed from power in 2001 and driven from Afghanistan's larger population centers such as Kabul and Kandahar—was reemerging, particularly in the southern province of Helmand. There, a dearth of NATO forces allowed insurgents to sell heroin processed from the vast poppy fields they cultivated, smuggle weapons, intimidate the local population, and plan terror attacks in other parts of the country.[4]

For several months, Pentagon strategists had been developing options for a surge of up to thirty thousand troops in Afghanistan. The chaos in the country made CAG Marines an obvious choice to be part of that force. Our unit's Marines had a diverse set of skills and experience, so it was no surprise when, in early February 2009, the CAG headquarters received orders to mobilize a detachment to deploy in support of the Second Marine Expeditionary Brigade.

Thirty-five Marines and sailors in the CAG detachment were divided into five teams, four of which were tasked to support infantry battalions. My team was assigned to the First Battalion of the Fifth Marine Regiment. Within a week of mobilizing, we joined 1/5 for an exercise at 29 Palms, the Marine Corps' training base in California's Mojave Desert. It was there that my team would meet the Marines with whom we'd spend months in a combat environment, and I wanted us to make a solid first impression.

We flew there in a military troop transport from Andrews Air Force Base near Washington, D.C. It was roughly ten hours in a no-frills prop-driven aircraft. Whatever I had eaten for breakfast was not sitting well in my guts by the time we disembarked at the expeditionary airstrip at the base, so I made a beeline for the bathroom. Our quarters had been built during the Korean War, and the spartan conditions there had seen few improvements since. The row of toilets in the ramshackle latrine had no doors or dividing walls, but I wasn't worried about privacy or modesty at the time. Soon after I took a seat, two other Marines came into the latrine and sat on the commodes on either side of me. To my left was the battalion executive officer (XO), Major Tom Lacroix, a friend from my active duty days, with whom I had been in touch since learning I would be joining the battalion.

"Fancy meeting you here, Gus!" Tom said to me with a laugh. Then he leaned forward so he could speak to the Marine sitting on my right saying, "Sir, this is Captain Biggio, the guy I was telling you about who's going to be our CAG team leader."

I turned to say hello (but not shake hands) and recognized the stern-looking major (now a lieutenant colonel) whom I had met about seven years earlier while working with the U.S. Congress, Bill McCollough. It was not quite the setting in which I had hoped to make that aspired solid first impression.

Modern warfare is not limited to conventional operations where the objective is "massing firepower at the appropriate place and time to destroy the enemy."[5] Instead, it focuses heavily on providing security to, and gaining the trust of, the local population, often in competition with insurgents who seek to fill the void left by absent government leadership. The evolution in 29 Palms included plenty of practice shooting and blowing things up, as would be expected. But it also included an equal amount of "nonkinetic" training—"what-if" scenarios with role players acting as tribal elders, refugees, or covert insurgents. Successful tactics in these scenarios consisted more of using proper body language and cultural awareness than of moving and shooting under fire.

The battalion received high marks from the training evaluators. When the three-week exercise ended, I was rounding up my team to head back to the East Coast for some final pre-deployment training when Lieutenant Colonel McCollough came to see us off. In his succinct, matter-of-fact tone, he said, "Your guys did well; we'll be glad to have you with us." The first impression my team had made was a good one.

Afghanistan continued to be an enigma for political and military planners. Questions about where, why, how many, and when to deploy additional troops persisted.[6] Even if numbers could be agreed upon, interservice rivalries caused headbutting about whether the majority of troops would come from the Marine Corps or the U.S. Army. Diplomats struggled to paint an optimistic picture of the country amid widespread claims of Afghan government corruption and incompetence.[7]

Amid all this confusion, one thing was certain: our CAG detachment was headed to Afghanistan. In early May, we assembled at our unit's headquarters hours before the sun rose to start making our way there. It would be the last time we would see our families until our return, which was expected to be in December.

My wife drove me onto the base while our son, now sixteen months old, snoozed in his jammies in the back seat of our car. Being in the military often requires an ability to be emotionally opaque. When saying goodbye, it's best to take the Band-Aid approach: just rip it off and get it over with. But at this moment, my guts wrestled with my feelings. I was leaving my wife and young son for a noble cause, yet I felt a tinge of doubt, nervousness, and even fear come over me. Military spouses also have to be stoic in the face of these sendoffs, and my wife maintained her composure as I unloaded my gear from the trunk of our car.

"I need you to do one thing for me," she said, looking me squarely in the eyes when I returned to the car after putting my bags on the bus that would take my unit and me to our plane.

"Yes?" I asked, bracing myself to hear something profound such as, "Come back with your shield, or on it," the tough counsel Sparta's wives and mothers gave their warriors as they went off to war centuries ago.

"Change his diaper," she commanded, handing me my son, who had just awakened from his slumber.

I did my duty with well-trained proficiency and strapped my son back in his car seat. Giving my wife one last kiss, I patted her belly and pocketed the picture of her ultrasound from the previous week, showing a healthy, potato-sized baby number two due in a few months.

And then I went to war.

CHAPTER 4
THE ART OF WAR BY POWERPOINT

There was such a dense concentration of American energy there, American and essentially adolescent, if that energy could have been channeled into anything more than noise, waste and pain it would have lighted up Indochina for a thousand years.
—MICHAEL HERR, *Dispatches*

MAY 20, 2009

MY FIRST FULL DAY IN THE WAR ZONE WAS FRANTIC. I WAS SLEEP deprived, disoriented, and separated from my Marines. I barely had any ammunition and was down to a quarter liter of lukewarm water in a dust-caked plastic bottle, certainly not enough to sustain me in the hundred-degree weather for very long. But I was mission focused, as I carried in my hand one of the most transformative innovations in war-fighting our military has seen in decades: a thumb drive with my contributions to a PowerPoint presentation that would be shown to the commanding general of the MEB later in the afternoon.

I was at Camp Leatherneck, an expeditionary Marine base rising out of the Afghan desert to serve as the hub for Marine operations in

Helmand Province. About a week earlier, General David McKiernan had been replaced as the commander of NATO forces in Afghanistan, serving in the job for just eleven months before receiving his orders to go home. With the war entering its eighth year and a new administration in office, many felt it was time to look at our presence in Afghanistan with fresh eyes. A new ground forces commander now rounded out the team executing America's war strategy.[8] From the shadows of "black ops" run by the Joint Special Operations Command came General Stanley McChrystal to take the helm of NATO operations in the country. An increased emphasis was being put on "civil-military" operations. This was no longer just a military campaign. Civilian diplomats were playing an ever-increasing role in visions for success in the country. General McChrystal was regarded as one of the savviest practitioners of COIN, and he had been given the herculean task of aligning the efforts of U.S. gunslingers and bureaucrats with those of their Afghan counterparts toward a unified strategy that had never been clearly defined.[9]

The development and construction of Camp Leatherneck began in late 2008 in anticipation of redirecting the war's efforts from Afghanistan's mountainous north to its southern provinces. If you were going to take the fight to the enemy, there was no better place to set up shop than in Helmand Province: "ground zero of everything bad in Afghanistan."[10] Brigadier General Larry Nicholson, commander of the Marine forces operating out of Helmand, seized the opportunity to make his mark on the war's new blueprints. The base echoed and thumped around the clock with the sounds of banging hammers, humming generators, and bulldozers and other earthmoving vehicles. Around the base, pallets of two-by-fours and plywood sheets were laid out next to concrete pads where new barracks, offices, mess halls, and "morale" facilities materialized daily. Mostly at night, for tactical security reasons, there was a steady roar of aircraft taking off and landing at Camp Bastion, the neighboring British base that had an airfield big enough for large multi-engine planes. Massive C-17 transports were delivering the brigade's fifteen thousand Marines from their bases in the U.S. via Manas Air Base[11] in Kyrgyzstan, each Marine lugging a deployment's worth of clothing and equipment stuffed into one backpack and a seabag. Helicopters buzzed through the sky, taking many of the newly arrived Marines on to austere outposts in the hinterlands. The occasional piercing shriek of rockets fired from a HIMARS—a truck-mounted mobile launching platform capable of accurately firing high-explosive rockets onto targets over a hundred miles away—reminded us there was a real war going on not too far away.

We stashed our gear in large rectangular nylon and canvas tents about the size of a circus tent, each capable of housing about one hundred Marines. Inside, foldable cots were spread out in orderly rows, the units assigned in each tent designated by the red and gold guidons posted outside the entrance. Late May temperatures in Afghanistan were always in the high nineties but often reached well above one hundred degrees by midday, and large air-conditioning units at either end of the tents were used to keep the inside temperatures bearable. The combined noise of generators powering the blowers on the AC units ensured a constant cacophony that sounded like the floor of a manufacturing plant.

A late-spring weather phenomenon called the "Wind of One Hundred Days" kicked up funnel clouds of the fine desert sand the base was being built upon. We constantly swept dust off the sturdy nylon tent floors, cleaned our weapons, swabbed Q-tips in our ears, and wiped Wet-Naps across our faces to fight the persistent mess. The roads throughout Camp Leatherneck were not yet paved, so the large vehicles always using them kicked up more dust. And it wasn't just armored Humvees or other military vehicles. Commercial vehicles hauling food, potable water, and other supplies necessary to sustain tens of thousands of Marines and contractors constantly roved around the base. A large fleet of tanker trucks affectionately called "honey suckers" hauled five-thousand-gallon tanks used to vacuum the contents of the hundreds of plastic porta-potties spread around the base, yet another Sisyphean ritual necessary to ensure a smoothly functioning (and hygienic) camp. Whether it was intentionally witty or just fortuitously ironic, one of the honey suckers' tanks had "*La Dolce Vita*"—"The Sweet Life"—stenciled on its side in large block letters.

Though Camp Leatherneck was still in early development, it was taking on the look and feel of a permanent facility. While many people back home thought of the war in Afghanistan as being waged in dingy and primitive mud huts and rugged mountains, builders were putting up air-conditioned fitness centers,barber shops, dining halls that had soft-serve ice cream dispensers, and a base commissary selling tax-free PlayStations, Xboxes, flat-screen TVs, and candy bars and potato chips in bulk containers, as well as souvenir war T-shirts with macho slogans and cool graphics such as eagles, American flags, and skulls. All these facilities were staffed by eager and often non-English-speaking "third-country nationals" (TCNs) from places such as the Philippines, Nepal, Bangladesh, and Sri Lanka—any place but Afghanistan, whose citizens were not permitted inside Camp Leatherneck's barriers for security reasons.

The "military-industrial complex" that President Dwight Eisenhower warned of in his 1961 farewell address was hard at work at Camp Leatherneck, and the private contracting firms that provided many of the supply and logistics duties on the base were well compensated for their efforts. The irony of not hiring any Afghan nationals—the very people we were in the country to serve and protect—was not lost on any of the Marines I served with.

If the base chow halls (there were more than one) didn't satisfy the cravings of the service members and thousands of contractors at Camp Leatherneck, they could get a taste of home at the base's Burger King, Pizza Hut, Baskin-Robbins, or KFC, each of which had opened in a portable trailer even before the MEB's permanent operations center was built. These fast-food joints were staffed by a cadre of TCNs who had likely never eaten the type of food they were serving before they came to Afghanistan.

It became clear to me that not every Marine who served in Afghanistan would do so from the austere environments in such places as Nawa, Garmsir, or Farah, where my fellow CAG members and I were headed. In fact, many service members who deploy to Afghanistan spend their entire time on bases like Camp Leatherneck and may never actually meet any Afghans while in their country. In many ways, this is no different from what U.S. service members have experienced in other wars. America's long and big wars have always required massive ecosystems of support that come to resemble factory towns as much as military operations hubs.

In Vietnam, there was Long Binh Post, south of Saigon, which was as big as Cleveland when its construction was completed. To a casual observer, Long Binh Post might have looked like a massive health club with its eighty-one basketball courts, sixty-four volley-ball courts, twelve swimming pools, eight softball fields, multiple weight rooms, and even two mini golf courses. Soldiers less physically inclined could sate their intellects at one of Long Binh's three libraries or party it up at forty different bars.[12]

A generation later, American service members again enjoyed many of the luxuries of home while serving in combat zones around the world, including in Iraq, where our military and State Department took over Saddam Hussein's palaces after he was overthrown in 2003, setting up a vast network of "morale, welfare, and recreation" (MWR) facilities in the dictator's former residences.[13] Camp Leatherneck was on its way to being a quasi-luxury posting as well.

There has always been a rift between the soldiers and Marines who spend their deployments in the mud and dirt of the front lines of America's wars and those who are tasked with supporting their efforts. As wars become more high tech, the ratio of front-line troops to support troops will continue to skew in favor of the support personnel, and the two groups will experience war from entirely different perspectives. Those on the front lines will see their uniforms bleached from sweat, their necks and hands become bronzed by the sun, and their boots worn flat from countless patrols. They will gain an intimate familiarity with the dirt of their area of operations and the people living there. The REMFs (rear-echelon motherfuckers), on the other hand, will spend their war in air-conditioned command centers, wearing clean uniforms that might start to get tight around the waist from eating too many regular meals and carrying weapons that may seem more like an ornament than an actual instrument of war. I was glad to be one of the former, but time in Camp Leatherneck was a necessary part of my movement to the front lines.

Clutching the thumb drive with my PowerPoint file, I found myself standing at the back of a side room in the MEB's operations center. In front of me were two dozen computers arrayed across several rows of folding plastic tables. Sitting in front of each of those twenty-four computers were twenty-four Marines, only one of whom was a captain. The rest were majors or lieutenant colonels, and each was diligently pecking away at their contribution to a PowerPoint presentation that someone at least one rank higher felt was vital to the war effort. None of these field-grade officers had a clear role in the chain of command, but they typed, nonetheless, with an earnestness that suggested whatever they were preparing was crucial to winning the war. A young sergeant and a corporal continuously weaved among the rows of tables to give the officers assistance with any graphics or fancy text they wanted to include in their slideshows.

So this is how we fight wars in the twenty-first century, I thought to myself, feeling a knot in my stomach as I looked at the colorful flash graphics on the screens in front of me. I had prepared just five slides with bullet-point black text on a white background. No colors, no flashing images, no buzzwords. Just what I thought was the basic information a general, with a limited amount of time, would want to know about my team's role in our upcoming operation.

It turned out that my worries about a subpar presentation were unfounded. General Nicholson's reputation as a straightforward, no-nonsense leader was evident about ten minutes into the day's first presentation after he interrupted the speaker to ask how many slides were in the deck being presented. When he was told, "Eighty-five, sir," he asked how many were actually important, which drew a blank stare from the unlucky lieutenant colonel leading the presentation and muffled laughter from other Marines in attendance. The general politely—but with obvious annoyance—told the presenter to get through the substance of the remaining slides in fifteen minutes. All that brainpower and effort from the field-grade officers I'd watched in horrified awe earlier in the day were apparently for naught. The insidious effects of PowerPoint were thwarted that day, but they would go on to pervade much of the war's operations and planning, even though its most senior commanders, including General McChrystal, often and publicly bemoaned its existence and the consequential waste of time spent viewing slideshows.[14]

There was much to do at Camp Leatherneck before I would join a small group of Marines in Nawa, as part of the battalion's first wave of Operation Khanjar. Besides delivering the PowerPoint presentation, I had further reasons for being at the MEB headquarters. Money was another key component of fighting wars in the twenty-first century. As the Civil Affairs team leader for the battalion, distributing money for battle-damage claims and small projects would be one of my duties. I needed to go through various training courses—presented with PowerPoint, of course—to be authorized to receive thousands of dollars of U.S. taxpayers' cash, which I'd carry in a Ziploc bag in my cargo pocket. Money was such an integral part of the war-fighting process that it even had its own acronym—MAAWS: Money as a Weapons System—and a two-inch-thick manual describing every form and authorization needed to obtain and use it.[15]

An Army major oversaw Camp Leatherneck's finance office, and the task of training and authorizing Marines in the use of this new "weapons system" fell to him. He looked exactly like what one would expect a REMF to look like: pasty skin, droopy eyes, a slack jaw, and a slightly hunched posture. His gait was more of a shuffle than a stride, and his speech was frequently interrupted with sniffles, as if he were battling allergies. In front of a room of about fifty Marines, the major began his presentation by saying how excited he was to be at Camp Leatherneck for his first overseas deployment. He went on to share his concern that so many of the Marines in the room who would be issued cash were "just sergeants," implying that they lacked the professional maturity or judgment to handle about $2,000 each. Most of the sergeants listening to the major's fretful speech were squad leaders, in charge of the lives and welfare of a dozen Marines. Each of them was on at least a third deployment in a combat zone. The major clearly didn't know his audience.

We endured the training and learned the distinctions among the different types of funds to which we had access and what each could and, more importantly, could *not* be used for. We learned there were

CERP funds, FOO funds, OMA funds, and POERF funds and received veiled threats about the long jail sentences that awaited us if we ignored the repeated admonishments to *never*, under *any* circumstances, comingle these different funds.[16] Most of the Marines in the class would just need a few hundred dollars to pay for battle-damage claims and small infrastructure projects, so the warnings about comingling fund types weren't relevant for them. My duties, however, required me to have some of each, so I paid attention. After our training session, I made my way to the disbursing office, filled out the required forms, and handed them to the disbursing clerk. Moments later, I was presented with one large bag filled with Afghani bills equivalent to about $50,000.

"Here you go, sir," said the young NCO disbursing clerk handing me the cash.

"Can you put this in separate piles for me? We were just told not to comingle the different funds," I said, looking incredulously at the single stack of taxpayer money lumped in front of me.

The clerk gave me an annoyed, almost insubordinate stare before saying, "Nah, you're good to go, sir. Just make sure you fill out your paperwork clearly."

I felt like this might have been a secret test to see if I had paid attention in the training session. But when the clerk pursed his lips, raised his eyebrows at me, and impatiently tapped his fingers on the counter between us as he waited for me to sign the receipt for the cash that he had put in front of me, I realized that it was just a test of my self-restraint. So I signed the necessary forms, put the bag of cash in my cargo pocket, and trudged out the door.

I had my rifle and my pistol, and now I had my cash. I was ready to get out into the wilderness and fight this war.

CHAPTER 5
CROSSING THE RUBICON[17]

You are about to embark upon the great crusade, toward which we have striven these many months. The eyes of the world are upon you.
—GENERAL DWIGHT D. EISENHOWER,
in his letter to members of the Allied Expeditionary
Force on the eve of D-Day, June 5, 1944

JULY 2, 2009

AT 1:00 A.M., A NOT-QUITE-FULL MOON EMITTED ENOUGH LIGHT to allow NVG-wearing helicopter pilots to discern the key features of landing zones in Nawa District, where they were dropping off hundreds of combat-loaded Marines. Several hundred more Marines were easing along the district's dirt roads in armored Humvees or large mine-resistant, ambush-protected vehicles (MRAPs). The Humvees and MRAPs were spread out in convoys, close enough to keep an eye on each other but far enough apart to ensure that the blasts from any improvised explosive devices (IEDs) would not hit multiple vehicles. Operation Khanjar was officially underway. In total, over four thousand Marines would push into Nawa and its neighboring districts, Garmsir and Khan Neshin, along with hundreds of Afghan National Army soldiers.[18]

A few weeks earlier, an advance wave of about three hundred Marines had deployed to this same district as part of the operation's first phase. That phase was intended to convince Taliban insurgents that the increase in NATO troops was limited only to a small contingent of Marines reinforcing the fifty British troops who had held Patrol Base Jaker for several months and who rarely ventured outside its relative security.

The second phase, which began in early July, had several other objectives. One was purely focused on combat: the Marines arriving by air and ground from all directions would certainly catch people off guard, particularly the insurgents who were not killed in the operation's first phase or who had not entirely left Nawa yet. Any who chose to fight the waves of Marines surging in would be overwhelmed and killed. The second objective was more nuanced but strategically vital: the Marines were coming to stay and provide a secure environment for the local population, which would enable the Afghan government to reestablish itself in the beleaguered district. The Marines were part of a counterinsurgency campaign (COIN in jargon-heavy military terms)—the new war strategy espoused by General Stanley McChrystal, the recently designated commander of all NATO forces in Afghanistan.

It would be an easy shortcut to summarize the objectives of COIN with a clichéd phrase about "winning hearts and minds." In some sense, that's an apt description. But a more detailed look is useful to grasp where much of the focus of twenty-first-century warfare is being directed and to appreciate the accomplishments of 1/5 and the other Marines of the Second Marine Expeditionary

Brigade (MEB) whose mission started in the summer of 2009. One former Army officer pointed out that the images most likely to make the evening news from the wars the U.S. military had been fighting for nearly two decades were not at all like those in the documentaries about World War II, Vietnam, or even Desert Storm. Instead, viewers would see as many images of military construction crews and clinics opening in remote villages as they would see of explosions and gunfire.[19] Those non-kinetic efforts were part of how COIN battles were won.

Warfare has evolved over centuries. No longer do masses of armies charge forth on open fields under the banners of their leaders and meet face-to-face to mutilate one another with maces, swords, and axes. And while it is important to have a strong navy and air force, as well as tanks and artillery to augment infantry troops ready to battle a conventional adversary, the post-World War II and Cold War eras have seen a (hopefully) reduced likelihood of major armed conflict between nation states.

The enemies in a COIN war look and fight differently from those in a traditional army. They often don't have uniforms and instead appear to look like typical civilians. In fact, when Marines arrived in Nawa in 2009, they were given vague warnings about how the Taliban preferred to wear white or black turbans, which we quickly realized was *not* a key identifying characteristic, as nearly all of the adult men in Nawa wore such an outfit out of practicality and convenience.

Nor will a typical insurgent be affiliated with a recognized state. Groups such as the Taliban, ISIS, and al-Qaeda have been notably opposed to any influence or control by recognized governments (and even though the Taliban and al-Qaeda have enjoyed financial backing and tacit support from Pakistan and Saudi Arabia, their leadership has consistently shunned directives from those countries). Identifying friend from foe in an insurgency can be a maddening endeavor. Indeed, many veterans who fought in Iraq and Afghanistan can relate stories about how after sitting down to have tea and a discussion with a group of locals, they exchanged gunfire with those same locals just hours or days later.

Insurgents will fight differently than a regular army, using tactics that are difficult to counter with traditional means. Surprise attacks in civilian population centers and remotely detonated IEDs are some of the more common insurgent tactics. A spray of AK-47 gunfire at U.S. forces in a crowded market-place can produce casualties and chaos, and the insurgent can simply drop the cheap and easily replaceable weapon and blend in with the fleeing crowd. The confusion he's created frees him to fight another day—and perhaps have a few cups of tea with his adversaries until that next fight.

COIN success is reliant on a population-centric approach. Gone are the days when victory was determined by who held the higher ground, often accomplished by killing more fighters than the enemy could. Instead, the critical "terrain" in a COIN fight is gaining the legitimate support of the local population. In an Area of Operations (AO) where there are cultural, religious, and ideological differences—not to mention language barriers—earning and maintaining this legitimacy among the locals is a never-ending ordeal. The *tactical* decisions of small unit leaders can have *strategic* implications, and the battle for support is constantly subject to manipulation and disinformation. Whatever support is gained can quickly erode with a single thoughtless mistake or clever propaganda effort.

The Marines of 1/5 knew these challenges long before they began hitting the trails and canal paths of Nawa. With their intense pre-deployment training regimen, they were ready to use the weapons at their disposal, but they were just as ready to, as General James Mattis frequently expressed, "engage your brain before you engage your weapon."

General Larry Nicholson, commander of the Second MEB and of all the Marines serving in Helmand Province, was an ardent supporter of General McChrystal's COIN strategy. Before the Marines from 1/5 began their push into Nawa, he assembled them for a pep talk, emphasizing that to be successful, they had to be out with the community. He said, "We're not going to drive to work. We're going to walk to work . . . . Get to know the people. That's the reason why we're here."[20]

The general knew how to fight a war, having done so several times over more than thirty years of service, including as a regimental commander in some of Iraq's most intense combat zones half a dozen years earlier. He presciently forewarned his Marines that they would win this war not only with aggression, guns, and bullets but also with patience and humility. They should expect to eat lots of goat meat and drink plenty of tea just as much as they should expect to get in firefights with the insurgents skulking around Nawa.

The Marines arriving in the district understood their orders. As they made their way there in the dead of night, they knew they would not be conducting this war from behind the bullet-resistant windows of armored vehicles. Instead, they would be putting miles on the soles of their boots, shaking hands, sitting on their haunches, and chatting up nearly every Afghan national they met.

Only the soundest sleepers in Nawa would not have known that something was happening in the wee hours of the morning on July 2 as the thumping crack of helicopter rotors and the growling rumble of diesel engines echoed everywhere. When the sun rose that morning, villagers looking into their freshly harvested and plowed fields saw squads of Marines fanned out, keenly scanning tree lines and village compounds for signs of trouble. We were not on a stealth mission and didn't make any effort to mask the noise of our movements or conceal our presence. In fact, we *wanted* the Afghans to know we had arrived—the patrolling Marines went out of their way to approach the locals they encountered to introduce themselves and explain our mission.

Every Marine in 1/5 told every Afghan he met the message the battalion commander, Lieutenant Colonel Bill McCollough, wanted them to relay: We were here to stay, and the Afghan government was on the way. This message was often met with skepticism that the Marines would indeed stay, and with clear disdain for the Afghan government, which had failed to protect them from the Taliban insurgency while many of its officials got rich from international aid intended to trickle down to people like those in Nawa. But when the battalion's company commanders organized *shuras* (consultations) with the village elders in their respective AO to reiterate this message, the audience at least politely listened, albeit with bemused interest.[21]

During the first weeks of Operation Khanjar, the heat and humidity were as much our enemies as was the Taliban, some of whom had blended back into the general populace or fled to neighboring districts such as Marjah, where there was not yet a NATO presence. Nevertheless, Marines trudging through the area in the early days of the operation got into their share of firefights each day, some consisting of sporadic harassing fire and others lasting for several hours.

Many of the locals who weren't shooting at us regarded the Marines with cautious reserve or even visible scorn. Foreigners had been passing through Afghanistan for centuries. Although our uniforms may have looked different than those of the Russians or Brits who had come before us, our promises probably sounded familiar to some of the older Afghans. They had seen foreign armies come and go over their lifetimes, and their grandfathers and great-grandfathers would have told them about the dismal fate those foreigners met at the hands of their Afghan tormentors. By talking more and shooting less, we had embarked on a new type of warfare in the earliest days of the twenty-first century.

In July 2009, with Operation Khanjar underway, the eyes of the world were upon us. It was our fight to lose, but winning was our only option.

CHAPTER 6
WHERE THE WILD THINGS ARE

There was much of the beautiful, much of the wanton, much of the bizarre,
something of the terrible, and not a little of that which might have excited disgust.
—EDGAR ALLEN POE, "The Masque of the Red Death"

JUNE 5, 2009

YOU NEVER REALLY WAKE UP IN A COMBAT ZONE BECAUSE YOU NEVER really sleep. Instead, you often just drift in and out of awareness. Sometimes, if you're lucky, you can snooze for a few hours at a stretch, but that's only on the good days. On my first morning in Nawa, after a fitful rest, I bolted upright at about 4:45 a.m. to the sound of the morning *adhan*—the first of five daily Muslim calls to prayer. It was being announced from a cheap speaker system at a mosque near the eastern side of the district center. The faint crow of a rooster, and the throaty growl of a British Army Land Rover's diesel engine as it fired up near the dusty patch where I had chosen to lie down for the night, signaled it was time to put on my boots and start the day.

About an hour after rising, I went up the steps of the shabby brick structure that was our headquarters and stood behind a machine gun placed among the sandbags in a parapet. I took out an MRE, laying out its contents for my breakfast, as I gazed at what would be my home for the next several months. It was like staring at a pastoral scene from a Van Gogh painting. A group of farmers was busy harvesting wheat in the field bordering the patrol base's barriers, slicing the dried, grassy stalks with handheld scythes. Dozens of swallows darted acrobatically through the sky, picking off the swarms of flying insects uprooted by the wheat harvest. The sun was creeping into the sky, painting the freshly cut field with shifting shades of gold and brown. A few locals pedaled rickety bicycles on the dirt paths near our base, emitting steady squeaks as their rusty chains moved them along. A flock of sheep bleated as a gaggle of teenagers guided them through the grassy patch on the base's northern edge. Small 120cc motor-cycles puttered by, some with just a driver, others with as many as four passengers on board, usually young kids holding tightly to one another. A few tractors and an occasional van or car bounced along uneven dirt roads. The Afghans were early risers—they had to be to beat the cruel summer heat—and so we rose early too.

"Let's get kitted up and take a stroll through town," suggested the captain of the British Army contingent that had held the patrol base for the last several months. Twenty minutes later, I took my first steps "outside the wire" into the district center of Nawa.

The district center was on the eastern edge of Patrol Base Jaker. Its "Main Street" was lined with mostly deserted one-story mud shacks that had been the hub of commerce in better days. Now they looked more like the setting for a post-apocalyptic sci-fi movie. Only a handful of the shops showed any signs of activity, selling a random mix of warm Pepsi and generic orange-flavored soda, batteries, secondhand cell phones, motorcycle parts, and plastic rugs imprinted with Arabic designs. A "pharmacy" offered a few bottles of "Advel" and "Baier Aspreen" in dirty plastic bottles loosely resembling the brand names they tried to imitate, as well as a handful of condoms whose foil packages looked to have spent the better part of their lives inside the pocket of someone's jeans. The proprietor of a veterinary supply store, who said he was also a veterinarian, showed off a collection of (relatively) clean and rust-free knives with twelve-inch blades as part of the assemblage of goods available at his shop.

"You're an animal doctor?" I asked him through one of our interpreters. "*Wuuh, wuuh,*" came his enthusiastic reply, "yes" in Pashto. The vet and our interpreter engaged in an animated conversation that included vigorous chopping and slicing hand motions until our interpreter turned to me and said, "And if you need a goat slaughtered, he can do that too."

I used my Pashto training to thank him, "*Deh-deh mahnana,*" placing a hand over my heart and nodding politely before continuing our walk.

A former livestock stable adjacent to the barriers surrounding the patrol base had been transformed into the local police station. We sauntered through the gate where about two dozen Afghan cops milled around, their unrushed and decidedly relaxed mood likely related to the distinct aroma of marijuana floating through the air. At 7:00 a.m., several of the cops were already nicely buzzed. Before heading back inside the gates of the patrol base, we chatted with Nafez Khan, Nawa's shifty-eyed police chief. Meanwhile, several of his officers—some comfortably stoned—loaded themselves into the back of a forest green Toyota pickup truck with their AK-47s in hand to take their posts for the day. Many of the police officers had adorned their rifles with shiny tape, stickers, or even flower petals, as if they needed some color in their lives to distract them from the mainly beige surroundings in which they found themselves.

About one hundred meters to the west of the patrol base's barriers was an unoccupied mosque, a ten-by-ten-meter mud structure nearly identical to every other building within view. The only characteristic marking it as a holy site was the speaker dangling from a pole on its roof, ostensibly used to announce the call to prayer, if its sound system worked and someone actually showed up to announce those calls. Next to the mosque ran the first of two tree lines exactly parallel to the barriers protecting our patrol base. The second was located another fifty meters beyond the first. Each tree line was nourished by a shallow canal that irrigated the fields they bordered.

Even with high-tech communications systems, advanced weaponry, and GPS trackers, the front lines of modern warfare are crude places. We had no sinks, running water, or vanity mirrors. We made do with a dented tin bowl and a handheld mirror to do a quick wash and shave in the mornings. When we took a rare shower, we stood on a wooden pallet while holding a water jug over our heads. We slowly trickled some of the water out, soaped up, and then rinsed off with the remaining water. A twenty-by-twenty-foot burn pit about five feet deep constantly smoldered with the trash we dumped there, mostly empty plastic bottles and MRE wrappers.

Tucked away from where we slept and ate was the latrine. Five long plastic pipes about six inches in diameter were driven into the ground at a thirty-degree angle—the "piss tubes." A roughly constructed plywood shed housed four doorless stalls. The "drop zone" under each stall was a section of a fifty-five-gallon barrel, whose contents were burned with a gas and kerosene mixture several times a day. Sometimes the wind would shift, and the acidic smell of melting plastic from the burn pit combined with the pungent stench of flaming shit would waft through the air. It was an odor no amount of potpourri could mask.

It was always too hot to take a seat and relax at the latrine, read a magazine, or work on a crossword puzzle, but some budding writers took the time to scribble words of wisdom or notices on the stall's walls. One classic note read: "In order to reduce the effects of excess splashing, all turds longer than six inches must be lowered by hand into the latrines." I'm not aware, however, of anybody taking that notice seriously. Even if you weren't in a rush to be done in the stalls, the creepy sensation of flies tickling your exposed buttocks made lingering on the commode unpleasant. Some Marines claimed they had the Zenlike skills of Ralph Macchio's character in *The Karate Kid*, but instead of catching flies with chopsticks, they caught them between their cheeks by standing up quickly when they were finished. I took them at their word.

The battalion's AO was about 350 square miles, roughly the size of New York City's five boroughs.[†] Other than that, there were few similarities between the Big Apple and Nawa. Mud huts surrounded by ten-foot-tall mud walls defined Nawa's architecture. Vehicles drove mostly on deeply rutted dirt roads. The few asphalt roads in the district, cracked and brittle, had succumbed long ago to weather and wear. We were as likely to see people riding on camels or mules as in (or on) any type of motorized vehicle. The Helmand River to the district's east filled the maze of irrigation canals that in turn watered the corn, wheat, and poppy grown by the majority of the ninety thousand Nawa residents who were farmers. To the west was an expanse of reddish brown desert called the Dasht-e Margo— the "Desert of Death." It was used by weapons and drug smugglers shuttling their goods between northern Pakistan and districts in Helmand and beyond.

In some ways, the rural areas of Afghanistan were untouched by modern progress and technological advances, and the sights I was seeing were probably not much different from those the first American in the country saw over 170 years earlier.

[†] The total land area of Nawa is about 950 square miles, but the habitable area is only about 350 square miles.

In the late 1830s, a Pennsylvania-born Quaker named Josiah Harlan boldly strode into Afghanistan with the ambitious, but naïve, vision of becoming the country's king. Harlan became a globe-trotting explorer around 1820 after his fiancée broke his heart by canceling their pending nuptials because a more handsome suitor came along. Despite not having any formal training, he became a surgeon in the army of the British East India Company, serving in Burma and India before making his way to Afghanistan. He eventually found his way into the confidence of Shuja Shah Durrani, an exiled Afghan ruler who had a propensity for maiming servants who disappointed him. Harlan convinced Shuja he was working for the U.S. government and was recruiting a mercenary army to help Shuja regain his rule. Shuja embraced the idea, and Harlan assembled a menagerie of troops to fight on his behalf in a country that seemed always to be at war with itself.

Harlan's recruits included Hindus, Muslims, Sikhs, and even two deserters from the British Army, which had a strong presence in Afghanistan in the 1830s. The big war in the country, at that time, was between the Durrani and Barakzai tribes, and Harlan set off with his band of hired guns to overthrow Dost Mohammed Khan, the head of the Barakzai tribe. In a comical twist of loyalties, Harlan soon met and befriended Dost Mohammed and switched sides. Between battles with Shuja's forces (whom Harlan had initially assembled and trained), Harlan and Dost Mohammed spent their evenings discussing the state of global affairs, including the similarities between the three-branch systems of government in the U.S. and Afghanistan. When they weren't having these discussions, Dost Mohammed immersed himself in drunken lasciviousness, entertaining with members of his court a small harem of prostitutes who always traveled with them. The Quaker Harlan observed the unscrupulous proclivities of his new Muslim friend with discreet indifference.

Harlan began to fancy himself a modern-day Alexander the Great and somehow was able to add an elephant to his arsenal of beasts and weapons fighting on Dost Mohammed's behalf. In 1839, after achieving some military and civic successes in the country, Harlan made his way to Kabul, where he was confronted by Shuja Shah Durrani, his original Afghan protector. By this time, Shuja had been restored to power with the help of the British Army.[22] Given his shifting loyalty, it is not surprising that Harlan was no longer welcome in the country. What *is* surprising is that he was not summarily executed by Shuja for his betrayal. The restored Afghan ruler merely directed the British military to expel Harlan from the country, but before he left, Harlan was able to take a long hike and raise the Stars and Stripes 12,500 feet above sea level at the Khyber Pass in Afghanistan's Hindu Kush.[23] Although Harlan never achieved his initial dream of becoming Afghanistan's king, he was immortalized in fiction, serving as inspiration for Rudyard Kipling's short story "The Man Who Would Be King."

The Brits who expelled Josiah Harlan from Afghanistan in 1839 and reinstated Shuja Shah Durrani as the country's ruler expected Durrani to serve as their imperial puppet. However, they soon found themselves on the receiving end of Afghan brutality. Following a series of mishaps and an increase in hostility toward them from the local population, the British Army began evacuating Kabul in January 1842. They headed to their nearest garrison in Jalalabad, ninety miles away, on the other side of the narrow Khyber Pass.

Led by General George Elphinstone, nearly 4,500 British and Indian soldiers began the arduous journey, accompanied by 12,000 camp followers, many of whom were wives and children of the soldiers. The Afghan promise of safe passage they'd obtained was honored until it became convenient to surround and gun down the nearly defenseless Brits and Indians in a narrow mountain gorge. There was no escape or shelter from the fire the Afghans rained on them from above. Of the more than sixteen thousand who began the trek from Kabul, only *one* man, Dr. William Brydon, a surgeon in the British East India Company army, made it to the garrison in Jalalabad, exhausted and bloodied by his ordeal.[24]

Afghanistan has been a strategically vital but geographically inconvenient, and often perilous, stopover since the days when Alexander the Great's army swept through Asia. Today, its border is framed by former Soviet Socialist Republics to its north and Iran to its west. Pakistan stretches along 1,500 miles (about 2,400 kilometers) of its southern and eastern frontiers, along a border that was arbitrarily drawn in 1893 (and viewed by many as illegitimate) known as the "Durand Line." It even shares a 47-mile (76-kilometer) border with China at its northeastern tip, an area designated as a nature reserve by both countries.[†]

For centuries, the country was a buffer zone between the British and Russian Empires and an important hub along the Silk Road. It had once been a great and expansive empire, reaching into Delhi and stretching as far as Tibet under the reign in the mid-1700s of its revered Pashtun king, Ahmad Shah Durrani (Shuja's grandfather), who was called the "Pearl of Pearls" because of the prominent pearl earring that usually dangled from one ear.[25] Foreign armies came and went, trying to impose their own rule and borders, but usually ended up with little more than savage wounds, depleted forces, and crushed pride. The Treaty of Rawalpindi, signed in 1919 by Great

---

† This border also marks the greatest terrestrial time zone difference on earth, with a 4.5-hour difference between Afghanistan's UTC+3.5 hours and China's UTC+8 hours.

Britain and Afghanistan, formally granted independence to the country. One would think that they'd have rejoiced and reunited upon gaining their own sovereign status; however, the Afghans fought among themselves throughout several decades of civil war.

Americans came back to Afghanistan in the 1950s and 1960s. Although they were not as flamboyant as Josiah Harlan, their ambitious plans would have made him proud. Since the signing of the Treaty of Rawalpindi, Afghanistan had seen little foreign interference, military or otherwise. But America's post-World War II vision recognized Afghanistan as the vital hub that others had seen for thousands of years, and thus, the U.S. decided to plant a metaphorical flag in its dirt. The prestigious engineering firm Morrison-Knudsen, builder of the Hoover Dam and San Francisco's Bay Bridge, was commissioned by Afghanistan's government to undertake a wide-ranging infrastructure development program. In addition to roads, schools, and clinics, the country's leaders envisioned the Helmand River Valley becoming an agrarian wonderland. The vast network of canals that sprawled through Nawa and other districts in Helmand were designed and dug by Americans who could never have imagined that a little over half a century later, their work would provide cover and concealment for American Marines being shot at and returning fire.[26]

Life for the American expatriates living in Helmand Province was good. Although there were some unavoidably harsh aspects to living in a landlocked country in the middle of Asia, they enjoyed the bonds of a tight-knit community and comfortable living, with pools, decent schools, and open-minded Afghans. But things started to deteriorate, and Americans began to leave the country in the 1970s, after a series of coups, regime changes, and assassinations left the country in the hands of the communist People's Democratic Party of Afghanistan (the PDPA). Just after Christmas in 1979, Soviet military advisors swarmed in, followed by infantry divisions and aviation squadrons. It was an invasion that Soviet premier Leonid Brezhnev claimed would last just four weeks, though the Russian war there continued for nearly seven years after his death in 1982.[27]

Afghanistan became the hub of a proxy battle in the Cold War between the U.S. and the Soviet Union, even though the revolt that put the PDPA in charge of the country was more the culmination of a feud between rural Pashtuns (who ended up in power) and urban Uzbeks than it was a rejection of capitalism and the embrace of communism by the coup's leaders, as one Soviet ambassador tried to claim.[28]

In early 1980, two months after the Soviets invaded Afghanistan, a young and inexperienced group of American hockey players pulled off a stunning victory over the heavily favored Russian team in the Winter Olympics in Lake Placid, New York, in what has been immortalized as the "Miracle on Ice." A few months later, American Summer Olympic athletes were robbed of a chance to rub their athletic prowess in the face of the Russians when President Jimmy Carter made the feckless gesture of leading a coalition to boycott the 1980 Summer Games held in Moscow in protest of the Soviet Army's invasion of Afghanistan.[29]

In 1980, the Russians had the same imperial aspirations as Afghanistan's other invaders through the centuries, and they were indiscriminately cruel to the Afghans.[30] Amid the chaotic violence of Russia's occupation, Americans once again came to Afghanistan. But instead of adopting Josiah Harlan's flamboyance or the relative comfort of the adventurers of the 1950s and 1960s, this new wave of Americans came into the country covertly. They embedded themselves with the Afghan resistance fighters (the *mujahideen*) and trained them in the use of guerrilla tactics and unconventional warfare. The CIA-led effort, dubbed Operation Cyclone, included shady arms deals, back-channel bargaining through Pakistan's anticommunist government, and congressional appropriations shenanigans that put Stinger missiles—shoulder-launched heat-seeking rockets capable of shooting helicopters out of the sky—in the arsenal of the *mujahideen*.[31] With the CIA's help, Russia was forced to make a humiliating withdrawal from Afghanistan in early 1989, an event seen as part of the beginning of the end of the Soviet Empire.[32] However, Afghanistan's victory over the Russians came with a stunning cost. More than one million of its citizens were killed and two million others were made refugees in neighboring countries.

The Soviet withdrawal from Afghanistan was a short-lived triumph for the country. With the communist threat in Afghanistan gone, the U.S. no longer saw a need for its presence there. In retrospect, the Soviet defeat became a shallow victory for America. With the absence of a great power in the country, Saudi Arabia and Pakistan saw an opening to arm and educate jihadist leaders under a perverted sense of Sunni Islam, using proxy actors in order to maintain a thread of deniability regarding their direct influence. As a result, Islamic fundamentalism swept through Afghanistan's provinces, and leadership voids expanded. In the decade after the Soviets left, the world turned its attention to other events, like the fall of the Berlin Wall and speculation about whether protests in China's Tiananmen Square would transform that country.

Meanwhile, Afghanistan continued to fester.[33] By the mid-1990s, a group of Sunni Islamic fundamentalists calling itself the Taliban gained power in the country. The Taliban's takeover caught the U.S. off guard, but was also largely dismissed, as it was seen as just a continuation of the country's centuries-old tradition of fighting along tribal and religious divisions. In the mid- and late 1990s, a ruggedly handsome and eloquent warlord named Ahmad Shah Massoud, dubbed the "Lion of Panjshir," led a large force of resistance fighters against the Taliban. He was murdered two days before 9/11.[34] In October 2001, a month after Massoud's death, Americans once again set foot in Afghanistan.

Seven and a half years later, I was one of them.

CHAPTER 7
BADGES? WE DON'T NEED NO STINKIN' BADGES![35]

At his best, man is the noblest of all animals;
separated from law and justice, he is the worst.

—ARISTOTLE

JUNE 8, 2009

I FIRST SAW THEM WHEN THEY WERE ABOUT TWO HUNDRED AND FIFTY meters away and had them in my sights by the time they'd closed the distance to about one hundred and fifty meters. They couldn't go very fast on the heavily rutted dirt road without their motorcycle tipping over, but they were cruising along at a steady pace, headed straight toward us.

They'd be on top of our position in twenty seconds, max.

The driver and his passenger had such a relaxed, almost distracted manner about themselves that it seemed inconceivable they were on a suicide mission. Yet there they were. The driver had an AK-47 slung over his chest, its pistol grip within easy reach of his right hand. Over his light green *shalwar kamiz*, the typical outfit of Afghan men, he wore a vest with multiple ammunition pouches, which I was certain were filled with extra magazines—or explosives he would detonate when he got close enough. The similarly dressed passenger grasped the driver's shoulder with one hand while his other held a loaded RPG. Their intent seemed clear to me.

The shit's going down, I thought to myself, instinctively checking that the magazine in my M4 was properly seated. I was determined to kill them before they got close enough to kill us.

Eighteen more seconds.

I had gone to this Afghan police outpost with another Marine, two British soldiers, and a squad of Gurkhas[†] who were part of the British Army contingent in Nawa. Their task that day was to provide some basic skills training to the dozen Afghan police officers assigned there.

The police outpost was a crude, almost primitive structure. It was roughly forty by fifty feet, surrounded by dirt-filled barriers standing about ten feet high, with heavily sandbagged wooden-framed guard posts in three of its corners. It was at the dead end of the road, close to the western bank of the Helmand River. Its northern edge looked over a large field that was irrigated by an array of canals. Those canals were the lifeblood of Nawa's farmers, who depended on them to water their crops, but they were also a great hiding place for Taliban insurgents, who took potshots at the

---

† The Gurkhas are a contingent of the British Army comprised of Nepalese nationals, analogous in some ways to the relationship between the French Foreign Legion and the French military. Boasting the motto "Better to die than be a coward," they are said to be some of the toughest and most fearless soldiers in the world (see, e.g., David Choi, "This is arguably the toughest soldier in the world," *Business Insider*, June 20, 2016).

outpost most nights. A few large trees butted up against the outside walls of the place, providing some natural shade over the mostly roofless structure when the sun was positioned just right. A simply constructed room used as sleeping quarters stood along one wall, with a dozen worn out cots splayed in disorderly rows inside. A cooking area was opposite from that. Pieces of worn cardboard and plywood scraps were strewn about the dirt floor in a futile attempt to keep the area free from Helmand's omnipresent dust and mud. Trash and food scraps littered the ground, accumulating in corners when swept up by the breezes that came off the nearby river.

The cops assigned to this outpost were, for the most part, an uninspiring bunch. They ranged from a husky older man, at least sixty, whose weathered face and pure white beard could have made him a contender in one of Key West's Hemingway look-alike contests, to a young man who claimed to be twenty but whose smooth, whiskerless face made him appear not a day over fifteen. None of them ever had much—if any—formal police training. It seemed that the main qualification for a Nawa cop was to be a friend of a friend of the shady police chief and to have an ability to withstand the mundane daily routine at this obscure outpost. Their daily wage was about five or six dollars, which was average for many rural parts of Helmand Province, for those who were able to get a job. There were widely circulated stories throughout the district that some of the more larcenous cops supplemented their income by imposing a "tax" on residents they encountered. Quite a few of them had homemade tattoos on their hands and forearms, and most smoked cigarettes at a steady rate. Several large marijuana plants growing on the outer edges of their outpost suggested that, when the sun went down and they were *really* bored, they passed the time getting high as well.

Most of them had been issued a uniform: matching bluish gray shirt and trousers and a pair of black leather boots. On that day, some of the uniformed cops had stripped off their uniform shirts and lounged around in sweaty white tank tops. They displayed varying degrees of attentiveness as the Gurkhas gave their lesson.

While the training was in progress, I had strolled about fifteen meters away to stand under a small tree that provided a bit of shade from the late afternoon sun. I was watching a swarm of ants devour the carcass of a small bird at the base of the tree when the sputter of a motorcycle coming in my direction on the long, straight road caught my attention.

Sixteen more seconds.

My eyes widened and my guts twisted with the realization of what was about to happen. Neither the motorcycle driver nor his passenger appeared to see me in the sparse concealment the tree's shade provided, so I was sure I'd be able to get a few shots off before they got much closer. Considering their direct angle of approach and knowing the power of my rifle's rounds, I thought I might be able to get them both with one rapid burst aimed at the driver's chest. The rounds would tear straight through his back and into his passenger's chest as well. Before dropping to one knee, giving myself a firmer firing position, I turned my head in the direction of the Gurkhas and screamed, "Heads up! Heads up! Heads up!"

Fourteen seconds.

Immediately after my shouting, I heard a scurry of activity behind me: running feet, clattering gear, frantic shouts. I paid it little mind, assuming the Gurkhas and Afghan policemen had seen what was bearing down on us and were bracing for the violence they were about to witness.

Twelve seconds.

Ignoring the commotion behind me, I pulled my rifle to my shoulder and peered through its scope. I found my target and aligned the red upside-down "V" to the middle of the motorcycle driver's chest.

Ten seconds.

I had my target in sight. By this time, they were no more than seventy-five meters away. Not quite "whites of their eyes" close, but close enough to shoot—indeed, closer than I would have preferred. I had flipped my safety switch to burst mode, which would fire three rounds in quick succession with each trigger pull. My trigger finger was primed to fire, and I was quickly exhaling through my mouth as I focused on the slow-moving target coming toward me.

Eight seconds.

At the moment I was about to pull my trigger and kill the oncoming suicide attackers, a heavy hand pushed the front of my rifle down. I heard a shout of "Stop! Stop! Stop!"

It was the Gurkhas' platoon leader. As I looked to him in bewilderment, I could see that his eyes were wide with panic as he yelled, "They're cops!" Then, seeing my confused stare and knowing that the danger had passed, he quietly repeated, "They're cops."

A few seconds later the driver cheerily tooted the horn on his motorcycle, drove past me, and parked the vehicle just inside the outpost's walls. He seemed oblivious to what had almost happened to him.

"We've got to get all these guys some uniforms," said Captain Pram, the Gurkhas' platoon leader, shaking his head with a relieved smile. "That was fucking close."

He had stepped away from the training his soldiers were providing to grab a smoke and had been standing just a few meters behind me when I first spotted the motorcycle ambling toward us. He'd recognized the motorcycle driver, one of the police sergeants, from other visits to the outpost. The two cops had gone out to buy (or more likely, steal) some food for the policemen's dinner that night. Now, as they walked into the compound, interrupting the

Gurkhas' lesson, the passenger proudly held up a small green canvas bag from which four confused chickens peeked out.

Inside the compound, the chickens were set loose, giving them a few more hours of free range before they became the evening's meal. A few of the other policemen chuckled as they spoke with the police sergeant and pointed in my direction, no doubt describing his close call with death at the hands of a newly arrived U.S. Marine.

The Gurkhas and I stayed for dinner that night, honored guests of the Afghan cops. The four chickens, their heads lopped off, had been diced into a mix of rice, onions, and spices. Out of a makeshift brick oven came big slabs of flatbread we used to scoop up our meal. Cans of lukewarm orange soda were passed around, and I savored the heavy sugary flavor and fizz amid the heat and humidity of the Helmand summer. One of the Gurkhas noted that most of the cops seemed to prefer the MREs we gave them to the meal their colleagues had prepared. He also predicted the inevitable diarrhea many of us who were eating the Afghan-prepared meal would experience in a few hours.

Before the sun set, we loaded ourselves into our vehicles to drive back to Patrol Base Jaker. The police sergeant whom I had mistaken for a suicide attacker and had almost killed just a few hours earlier was perched in one of the outpost's guard towers, puffing on a cigarette and placidly staring off into space, his AK-47 slung across his chest as it had been when I first saw him.

I shouted up to him, "*Hodai paman*," patting my hand across my heart in a typical Pashtun farewell.

Blowing out a lungful of smoke, he looked at me and smiled, made his hand into the shape of a pistol, and said, "Bang, bang!"

I repeated the gesture back, smiling to myself at this story's happy ending.

CHAPTER 8
THAT FIRST NIGHT

The Army might screw you and your girlfriend might dump you and the enemy might kill you, but the shared commitment to safeguard one another's lives is nonnegotiable and only deepens with time. The willingness to die for another person is a form of love that even religions fail to inspire, and the experience of it changes a person profoundly.
—SEBASTIAN JUNGER, *War*

JUNE 21, 2009

THEY KNEW WE WERE COMING. IN FACT, WE MADE A POINT OF making sure they knew we were coming. Before the Marines from 1/5 arrived, the fifty British Army soldiers at Patrol Base Jaker, whom we'd soon relieve, told the Afghan locals they met that more NATO troops were headed to Nawa to make the district safer. They said another fifty—possibly one hundred—would come, deliberately keeping the number much lower than the number that would actually arrive.

"Watch yourself," the patrolling Brits said with a coaxing wink to the locals, knowing that even if they weren't talking to an insurgent, word would probably get back to one. "These new troops are Americans, part of their military called 'Marines.' They might be a bit rough around the edges, but they like to fight, and they're pretty damn good at doing that."

If that message didn't get through, the one delivered on a partially moonlit June night a few weeks later did. The thump and rattle of helicopters punctured the night silence as they hovered, touched down for a few moments and jerked skyward again, dropping high-temperature flares behind them before banking right and then left to avoid fire from an insurgent lurking in the trees near our patrol base. Those helos' presence made it unmistakably clear that we were coming.

Only the lead element of the battalion had landed that night, joining a handful of Marines who had come to Nawa a few weeks earlier. They included the headquarters staff, communications technicians, an intelligence team, a few administrative clerks, some snipers, and a handful of other Marines such as my Civil Affairs team. At Camp Leatherneck, or back home in the U.S., most of these Marines might be referred to as "pogues," especially by the grunts in the rifle companies who puff up their chests and often joke about those who do desk jobs in air-conditioned offices well away from the front lines. But in reality, and especially in a war zone, every Marine, no matter what their role, is a rifleman first. The operations plan called for the battalion's lead element, composed mostly of these pogues, to get settled at Patrol Base Jaker in order to set the stage for and support the multipronged push into Nawa and other districts in Helmand Province that would occur a few weeks later. We knew the insurgents couldn't ignore the all-night rumble of dozens of helicopters dropping off the 150 Marines and their combat equipment in the middle of the district center. The message would spread: the Marines are here.

Even at midnight, the oven-hot, mid-June air, moist from the vapor sweating off the Helmand River two kilometers to our east, embraced us and gave the fine, sandy dust kicked up from the helo rotors something to cling to. As the last bird banked away just before 5:00 a.m., the sun peeked over the treeless rust-colored hills east of the river, revealing, for the first time to most of the Marines, the village and fields surrounding the patrol base.

There was little time for idleness. The practice of warfare in the twenty-first century is as much a technological as it is a human endeavor, even on the front lines. In that first light, Marines set about making the place their home. Satellite transmitters and radio antennas needed to go up, a motion-sensing device with an infrared camera fixed atop a fifty-foot-tall tower—called a G-BOSS—needed to be assembled, and GPS links to a troop-monitoring system called a Blue Force Tracker needed to be synchronized. Diesel-fueled generators hummed around the clock, keeping all this technology running.

We moved around the patrol base with rifles strapped across our backs and pouches with a few extra magazines of ammunition on our hips. The Marines not working a radio or running wires, setting up antennas, or tweaking satellite beacons wore their battle gear and stood behind a machine gun in one of the towers or other posts around the base, keeping a focused eye out for any threat that might come our way. The Taliban knew we were here now, and we were ready for them.

"Keep eyes on the tree lines," ordered a senior NCO to the Marines manning the west-facing posts late in the afternoon of that first busy day. He knew his tactics, honed during prior tours in Afghanistan and Iraq. He also knew the Taliban weren't fools and had some tactics of their own as well. The late afternoon sun was two fingers above those tree lines to the west, causing a blinding span of light to ripple through their leaves and create a perfect screen for a fleet-footed insurgent to settle into a good firing spot, relatively obscured from view.

A rocket-propelled grenade (RPG) moves fast. By the time you see its contrail, it has usually hit or sailed past its mark. The guy who shot the first one at us—the signal to his buddies to light up our patrol base—had bad aim or a faulty launcher. Whatever the case, that initial RPG, which was fired at about 6:00 p.m., went high and wide of its intended mark. The distinct whistle-and-rip—*shhh-hhrrreeeeeeeeettttt*—may have zipped over our barricades, landing in an empty compound on the other side of the patrol base, but it set off the team of AK-47 gunners hunkered in the canal by the second tree line. Those gunners fired away at our patrol base, not so much with deliberate aim, but to hurl rounds at our barn-sized structure and dirt-filled barriers. The spray of bullets smacking against the walls inches from our heads brought to mind a remark a Desert Storm veteran made to a reporter inquiring about the fear of impending combat. He said that he wasn't worried about the bullet that has his name on it. "It's the one addressed 'to whom it may concern' that bothers me."[36]

The insurgents in the tree line certainly knew the troops who had been on the ground for less than a day would respond, but they likely hadn't anticipated the intense martial spirit of a Marine. While some Marines had spent their day setting up antennas and satellite receivers, others had confirmed the sight pictures of the .50-caliber and MK19 machine guns emplaced around the patrol base, noting the range and direction to key target points in our fields of view. Three 81 mm mortar tubes were oiled and calibrated to drop high-explosive rounds along the second tree line. Two of our snipers were perched in what looked to an unwitting observer like an empty guard hut at the far end of the LZ. We were ready.

Seconds after that first RPG round screamed over our heads, two .50-caliber machine guns began dancing their rounds into the base of the far tree line, mincing their way through branches and tossing up the dried mud berm of the canal as if it were made of brittle clay. A moment later, the MK19s began belching 40 mm grenades along the same path. The metallic *chinka-chinka-chinka-chinka-chinka* of five-round bursts leaving their muzzles was followed seconds later by the *crump-crump-crump-crump-crump* of their explosive-tipped rounds finding their mark. The big guns weren't going to get all the action, though. The green tracers from each fifth round in the belts of the 7.62 mm M240G machine guns traversing the width of the canal marked a point for any Marine with an M4 to aim his fire. For good measure, the mortar squad started dropping high explosive rounds on their preset targets, the whistling shriek of the rounds on their descent adding their distinctive tone to the clamor around us.

And that was just the commotion to our west. The insurgents had put a few teams to our north and south, tucked into the walls and corners of some abandoned mud huts. A few of the bolder ones took positions on the roofs of the huts, not realizing that the slightly higher perspective of the Marines on post and the sun's direct glare from the west provided a crystal clear view of them. The insurgents' harassing fire was returned at least tenfold. A few of them, who sensed they were outgunned, ran from their firing positions, some not far or for long.

"Take him, take him, watch my tracers!" shouted one of the junior officers as he fired downrange. The first five rounds in his magazine, loaded with tracers, pinpointed where the other Marines should aim. The insurgent in the Marines' sights sprinted away from the tree line clutching an RPG. He was one of those who didn't get very far.

A rifle platoon from Charlie Company, which was part of the first wave into Nawa, had set up in an abandoned school five hundred meters southeast of the patrol base and was engaged at almost the same time. They, too, had begun setting up and reinforcing their positions before the sun rose. The insurgents who attacked the school grounds waited for the fight at the main patrol base to reach a fevered pitch before making their play. Perhaps because of the Marines' nearly immediate response and its sheer ferocity, the fight by the school lasted only about twenty minutes. Then the attackers wisely decided they would prefer to fight another day and hastily made use of the lush foliage and orchards they were firing from to retreat.

As the sun sank below the tree line, we donned NVGs to look for remaining targets. The insurgents slowed their onslaught, taking more deliberate and less frequent shots at us. Thermal sights on a Javelin missile picked up a cluster of three or four men with weapons planning their next move a few hundred meters from our patrol base. They were in some bushes about twenty meters away from an abandoned compound close to the tree line from which we had been taking fire. They would have heard the hiss-like *shhhhwwwwwooooottt* from the rocket's launch and the rhythmic *thwock-thwock-thwock* of the charges detonating off its wire-guided system as it raged toward them. But it's doubtful they had time to think about much else, as the ground beneath their feet swelled and churned from the impact of the Javelin's explosion. One or two might have limped away, but none ran.

Potshots continued throughout the night. We popped up an occasional illumination flare to keep the insurgents wary and to watch for any suspicious shadows in the tree lines and the grooves of the recently plowed wheat field bordering the outer wall of the patrol base. Watch rotations were assigned to pick up on the next attack. It never came, but we were ready if it did. No Marine was far from a weapon or a firing position. We propped our heads against our Kevlar helmets for pillows. Our flak jackets, spread out on the concrete floor, sufficed as mattresses. Captains and corporals, lieutenants and sergeants, lay side by side at various posts, catching what little well-deserved sleep they could.

The nighttime humidity swept in and over us, pushing the cordite smell from thousands of spent rounds into our sweat-soaked clothes. The night turned silent, interrupted only by the occasional pop of an 81 mm flare round or boots scraping across the rough concrete floor, jingling spent brass rounds that littered the ground. A few Marines snored.

The next morning began like the one before. We still had to get settled in our new home and prepare the place and ourselves for the bigger operation planned to occur in early July. But there was a swagger now. The insurgents had tested us, and we had shown them we knew how—and would never hesitate—to respond.

"That first night . . ." became the baseline for just about every other engagement we had. It served as a barometer for the Marines who joined us later and a story to tell the clean-uniformed "combat tourists" arriving on a short trip from Camp Leatherneck, or the journalists and dignitaries who wanted to get a peek at the pointy edge of the spear we commanded months later. Those three words were a code phrase for pride, belonging, and brotherhood among those who were there. Some wouldn't have the chance to get outside the wire many more times on this deployment because their skills were required in different ways. But they were there that first night. The night the Taliban knew we were coming. The night they wanted to test us. The night we let them know the U.S. Marines had arrived.

That first night.

CHAPTER 9
ENVY

He was frightened beyond any fear he had ever known. But this brilliant and intense
fear, this terrible here and now, combined with the crucial significance of every
movement of his body, pushed him over a barrier whose existence he had not known
about until this moment. He gave himself over completely to the god of war within him.
—KARL MARLANTES, *Matterhorn*

JUNE 24, 2009

WITH THE BENEFIT OF HINDSIGHT, IT MADE SENSE THAT WE WOULD
get hit when we did. For the past week, we'd been pushing the "security bubble" around Patrol Base Jaker farther than the platoon of
Brits who manned the remote outpost had in months. Each day, we
pushed out another thousand meters or farther, in every direction.
We were sort of itching for a fight. We were Marines, after all, and we
wanted to force the local insurgents either to engage us or fall back
to areas where they thought we wouldn't venture. There, the rest of
our battalion would catch up to them in another week, when our
major operation kicked off in full force. Most days we got the fights
we were looking for, though they were often short and sporadic,
more like harassing sniper fire than decisive engagements.

At 4:00 p.m., Lieutenant Shawn Connor, a former sergeant who earned his rank through a highly selective commissioning program, gave a patrol brief to his platoon and the "straphangers" joining the patrol, which included my Civil Affairs team. Several of the platoon's NCOs were on their second or third deployment, but many of the Marines listening to the brief were eighteen, nineteen, or twenty years old—not yet of age to legally buy a beer, but old enough to wield and use the armaments of war. Most of them had never been outside the United States, let alone to a place like Afghanistan. They were from Texas, California, Ohio, Arizona, and Connecticut—from big cities, rural farmlands, and quaint university towns. A few had some college credits; others had shipped off to boot camp the day after their high school graduation. They were jocks, geeks, hipsters, surfer dudes, and rednecks. The assembled group was mostly white, but with a sizeable number of blacks and Hispanics too. They chose to serve for a variety and a combination of reasons: patriotism, adventurousness, economic necessity, and family tradition. But the fact was they had *chosen* to serve, and they now found themselves part of the tight-knit cadre of warriors fighting in one of their country's wars. A casual observer might suggest they represented a cross section of America, and in some ways that was true. The difference was that these Americans were tightly coiled and keenly observant trained killers. In fact, in a week's time, several of them had proven to be more than just *trained* killers. When their presence of mind mattered most and their adrenaline-fueled bodies needed them to shoot straight and true, they did so unhesitatingly. I was in good company.

When the lieutenant finished his brief, the sounds of our prepatrol rituals filled the air with a snappy cadence. There was the rip of Velcro as Marines adjusted their body armor; the tap and thunk of loaded magazines knocking on a Kevlar helmet to seat the rounds; the hissing, beeping, and squawking of handheld radios; the snap of carabiners securing rifle straps to our gear; the high-pitched whine of a minesweeping detector starting up; and the oily, metallic slide and click of a machine-gun charging handle securing a belt of ammunition in place all made it clear we had serious business ahead of us.

Five minutes later we were given the order, "Let's go!" Forty young men who were loaded up with testosterone and firepower stepped through the gate of our patrol base and into the quasi-medieval terrain of the district we had come from the other side of the world to protect.

We headed north from where we were, then wound our way through narrow pathways between the tall mud walls surrounding residential compounds along the small irrigation canals branching off the Helmand River. We skirted fields whose winter crops of wheat or poppy had recently been harvested. The platoon's tactics were tight and smart: eyes and ears alert for anything out of the ordinary. We kept our distance, not bunching up, moving like the ebb and flow of an accordion as the terrain required. When we came to an open field, we crossed in a "bounding overwatch" where the first Marines at the crossing took a knee and observed the site while other Marines ventured through the open area, then turned to secure the path of the Marines coming their way. It was a leapfrogging technique, but with guns, and where the consequences of fucking up were far more dire than in any playground game.

The local kids we encountered greeted us with curiosity and good cheer; many of the adults displayed indifference or even a sneer of derision. These reactions were probably the same as what the Brits and Russians who had come and gone in the decades, even centuries, before us had experienced.

Part of our patrol mission was to engage with the locals. I had a chance to break the ice with some leery farmers by showing them the magic of the Polaroid camera I carried with me, leaving them with an instant photo that I would sign and date in the big white space on the picture's bottom edge. For those we stopped to chat with, we were an excuse to take a much-needed break from the arduous task of plowing and churning their fields by hand. There were few tractors or plows in Nawa, so farmers worked in pairs or groups of three, breaking up clumps of soil and tamping down small paths of mud to create ten-by-ten-meter grids for their crops. The grid system facilitated efficient irrigation and movement among the plantings. Building the mud paths was grueling: one man drove a shovel into the dirt, and his partner helped him lift it once it was filled, using a rope tied to its shaft. Together they would dump the load onto the path, where another farmer tamped it down with a trowel or just his bare hands.

Ninety minutes into the patrol, the heat, humidity, and strain of carrying sixty or more pounds of gear on our backs had every Marine's uniform soaked through. Streaks of sweat trickled down our arms, necks, and faces. The rim of my glasses repeatedly caught a bead of perspiration from my brow, which then rolled down my lenses and blurred my vision before I could wipe it away with a dirty, damp cloth. We were still about three kilometers from our objective, where we would spend the night. It would take us another hour to get there. We kept a rhythmic sequence in our step, and maintained our sharp senses, but if the Taliban were watching, they could see fatigue setting in.

The sun was beginning its descent, giving us a reprieve from its direct rays. The half-light noticeably cooled the air a few degrees. Puffs of steam rose off the bodies of the patrol team due to the temperature change. It lent us an ethereal look as we trudged toward our bivouac site. We came to the western edge of a large square field, about 150 meters on each side. We needed to cross its southern fringe to reach a dirt road that ran north and south. The grid pattern of the recently harvested and plowed field indicated that its owner was ready to plant corn soon. Several piles of wheat chaff as big as cars dotted the field. Very little went to waste in Afghanistan: this chaff would soon be collected and mixed with mud and mortar to make bricks and to patch up walls around the village compounds. When dry, the mixture was as solid as concrete.

A compound sat on the northern edge of the field, its long outer wall stretching much of the field's length. A grove of trees on its southern border, lushly green from the water in a narrow irrigation ditch, provided a shady respite for three young boys tending a pair of cows and a herd of about a dozen goats. They stared at us with placid eyes and almost aloof expressions. A neglected mud wall about three feet high, which appeared to have been part of a goat pen in better days, was on the far side of the field.

The squad leader I was with motioned to me and three others to take a knee and cover the movement of the first group of four Marines as they crossed. I squatted by one of the small berms that formed the grid in the field, reflecting that it only provided about twelve inches of cover. The first group of Marines reached the thick mud wall on the other side, posted themselves safely behind it, and motioned for my group to head their way. I stood and began to move toward them.

When I was about a third of the way across the field, moving along the crest of a mud-packed berm, the three young shepherds, who moments earlier had idled lazily in the shade of the trees, began earnestly swatting the rumps of their livestock with saplings to move them in the opposite direction from where we were headed.

My translator, Hank, shot a question their way. They replied, and he spun to me and said, "Jagran Gus, we should move faster there," pointing to the low wall where the Marines covering our movement were crouching behind.

"Huh?" I replied, but before he could repeat himself, the air around my head suddenly heated up. I heard zipping noises as something streaked by my face. They were followed immediately by the crackling snaps of AK-47 shots. I stood in place and watched Hank dive facedown into the lowest groove of dirt he could find. His backpack was stuffed with a down sleeping bag that was slightly visible even if he wasn't. I turned to look at the Marines who had my back as they unleashed a fusillade of rounds toward the compound where the fire was coming from. My corpsman, Doc Velez, scampered toward the nearby grove of trees to take cover.

My senses instantly became more acute, and I could smell the fresh dirt being kicked up around me from the impact of bullets. My exhaled breath sounded like a gush of wind coming from my throat. I saw Marines around me moving swiftly into positions from which they could take cover and return fire. While they appeared to be effortlessly gliding, I somehow felt heavy and immovable. The sweat that soaked my uniform from the intense heat we had been contending with suddenly seemed to chill me.

I vividly remember that one of my first thoughts was about statistics. Specifically, whether I was about to become one. I reasoned that if I stayed put, I would die. If I moved, I might not. So I decided to move. Just then, a man's torso popped above the top of the compound wall. He hoisted an RPG to his shoulder, and a thudding clap followed by a shrieking bolt headed my way. I was already running when the rocket careened into the soft muddy dirt behind me, and maybe I just tripped, but the explosion seemed to toss me into the air before I landed squarely on my side, my left elbow absorbing my full weight. It felt as if my shoulder had been jolted out of its socket. My entire left arm filled with a queer tingly sensation. Rolling onto my back, I looked toward two Marines well positioned behind the safety of a downed tree about thirty feet behind me. I tried to make myself small, as more hot zipping rounds flew over my head.

"Can you see those fuckers?" I shouted, jerking my thumb in the direction of the compound just as I felt a piercing heat smack my right hand. I blinked, then looked dumbstruck at the small hole in my flesh, but I was relieved to see that there was no exit hole. It was a ricochet. A small piece of twisted metal stuck out of the fresh wound as it started to throb and ooze blood. I needed to keep moving.

I ambled to my feet, my legs rubbery from fatigue and fear, and hustled over to where Hank had been lying in the dirt.

Before becoming a translator for us, Hank had been a judge in one of Afghanistan's northern provinces. That was, until being a government employee became a death sentence. In the short time we had worked together, he had already proven himself unflappable and poised, even if his English phrasing was occasionally a bit awkward.

"Are you okay?" I asked, sprawling on the ground beside him.

"I'm no problem, but is not good time right now . . . ," he managed to say just as more bullets came our way. *Zip-crack, zip-crack, zip-crack, thwack-thwack-thwack.* They made contact with Hank's exposed backpack. A cloud of gray and white down feathers drifted above us. His sleeping bag had been shredded by a burst of rounds intended for our heads.

"Go to that wall, *NOW!*" I shouted at him, jumping to my feet and extending my left hand to help him up.

"Is good plan. Yes, I go there," he replied, grabbing my wrist. His grip sent a jolt of pain through my already tingling shoulder as he heaved himself up and ran toward the safety of the mud wall where a team of Marines was still laying down fire. A trail of down feathers wafted behind him as he moved.

As Hank reached the wall, I saw that about six other Marines had made their way behind its thick safety too. They took turns popping up and firing bursts at the flash points coming from the small openings in the compound wall. Then they'd duck back down to take a breath and move to a different firing point. As long as they were behind that wall, they were bulletproof. Covered in sweat, mud, and some stray goose feathers, I stood exposed in an open field while some assholes seemed intent on killing me. I envied the Marines who were safe behind the cover of that thick wall as I'd never envied anyone in my entire life.

At some point in the chaos, Doc Velez crawled to where Hank and I had been standing. "Sprint to that pile, Doc!" I told him, pointing to a heap of chaff midway between us and the wall where our fellow Marines were. We both darted as fast as we could toward it, though I paused momentarily after seeing a bearded head pop up over the opposing wall. Armed with an AK-47 he sent a wild spray of rounds in our direction. I squeezed off five rounds back at him and thought briefly of the cliché about the guy who couldn't hit the broad side of a barn. My heavy breathing and mud-caked glasses threw off my aim, but thankfully my assailant ducked his head down long enough for me to finish my sprint to the chaff pile. I rolled into its soft mass and was instantly covered by dry, scratchy wheat scraps that clung like burrs to my sweat-soaked uniform and sank inside my shirt and boots.

I took a smoke grenade from my hip pouch and told Doc Velez to get ready to run. He looked at me dubiously as I pulled the pin on the grenade, tossed it to the far side of the chaff pile we were hiding behind, and waited for the heat from the grenade to ignite the dry wheat scraps. I expected the combination of smoke from the grenade and burning chaff pile to provide dense enough concealment for us to run the last fifty meters from where we were to the wall where the other Marines were posted.

The chaff pile ignited quicker than I had expected, and a beautiful dense cloud of gray smoke, tinged purple from my smoke grenade, drifted gently *west* on a mild breeze coming off the nearby Helmand River. The wall we needed to get to stood fifty meters to the *east*.

"Fuck it, Doc, let's go!" I ordered, and we dashed away from the flaming smoke pile. My left arm was numb, my right hand was throbbing, my legs felt like Jell-O, and the sixty pounds of gear I carried on my back made me feel like an oaf lumbering through mud clods, but nothing was going to stop me from getting to my destination. I gritted my teeth and ran as if my life depended on it—which it did. When I reached the wall, I hurdled over the lowest spot I could find, took a knee and a long pull of water, squeezed the small piece of metal out of the swelling hole in my hand, and watched the Marines trade potshots with the insurgents still holed up in the compound.

"Sweet fire, sir," one of them said to me with a sly grin, nodding his head toward the flaming mass of wheat chaff I had torched. As he held his fist up for a bump, I thought to myself, there was no other place in the world I would rather be.

I was in good company.

CHAPTER 10
THE GOVERNOR ARRIVES

Citizenship is an attitude, a state of mind, an emotional conviction
that the whole is greater than the part . . . and that the part should
be humbly proud to sacrifice itself that the whole may live.
—COLONEL DUBOIS, in Robert A. Heinlein, *Starship Troopers*

IN THE SUMMER OF 2009, NAWA HAD BEEN VIOLENT, UNGOVERNED, and lawless for nearly five years. Thirty miles southwest of Helmand Province's capital, Lashkar Gah, and home to about ninety thousand Afghans, Nawa was part of what was once, in the 1950s and 1960s, called "Little America." But in more recent times, it had seen the exodus of the Afghan government officials living there and others with the means to leave for safer places. Taliban-led insurgents were well entrenched, bullying the remaining residents out of their meager livelihoods, imposing "taxes," and threatening or inflicting violence on anyone who questioned their legitimacy.

The insurgents in Nawa operated logistical supply lines that funneled weapons and IEDs to other terrorists in Afghanistan and beyond. They also operated an extensive heroin production business with near impunity. The Taliban's strict piety frowned on drug use, which was an offense punishable by death. But they had a sense of capitalistic opportunism as well and thought nothing of concocting a religiously justified rationale for *selling* heroin while not using it themselves. In their view, the ends justified the means, and the money raised from their drug trade would be used for other "holy" purposes such as buying guns and making explosives to kill their enemies.

The fifty British and thirty Afghan Army soldiers manning the patrol base in Nawa's district center since mid-2008 could only venture a few hundred meters from its relative security without being engaged in a firefight. Insurgent gunmen ready to attack kept a constant watch on their movements from nearby tree lines or empty compounds.

In July 2009, the arrival of a reinforced infantry battalion of nearly one thousand Marines brought a much-needed peace to the district, allowing Nawa's residents to reengage in commerce and travel about more freely. One of the Marines' objectives was to set the stage for GIROA, the Government of the Islamic Republic of Afghanistan, to establish itself as leading the district. A district governor in Nawa was one of the first critical actors needed to help achieve this objective.

Haji Abdul Manaf was appointed Nawa's governor by the Karzai government under a cloud of mystery and with a questionable résumé that included an abrupt dismissal as the governor of another district in Afghanistan for unknown reasons. In mid-July 2009, Manaf stepped off a NATO helicopter that could land only under the cover of darkness because of the continuing threat to low-flying helicopters from machine-gun and rocket fire. He was not just arriving, he said, but was in fact *returning* to Nawa, claiming to have spent time in the district fighting Russians among its vast canals in the 1980s. His claim was impossible to verify but we accepted it at face value, with a bit of skepticism.

His appointment came with many risks and little material reward. The "governor's mansion" was nothing more than an old and crumbling cement goat barn with some hasty patches and strings of generator-powered lights duct-taped to the walls. It was sparsely furnished with cracked and mismatched plastic tables and chairs, and thin, dirty mattresses on the floor in the "bedroom suite." He traveled constantly with the Marines—usually on foot, but sometimes in their armored vehicles—to attend meetings at the outer reaches of the district.

Despite the initial reservations of the NATO staff and Marines about Manaf's qualifications and background, he soon proved himself to be a trusted and dedicated ally. Though not entirely effective or organized, he was always optimistic and engaged. Gregarious and avuncular, he was a natural politician, enjoying the attention and well-wishes of his constituents as he traversed the district. He enthralled the generals, congressional delegations, and reporters who flocked to Nawa to witness firsthand an Afghan success story. Manaf often held court over dinners of lamb or goat cooked over rice and eaten by hand while seated on the ground. He was always beaming and backslapping amid the raucous jokes and comments typical of men-at-arms serving in harm's way. His English was limited, but one phrase he uttered frequently, without the aid of an interpreter and with true sincerity, always flattered the Marines around him: "You are like my brother."

Even with his jocular demeanor, he understood the gravity and strategic significance of his role and his district. He worked tirelessly with the Marines and NATO civilian advisors, local tribal leaders, merchants, mullahs, and citizens, hearing out their concerns and promising (perhaps sometimes overpromising) his best efforts to continue Nawa's progress.

Manaf particularly loved the Marines and was awestruck that these young warriors had left their families to fight for people they had never met in a foreign land. So it was no surprise that when a young Marine was killed by an IED, Manaf asked to come to the field memorial service and say some words of thanks, translated by one of our interpreters, for the sacrifice made by this young man for the people of Afghanistan. After Manaf made his comments, he turned to the helmet, boots, and bayoneted rifle signifying the presence of our fallen brother, straightened his back, and made a crisp, solemn salute. Earlier in the day, he had asked for and received a lesson in military saluting protocol from one of the battalion's sergeants.

I saw that salute again a few months later. As my tour of duty came to an end and Nawa continued to thrive, the helicopter that would take me on the first leg of the long trip back home landed in the middle of the afternoon in an open field outside our patrol base. Haji Abdul Manaf joined a group wishing me well. He grasped my hand and held it as I lumbered along, carrying seven months of equipment and memories to the waiting helicopter. Stopping outside the range of the helo's rotor noise, he turned to me, grasped my shoulders, and said in his best broken English, "Jagran Gus, you are like my brother." Then he stood tall and saluted with perfect precision.

CHAPTER 11
LINGUA FRANCA

Come, let us go down and confuse their language so they will not understand each other.
—GENESIS 11:7

THE U.S. MILITARY DEPLOYS WITH SOME OF THE MIGHTIEST WEAP-
onry, technically advanced communications systems, innovative
vehicles, and best-trained personnel of any nation in the world.
This arsenal of weapons, equipment, and warriors has served it well,
especially since the beginning of a century that has seen U.S. forces
deploy to scores of countries. These deployments include peace-
keeping operations, combat missions, humanitarian relief work,
postings to permanent bases outside the U.S., and port calls to
friendly host nations. The list of countries where U.S. forces have
roamed reads like the final exam from a geography bee: Afghanistan,
Bosnia, Djibouti, East Timor, Georgia, Haiti, Iraq, Jordan, Kenya,
Kosovo, Lebanon, Nigeria, Panama, the Philippines, Sierra Leone,
Somalia, Sudan, and Thailand, to name just a few.

In this globe-spanning presence, there is one critical absence
in the arsenal of equipment and skills of deployed units: the ability
to speak with the locals. The languages spoken in the places where
U.S. forces have served in the last decade include Arabic, Amharic,

Creole French, Dari, Dinka (yes, that's a real language), Farsi, Pashto, Russian, Serbian, Spanish, Swahili, and Tagalog, among others, each with various dialects. A typical Marine platoon might have a bevy of northeastern brogues, southern drawls, or midwestern twangs, but it's all English. And that's why we need people like Hank, Yah-ya, Wally, Chris, and their colleagues.†

Hank came from one of Afghanistan's east-central provinces. The country's best schools in its capital were just fifty kilometers from his childhood home, so his father sent him to Kabul University, where he studied law and learned English. After earning his degree, he returned home and worked for the national judicial system, eventually becoming a judge. The security situation in his province had been tenuous since the Taliban's emergence, but by the middle of 2008, the Taliban had entrenched itself as the de facto authority there, and being a government official, such as a judge, was a death sentence for anybody foolish enough to stay in the job. Like many Afghans in the ranks of interpreters working with NATO forces in Afghanistan, Hank was driven by a combination of financial necessity and a sense of duty to help wrest control of the country from the Taliban insurgency that was dominating many parts of the country.

Yah-ya was the nickname for an Afghan American who had lived in the United States for over thirty years before joining the crew of interpreters serving alongside Marines in Helmand Province.

---

† Being an interpreter has its risks, both during and after serving in a combat zone. Accordingly, I have changed the names of the interpreters mentioned in this book for their personal privacy and protection.

Yah-ya's grandfather was a senior minister for Afghanistan's first president, Mohammad Daoud Khan. In 1973, Khan overthrew the Afghan monarchy of his cousin, Mohammed Zahir Shah, and then led the country in a progressive direction until his assassination in 1978 at the hands of a Soviet-led military coup. Yah-ya was a preteen at the time, and his grandfather and parents wisely chose to leave the country before the same fate befell them. He eventually found himself in Arizona, where he was a successful small business owner, proud husband, and father. Though he became a naturalized American, Yah-ya never lost his love for his home country. The Pashto skills he maintained through his formative years as a teenager and young adult in America enabled him to serve both his ancestral homeland and his adopted country.

Wally was another Afghan American who wanted to serve both countries in their efforts to root out the Taliban from Afghanistan. Like Yah-ya, he and his family left the country in the late 1970s, making their way to the United States via Pakistan, Egypt, and Europe. He ended up in Washington, D.C., where he had been a taxi driver for nearly twenty years before one of his fares, a military officer recently returned from a tour in Afghanistan, struck up a conversation with him about the important ways Pashto speakers could help the U.S. military do its job in his country. A few introductions, applications, and language competency tests later, he found himself pounding the dirt of Helmand with the Marines. The quiet and patient observational skills he'd developed as a taxi driver served him (and the Marines) well as he parsed and explained the jargon and hyperbole that often got lost in translations between two completely distinct languages. He implicitly trusted the Marines but for good measure always carried a small .38-caliber pistol in the front right pocket of his trousers, a gift passed on by an interpreter friend who was leaving the country around the time Wally arrived.

Chris hailed from Afghanistan's western region near the Iranian border, but he had spent enough time in the U.K. and U.S. to develop a crisp and distinguished American/British accent. He wasn't quite movie-star handsome, but he had a lush head of velvet-black hair reminiscent of Ronald Reagan's that defied his age. It seemed to remain perfectly coiffed, despite the heat and humidity of Helmand, even when he took off his helmet after a long patrol. He had the smooth poise and confidence of a salesman and easily ingratiated himself with the Afghan leaders we met and worked with. His Dari language skills were crucial to our collaboration with the Afghan National Police officers assigned to Nawa, many of whom came from the country's northern and western provinces and spoke no Pashto. His speech was liberally vulgar at times, yet paradoxically he was always formally polite and deferential. He addressed every Marine as "sir" and responded to orders with "as you wish" and "it would be my pleasure." A confident storyteller, he had a tendency to illustrate his speech with vigorous gestures and facial expressions, making him seem at times like a stereotypical Italian, incapable of speaking without using his arms and hands.

These were just a few of the dedicated professionals who helped 1/5 succeed in Nawa. Each platoon had at least one interpreter serving alongside its Marines throughout the district. They were drawn to the work, which they knew would be performed in austere and dangerous conditions, for some of the same reasons that the rest of our team was drawn to join the Marine Corps: national pride, desire for adventure, or economic necessity.

Like Marines, the cadre of interpreters serving with the battalion came in all shapes and sizes. One was a former bodybuilder with a physique like an NFL linebacker. Others bore the signs of excess exposure to time and gravity, with thinner hair and paunchier bellies than their younger counterparts. Some of the younger ones hoped to earn enough money to go to school in Europe or the U.S., while others looked like college professors, with their sleek silver hair and bifocals. I suspect these elder ones may have been augmenting their retirement income. In every case, however, they were an essential bridge between the Marines and the residents of Nawa. They wore our uniform in a combat zone, and despite not having gone through boot camp or officer candidate school, they took on the confident strut one would expect of a Marine.

Effective COIN operations depend on winning over the trust of the local population. Without our interpreters, this could never have happened. As one Army officer noted, "Your interpreter is more important than your weapon."[37] Our interpreters enabled Marines to navigate the nuances of Afghan culture and colloquialisms. Oftentimes, they would deftly interrupt when Marines became too passionate or aggressive while speaking to an Afghan, suggesting alternative phrases to ones that, if translated verbatim, could have cracked already-strained relations.

The interpreters became the voice and ears of the battalion and gained as much trust among the local population as did the Marines. In fact, it was common for locals to come to a patrol base and ask to speak to one of the interpreters rather than to a Marine to pass along some critical bit of information. Sometimes, that information related to the location of an IED or a weapons cache. In this sense, our interpreters were as valuable an asset as any high-tech equipment we had, and it could be argued that they saved as many lives as our mine detectors and bomb-sniffing dogs. They endured the same hardships as the Marines they stood beside, all the while taking on the emotionally and mentally draining task of constantly thinking and speaking in two different languages in real time.

Many factors play into fighting and winning wars in the twenty-first century. The right weapons and warriors are just a few. With a gun and a radio, you can *fight* a war. With a Hank, a Yah-ya, a Wally, or a Chris, you can command hundreds of Afghan soldiers, have a teatime conversation with a tribal leader, or understand what makes a local farmer tick. And you can *win* a war.

CHAPTER 12
KILLING MIR WUT

*What a cruel thing is war: to separate and destroy families and friends, and
mar the purest joys and happiness God has granted us in this world.*
—Confederate General Robert E. Lee, letter to his wife, 1864

June 24, 2009

"OH FUCK! HOLY FUCK! THAT DUDE JUST GOT SHOT!"
    I had just ducked behind the safety of a thick mud-brick wall,
keyed my radio handset, and started blurting out a message to the
squads on my patrol that a civilian was bolting out of the compound
from where we were taking fire. I got as far as "all units be advised,
unarmed male running east to west on the south side" when three
distinct cracks interrupted my transmission and one of my team-
mates shouted that blunt observation. He might actually have started
with "FUCK! FUCK! FUCK!" or "HOLY FUCKING SHIT!" The
noise and tension limited my ability to remember his exact words.
But the message was unmistakable. As I peered over the four-foot
wall protecting us from the AK-47 rounds coming at us, I made out
the image of a writhing figure, felled to his knees in the tall grass
bordering the compound. Staggering to get up, he fell back again,

then hunkered down on all fours, clutching his midsection. I could see him grimacing in shock and pain before he crawled out of sight. I knew he was still there. I saw frantic movement amidst the blades of grass, as if he had decided to try to return to the compound from which he'd run but could only thrash about in agony.

I can get to him, I thought, looking at a path along the tree line to my right that would provide some cover and concealment from the insurgents who were still shooting at us. I duckwalked to the end of the wall and then began inching toward the first of the trees ten meters away when the dirt in front of me kicked up from a spray of bullets. For a moment, I thought about thrusting myself toward the shelter the tree might provide, but a second later its bark and branches snapped and shredded from two well-aimed bursts of fire. It was as if the shooter had read my thoughts and was daring me to use it for cover. Naturally, I scampered back to the comfort of the wall.

My breath heaved as I tried to think of a different way to get to him. The adrenaline-amped Marines around me fired copper-jacketed rounds at the shooters, who were poking their heads and rifle barrels out of small windows and cracks in the compound that was shielding their movements. Another squad of Marines laid down suppressive fire to protect their brothers moving toward the compound in an effort to catch any shooters escaping out the back. A third squad was pinned down by an unseen shooter to our west.

The grass where the man had gone down kept thrashing.

I stayed put.

Twenty minutes later—or it might have been only a minute; time both drags and flies when you're being shot at—the firing stopped. The insurgents slipped away into the grass and canals behind the compound. The patrol leader radioed for all squads to fall back toward the wall I was behind. We would move from there to our planned rendezvous site for the night—a small, undermanned police post. The Afghan officers on duty there had been expecting an assault from the local insurgents that night based on some vague rumors making their way through the district center. Our mission that day was to get to the police post and beef up its security, not get into protracted fights along the way. I looked at the spot in the grass that had been thrashing about moments before, but it was now still. As I turned my back and joined the platoon's march out of there, I thought to myself, *Fuck it, he's not a Marine.*

About two hours later, as we were setting up our positions at the ramshackle police station, one of the Afghan officers frantically asked us to call in a helo for a medevac. A local resident had run to the station to tell the police that a villager with gunshot wounds needed help. Minutes later, two men pushing a wheelbarrow raced up to the dilapidated gate of the police station, shouting for help. Slumped into the wheelbarrow was a barely conscious, panting, quivering man—a teenager, really. His attempts to grow a beard had yielded only a few random wisps and patches of whiskers on his otherwise smooth face. His skin color should have been the sunbaked tan of a typical Afghan, but it was a clammy bluish gray instead, fading from the loss of blood. His *shalwar kamiz*—the robelike shirt and trousers that is the standard Afghan outfit—was sky blue, just like the clothes of the person I had turned my back on as he lay thrashing on the ground a few hours earlier. But now it had a heavy, wet burgundy hue at the midsection and was caked with dirt and grass.

Remarkably, a helo was already in the air nearby as we made the medevac call, and the boy was picked up minutes later in an open field next to the police station. The Air Force medic team on board strapped him down and started cutting off his clothes, sticking in an IV, and putting an oxygen mask on the patient even before the helo lifted off. As it banked away and its rotor wash settled, a piece of fabric flapped across the ground and wrapped itself to my leg. Reaching down, I saw it was a *shemagh*, the scarflike sheet of cloth

Afghan men wear on their heads like a turban or drape over their shoulders, which is sometimes used as a makeshift satchel. This one was caked in blood; it had fallen off the young man's stretcher. I wadded it up and shoved it into my cargo pocket. Then I noticed the blood streaks on my hands. I dully took in the message of the image and felt the first stabs of guilt. Our job—*my job*—was to help the Afghans, to make them safer, and protect them from the violence of the Taliban. When I had a chance to do just that, I had turned my back, rationalizing that the Afghan writhing in agony after being shot in the guts wasn't a Marine, not one of us, and therefore not worth the risk of helping when *helping* was the very thing I was here to do.

The medics did everything they could, but time was their enemy. The blood loss, shredding of internal organs, and depleted oxygen to the brain killed the boy soon after they touched down at the hospital at Kandahar Airfield, about a thirty-minute flight from Nawa in a fast-moving Black Hawk helicopter. They said that if they had had just thirty more minutes, they could have saved him. With some patching up and a hospital stay, he would have been back to normal.

Thirty minutes.

After I turned my back on him, he had bled out for at least an hour before the Afghans who found him dumped him in a wheelbarrow and rushed him to the police station.

Thirty minutes, and he would have made it.

Instead, he died. He was put in a plywood casket, strapped as cargo into another helo, and brought back to our patrol base, where he spent the night in a small tent, watched over by a team of Afghan soldiers. At first light, he was loaded into an Afghan Army pickup truck that bounced along the road back to the village where he was killed. A squad of Marines and I went with them.

Greeted by the village elders, I hung back, taking in the event. I knew what was being said, even if I couldn't catch the words of the conversation. My interpreter, Hank, whispered a summary of the conversation, and I was relieved to hear that this death was being blamed on the Taliban. Everyone believed that if they hadn't started shooting at the Marines, if they hadn't taken over Nawa, it would never have happened. Nothing was said about his being left to die in the grass along the canal when a Marine captain could have made the call to get to him.

A wrinkled, leathery-faced man shuffled up to the coffin, looked inside, and with a dazed, trembling stare at the sky, mumbled "Wah-Allah?" Then two more times, each successively louder: "Wah-Allah? Wah-Allah?" Then his shoulders collapsed, and he sank to the ground, as if the weight of all his life's troubles had just smothered him. It was the boy's father. He had asked "Why, God?" and then, as if feeling ashamed to have questioned God's will, sank into a cocoon of solitude. The blood-soaked *shemagh*, by now brittle and dry, bulged in my cargo pocket. As I pulled it out to fold and hand to the father of the young man, whose name I learned was Mir Wut, a biting rusty odor wafted to my face, and some of the dirt and grass, clumped together with dried blood, flaked off in my hands.

We came back two days later to meet with the village elders and the father, to make amends and pay our condolences, in the administrative manner in which we were authorized. If a civilian was hurt or killed in a firefight involving Marines, we could pay the victim's family for their loss. I handed the father a neatly stacked pile of Afghani bills—equivalent to $2,500 in U.S. dollars, the cost of an Afghan's life according to our rulebook. Then I had him make an "X" in lieu of his signature on the receipt form next to where I had written his name. For good measure, and to meet the administrative requirements of the cash disbursement office at Camp Leatherneck, I had him ink his thumb and stamp it next to the "X" as well.

We sat in a circle in the dirt of a recently harvested wheat field. I faced the men of the village and nodded at their comments as they thanked me for our efforts to save Mir Wut, and the Marines for having begun to make the district safer. We drank a cup of tea, had a second cup, and made small talk. Politely declining a third cup of tea, we stood, placed our hands across our hearts, and murmured "*Deh-deh mahnana. Hodai paman*"—"Thank you. Go with God"—and marched out, casting a last glance at the fresh pile of dirt and rocks covering Mir Wut.

CHAPTER 13
BOLO

Just because you're paranoid doesn't mean they aren't after you.
—JOSEPH HELLER, *Catch-22*

JULY 15, 2009

THE INFORMATION COMING FROM THE BRIGADE HEADQUARTERS WAS judged fresh and reliable, so the intelligence section made sure it went to all the units in the field for action. By early morning, every squad had been issued a be-on-the-lookout order (BOLO in Marine speak) for the leader of the Taliban insurgency in Nawa. He was the man responsible for the manufacture and placement of the IEDs instilling fear among the locals and disrupting our efforts to establish a sense of normalcy in the district.

First Sergeant David Wilson, a battlewise career Marine on his seventh deployment over fifteen years of service, barked out the news during our patrol brief: "Listen up, we've got a BOLO. The main dickhead running the Taliban in Nawa is named Abdul Rahman."

Reading from his notebook, he continued, "It says here he's a fighting-age male, might be traveling in a white Toyota van or a

Corolla, has a beard, and wears a dark-colored turban . . . but sometimes a white one. Usually wears a watch on his left wrist."

This described most of the male population and vehicles in Nawa. The name Abdul Rahman—meaning "Servant of the Merciful"—dates to Islam's earliest days and is one of the most common boy's names in Muslim populations, just behind Mohamed and Abdullah. It was as if we were somewhere south of the Mason-Dixon Line and had just been tasked with finding a guy named Bubba who loves his momma, cheddar cheese grits, and his pickup truck, which happens to have a Confederate flag bumper sticker.

"Let's go find this fucker and win this war," barked First Sergeant Wilson.

The assembled Marines responded with a sarcastic and hearty "Hoo-rah!"

About thirty minutes into our patrol, we had found our man. Or at least someone named Abdul Rahman. A white Toyota passenger van slowly bumped down the road toward us, and one of the Afghan Army soldiers flagged it down. With my basic Pashto skills, I said hello and asked the driver his name.

"*Sta num zih dai?*" I inquired.

"*Zma num zih Abdul Rahman,*" he replied.

I asked with a smirk if he was the Abdul Rahman who was head of the Taliban in Nawa. My interpreter conveyed my question, to which Abdul Rahman answered, "No, but my sister's husband is."

Can it be this easy? I thought, until my interpreter continued translating, reminding me that *talib* in Pashto means "student" and Abdul Rahman's brother-in-law, who shared his name, was the head teacher at one of the schools in Nawa. The term "leader of the Taliban" had very different meanings for the cluster of Marines and Afghans crowding around Abdul Rahman's van.

I nodded my head toward the back seat of the van where a *burkha*-clad woman sat silently holding a child about one year old in her lap.

"Is that your son?" I asked.

Abdul Rahman, like proud fathers everywhere around the world, beamed as he said, "*Wuuh, hamdullah*" ("Yes, praise to God").

Knowing what the answer was likely to be, I asked the boy's name.

"Abdul Rahman," Abdul Rahman replied.

After a bit of small talk about farming and the summer heat, I apologized for delaying his travel and waved goodbye as he resumed his drive home.

We continued our patrol for several more hours. Along the way, we met many Mohameds, several Saed Ghuls, and five Abdul Rahmans, three of whom were about ten years old or younger, one who looked like a wannabe wizard from a *Lord of the Rings* casting call, and one who used a crutch to make up for his missing leg. We never did find the Abdul Rahman who was the leader of the Taliban in Nawa. It's possible he never actually existed. But we met a lot of nice people while looking for him.

CHAPTER 14
THE COST OF CONFLICT

I am sick and tired of war. Its glory is all moonshine. It is only those who
have neither fired a shot nor heard the shrieks and groans of the wounded
who cry aloud for blood, for vengeance, for desolation. War is hell.
—General William Tecumseh Sherman

"The Secretary of Defense regrets to inform you that
Sergeant William J. Cahir was killed in the line of duty while serving
in Afghanistan."—August 13, 2009

"The Secretary of Defense regrets to inform you that Lance
Corporal Donald J. Hogan was killed in the line of duty while
serving in Afghanistan."—August 26, 2009

"The Secretary of Defense regrets to inform you that Lance
Corporal David R. Baker was killed in the line of duty while serving
in Afghanistan."—October 20, 2009

"The Secretary of Defense regrets to inform you that Lance
Corporal Justin J. Swanson was killed in the line of duty while
serving in Afghanistan."—November 10, 2009

We choose to serve. And when we choose to serve, sometimes chance chooses us. Every service member who deploys overseas leaves behind someone who cares. Someone who, when giving that last hug before their warrior ships out, feels their pride clash with the fear that this last hug might in fact be the *final* hug. After that, every call from an unknown number, every unexpected knock on the door reignites the constant worry in the daily lives of those on the home front, making them shudder at the prospect of what might be.

When an American service member is killed overseas, a Casualty Assistance Calls Officer, or CACO, bears the burden of informing the family. They try to reach family in the morning, in the relative privacy of their home, rather than making a call to an office or lingering in the neighborhood waiting for a spouse or parent to come home.

The families might hear the closing thud of car doors—CACOs always travel in pairs—then see two service members in dress uniforms exit a government vehicle and approach their door. A chaplain is often with them. Sometimes the family greets the CACOs on their doorstep, after their peek out the window dropped a stone of dread in their gut. They know there is only one reason anybody wearing that uniform would be visiting. Other CACOs are met with doors slammed in their faces, shouts, outbursts, denials, and even forceful confrontations. It takes a heart of steel, edged with compassion, to ask: "Are you . . . ?"

Some have tears welling in their eyes; some stand with stoic poise; others are in dumbstruck shock; but when they reply, "Yes," the next words deliver the crushing news: "We regret to inform you that . . ." They hear the name and the word "killed," but everything else comes as a blur of noise and fury.

Thousands of miles away, other service members prepare for the homecoming. Packed in ice in an airtight aluminum casket that is covered by an American flag secured with the blue star field at the head, the fallen warrior is marched up the back ramp of a military cargo plane. Comrades stand at attention, saluting as their brother- or sister-in-arms passes them a final time. When the plane arrives at a U.S. air base, the awaiting family is given some moments alone with their loved one before the journey to a final resting place begins.

For some, that place is a small plot in their hometown. For others, it's one of our national cemeteries. The most famous is Arlington, across the river from our nation's capital. Once the home of Robert E. Lee, Arlington has seen the burial of thousands of our nation's heroes. They lie under symmetrically sculpted headstones, simply engraved and aligned with the markers of the others resting there, who were buried after a somber and precise ceremony.

The family is seated, and a subtle signal is given to an awaiting team who lead a horse-drawn caisson transporting the coffin to the gravesite. Other soldiers, sailors, airmen, or Marines march in front of and behind the carriage, to the quiet cadence of an NCO. Once in front of the gravesite, pallbearers smartly raise the precious cargo from the caisson and seem to glide effortlessly toward a platform where the casket will sit during the ceremony. A chaplain reads a prayer, friends make tear-choked speeches, and, behind the crowd, a seven-man team raise their rifles and fire into the air three times, the sudden crack of rounds jolting the senses of the mourners. "Taps" plays while the flag that was draped over the casket is tightly folded and handed to an officer or senior NCO, who then approaches a spouse, a parent, or a child, kneels, and says, "On behalf of the president of the United States, the commandant of the Marine Corps, and a grateful nation, please accept this flag as a symbol of our appreciation for your loved one's honorable and faithful service."

In an era when military service is an exception rather than the norm, the deaths of our service members in combat is as distant a concept as the lands where they fought. Local papers may run a story about the hometown hero, but usually little attention is paid to a life cut short in service to our country, and the loss is drowned out among news of celebrity gossip, political shenanigans, or other minutiae that consume our lives. The families of those killed in action are soon left to face their grief as well as they can, often alone. For them, the final ceremonies honoring their loved ones is a stark reminder that one of the constant realities of war throughout history is that bad things will happen to good people. The four Marines from 1/5 who lost their lives in Nawa were some of the absolute best of those good people.

William J. Cahir. Bill Cahir finished his run and stared into the mirror, asking himself, "Is there a Marine in there somewhere?" Even years before hijacked planes demolished New York's Twin Towers, hit the Pentagon, and crashed into a field in western Pennsylvania in September 2001, he had reflected on the notion of service and commitment. He felt that, despite a degree from Penn State, a stint as a policy advisor in the U.S. Congress, and a successful career as a journalist, something was lacking in his life. In that regard, he was not too different from the thousands of Americans seeking to serve their country in its armed forces after 9/11. What was different was that Bill was thirty-four years old. Most Marines that age have either long since left the service or have climbed through the ranks to positions of significant responsibility. After going through the physical and adminis-trative screening process, including getting an age waiver, thir-ty-four-year-old Bill Cahir stood at attention on Parris Island's infamous "yellow footprints" along with dozens of recent high school graduates, barked at by drill instructors who, for the most part, were nearly a decade younger than Private Cahir.

During boot camp, he never sought any special treatment based on his age, education, or former professional status. In fact, he worked harder, got dirtier, and endured more than many of his platoon mates. Buoyed by the supportive letters he received from his girlfriend of a few months, he thrived in boot camp, reveling in the training, particularly the grueling "Crucible," the final fifty-four-hour nonstop evolution that leaves recruits physically and mentally exhausted and wretchedly filthy. Those who finish will have earned the title "Marine."

As a reservist, Bill was obliged to spend one full weekend and two full weeks each year with his unit. But he signed up to serve overseas and deployed to Iraq with the CAG, first to Ramadi in 2004 and then to Fallujah in 2006. On each deployment, Bill's commanders and peers recognized his personal savvy and tactical prowess, and it was common for him to be tasked to meet directly with generals, diplomats, tribal leaders, and senior State Department officials, despite his junior rank.

Bill had been through some of the roughest fighting Marines saw in Iraq. He was battlewise and experienced and had earned the respect and trust of his fellow Marines. He was near the end of his required service commitment in the Reserves when he was asked if he wanted to do one more deployment, this time to Afghanistan. There was no obligation; he could have said, "No, thank you," and served the remaining few months of his Reserve duty in relative ease. Bill wrestled with the options facing him, but ultimately his sense of duty to guide and mentor the younger members of his team, who saw him as a leader and an inspiration, pushed him to say yes.

So Bill Cahir, forty years old by then, went to war for the third time in less than six years.

When Afghanistan's national elections were scheduled for late August 2009, the Marines of 1/5 were tasked with securing critical travel routes to polling stations in Nawa to ensure its residents could vote in safety. Every Marine is a rifleman first and foremost, and Bill was engaged in clearing operations in the northern villages of Nawa when a sniper's bullet struck him.

On August 31, two days after Senator Edward Kennedy, Bill's former boss, was laid to rest in Arlington National Cemetery, dozens of Marines led the caisson carrying Bill Cahir to the cemetery's Section 60. At the end of the ceremony honoring his life and service, the girlfriend who had written uplifting letters to Bill during boot camp and who had since become his wife, clutched the folded American flag that was presented to her across her chest and next to the twin girls growing inside her—the twins Bill had beamingly told me about the day before he died.[38]

Donald J. Hogan. The five-week battle for Iwo Jima was an epochal event in Marine Corps history. Between mid-February and late March of 1945, thousands of Marines fought against heavily fortified, well-trained, and zealous Japanese soldiers defending the island and its strategically placed airfields. The fighting on Iwo Jima was fierce, often in close quarters, where the smells and sounds of combat punctured the senses. One of the Marines who fought on Iwo Jima was named James Hogan. Wounded by a sniper's bullet, Hogan went on to serve in two other wars, Korea and Vietnam, before retiring as a gunnery sergeant with over twenty-two years of service in uniform.

Just over six decades after the elder Hogan fought in the South Pacific, his grandson Donald signed up to be a U.S. Marine. After graduating from Tesoro High School in Rancho Santa Margarita, California, in 2007, Donald Hogan gave college a try but dropped out after a few months to pursue his childhood dream of becoming a Marine. His parents were understandably concerned. The country was at war, and living relatively close to several Marine bases in

Southern California, they couldn't help but notice the frequent news stories about units shipping overseas and about those who died while serving with them. But like all Marine parents, they were also proud of their son and the way he identified himself as one of the Corps' warriors. With just under two years of service, Donald was certain the Marine Corps was where he would make his career. He told his parents he wanted to retire at an even higher rank than his grandfather.

Donald's platoon mates saw in him a devoted comrade whose can-do attitude was contagious. He had an almost obsessive attention to detail, going through pre-patrol rituals inspecting his and his fellow Marines' equipment and weapons, always focusing on accomplishing the mission no matter how routine it may have seemed at the time.

On the morning of August 26, a local Afghan boy tipped off Donald's platoon that an IED with a pull-string detonator was planted somewhere along a frequently traveled dirt road. Donald took point on the patrol that went to look for it, leading the unit by several meters while sweeping a metal detector along the path he traveled. By late August, the corn in Nawa had grown to about chest high, enough to conceal anybody crouching among its stalks. The patrol had taken a halt to orient itself and check in by radio with its headquarters. Scanning the area around him, Donald spotted an odd clump of dirt next to the road with a thin, almost transparent string coming out of it leading into the cornfield. Suddenly, the string was being pulled taut. Someone in the cornfield chose this moment to detonate the explosive buried under mud, laden with jagged metal. Donald was the only person to see it, and he could have easily taken cover on the berm opposite the IED.

Instead, he rushed toward the Marine closest to the bomb, tackled him to the ground, and shouted to his squad mates, "Wire, get down!" giving them invaluable seconds to take cover before the hidden insurgent detonated his deadly charge. A deafening jolt hit the Marines, and when the smoke settled, one was frantically applying a tourniquet to his upper thigh to staunch the bleeding from his femoral artery, while others treated their own and others' wounds. Donald Hogan lay motionless next to the Marine he had shoved out of harm's way. He was killed instantly by the IED blast, his last thoughts and actions focused on his fellow Marines rather than himself, choosing to sacrifice his future to ensure one for them.

No one can be sure of the exact toll the IED Donald Hogan warned his platoon mates about could have taken, but it is certain several Marines would have been killed and others more severely wounded but for his actions. He was buried with full military honors at Fort Rosecrans National Cemetery at Point Loma in San Diego and was awarded the Navy Cross, the nation's second-highest award for valor, for his swift and selfless decisiveness. On August 29, the Marine who Donald Hogan had pushed out of harm's way three days earlier received a message that his wife had given birth to their first son.[39]

David R. Baker. Painesville is a small town of just under twenty thousand residents east of Cleveland, Ohio. From its founding in the early 1800s, Painesville has sent its sons to war. The city's namesake, Edward Paine, was a Revolutionary War general, and two of Paine's descendants served as generals in the Army of the Potomac in the Civil War. David Baker followed in the footsteps of his hometown's forebears.

David had a quiet good-old-boy demeanor that belied his mischievous side, always ready to pull a prank on a sibling or a friend and quick to tell a joke. He joined the Marine Corps soon after graduating from Riverside High School, where he was a standout on the baseball diamond and a memorable and amiable student among his classmates, even though he was fairly shy. He arrived at Parris Island for boot camp in 2006 after graduating high school, and soon after, he began to express doubts about his choice. But those doubts faded once he joined his fleet unit. It was then that his parents saw the distracted mannerisms of a teenage boy change to the focused intensity of a young man—the same transformation thousands of other parents had witnessed in the process of their son or daughter becoming a Marine.

David maintained a soft spot for his home and family, even while immersed in the Marine Corps' vigor. Before deploying to Afghanistan, he gave his mother a stuffed teddy bear that played a recording of his reassuring voice each time she squeezed it. He called home on October 1 to hear his family wish him a happy twenty-second birthday. When his father asked why he chose to walk in the point position—the most dangerous—on his squad's daily foot patrols, David replied, "That's my job."[40] Talk soon turned to Christmas plans in Ohio, since the battalion had just learned it would be home in time to celebrate the holiday with families.

On October 20, David Baker was killed in an IED explosion that also injured several of his platoon mates. He began his journey home that evening, making his way to rest forever in Arlington National Cemetery two weeks later, buried two headstones away from Bill Cahir. David's family, friends, and community members continue to remember his life and service, whether through ceremonies at his former high school or honoring his birthday with his favorite meal of pork chops, mashed potatoes, and Mickey's beer. In 2011, David's sister named her son after the uncle he was never able to meet.[41]

Justin J. Swanson. The United States Marine Corps was born in a bar on November 10, 1775. Since that date, Marines have proudly celebrated its birthday wherever they are. Honoring the day in the dust and heat of a combat zone has a special significance. The sparkle and glitz, fancy meals, and fluffy cake cut with a ceremonial sword at a formal event in a hotel ballroom are replaced by grimy uniforms, lukewarm field rations, and crusty, tasteless cake cut with an oily Ka-Bar knife. But Marines relish the moment, the sense of camaraderie never more powerful as they perform these birthday rituals with rifles slung over their shoulders and their boots in the dirt. On November 10, 2009, the Marines of 1/5 tempered their enthusiasm for their 234th birthday with sorrow as they saw one of their own killed.

Justin Swanson was a charmer. He could talk his way out of trouble or win the attention of just about any girl he chose with his good looks and swagger. Born in Southern California, he attended Buena Park High School, played sports, and participated in the school's Peer Assistance Program, which matched students with others who might be struggling socially or academically. Never a strong student himself—some of his report cards bluntly stated that he was "in danger of failing"—he was nonetheless a widely recognized leader among his peers and a favorite of many teachers. The same report cards stated that Justin was "a pleasure to have in class." He always told the students he mentored that "I got your back."

The Marine Corps first piqued Justin's interest when he met a recruiter soon after he was old enough to drive. With a father in prison, the Corps offered options that his mother felt she couldn't give him. She had been working three waitressing jobs in order to raise Justin's younger siblings. She signed the papers allowing Justin to enter the Corps' deferred-entry program at seventeen. He headed to boot camp shortly thereafter.

His mother said he was high energy, confident, and that he thrived on camaraderie. The Marine Corps was where he belonged, and it was no surprise that he excelled. He had already done one deployment with 1/5 when the battalion turned its attention to its next tour in Afghanistan. His unit leaders recognized Justin's technical prowess and tactical savvy. It was common for him to be called on to fix glitches with the unit's radios or to walk point on a patrol.

As the Marines of 1/5 planned to have a field celebration of their birthday, Justin was driving an armored Humvee that rolled over an IED. The explosion was so powerful that it flipped the two-and-a-half-ton vehicle onto its roof. Justin was killed instantly. The Marine in the Humvee's turret was thrown from the vehicle, breaking his neck but miraculously surviving.

Justin's mother was roused from sleep by her daughter early in the morning of November 11 with the news that two men in uniform were at the door. A week later, Justin returned home to Los Alamitos Airfield as the sun was setting over the Pacific Ocean. As he was brought to his final resting place in Westminster Memorial Park, his funeral procession passed hundreds of bystanders along the way who came to pay their respects to Justin's service, including a class of preschool students, standing at attention with their hands over their hearts.[42]

CHAPTER 15
CONVERSATIONS WITH GOD

Every day above earth is a good day.
—ERNEST HEMINGWAY, *The Old Man and the Sea*

AUGUST 20, 2009

IT WAS HOT, THE SUN'S RAYS PULSING AGAINST US LIKE A PUNISH-ment for the folly of being outdoors. As we patrolled along an uneven dirt path next to an irrigation canal, we walked into a blanket of humidity that seemed to add even more weight to the sixty or seventy pounds of body armor and gear we wore. The steam from the nearby Helmand River embraced us and joined the sweat we had been drenched in for nearly the whole time since leaving the patrol base at sunrise three hours earlier.

I should have been alert, my eyes inspecting odd clumps of dirt and any other telltale signs of an IED along our route. I'd seen the random savagery those wretched explosives could wreak, and I owed it to my squad members to pay attention. But, goddamn, it was hot, and my mind wandered. The humidity fogged my glasses, further degrading my attention. It had been a week since my team chief had been killed by a sniper's bullet, and I rehearsed the letters to his wife and parents that I had written, thrown away, rewritten, and thrown away again. I thought of the last "normal" conversation (one that didn't involve current operations and plans) we had. It was when he told me with a beaming grin that during his last call on the satellite phone with his wife, she surprised him with the news that the pregnancy he knew about before we left for Afghanistan was going to give them *twin* daughters. They were due a week after our planned return from deployment in December.

I thought of those unborn girls and their widowed mother and cursed God's arbitrary cruelty. *Fuck you, God, for what you do!* I said to myself as I wiped my thumb across my glasses, replacing the humid fog with a dirty, sweat-streaked smudge.

A teenaged boy emerged from a compound we were walking past, carrying his younger brother in his arms, and darted toward the first person in our group not carrying a rifle, our interpreter Yah-ya. The boy implored Yah-ya to ask our corpsman to help his brother. He had heard that the Marines could help anybody with a medical problem and that they had a clinic on their base where they treated locals needing aid. The boy in his arms looked about two or three years old, and it was clear there was nothing that could be done for him.

The boy hadn't been injured in the crossfire of a gunfight or hit by the fragments of an IED. Instead, he had been born with a birth defect that left him with what appeared to be hydrocephalus. He had an abnormally large head and deformed, useless appendages. He didn't seem to have any sentience; his eyes stared vacantly past attempts to make contact with him. He was a living being, but with no ability to do anything more than breathe, twitch involuntarily, or make an occasional guttural and incomprehensible sound. That he had lived as long as he had was incredible. He had endured both the harsh circumstances to which he'd been born, with no chance of any modern medical care, and the risk that his family might have smothered him out of pity or financial necessity.

We explained to the brother that this was not the type of medical condition we could help and began to leave. He stood there with a surprised and desperate look. Whatever superpowers he may have thought we had, we didn't, but he seemed unwilling to believe that, insisting that if we just flew his younger brother to a bigger base in Kabul or Kandahar, the boy could be cured. We had no choice but to continue our patrol. His expression turned from hopeful urgency to resentful scorn as I placed my hand on my heart and muttered, *"Hodai paman"*—"God be with you"—and continued humping along the dirt trail where the rest of the patrol waited for us.

Again, I should have been alert, focused outward, but instead I resumed my musing on God and his absurd cruelty as I considered the impoverished boy I had just left, holding the helpless being that was his brother. That family had no hand in their tragedy. They were farmers, a hardscrabble profession in Helmand Province, where the environment made outdoor work particularly brutal and a decade of warfare made daily existence a perilous challenge. To add a helpless child to the mix was unspeakably cruel, an undeserved additional test of faith for a family whose faith was probably already pressed to its limits. So I questioned and cursed God again, not expecting or receiving an answer.

An hour later we arrived at our patrol checkpoint, an abandoned school building in a village where nobody from the battalion had spent much time. The Afghan police detachment in Nawa was considering setting up a makeshift outpost near there, and my task was to gauge the "atmospherics" of the area, to assess the suitability of the nearby infrastructure of roads, trails, and canals as well as the mood of the local population. As I surveyed my surroundings, I stood atop a crossing over a five-meter-wide canal, one of the many roughly constructed bridges throughout the district: cement culverts packed around with rocks, blocks, and mud. Since the bridge seemed to be solid and wide enough to withstand the weight of an armored Humvee or an MRAP, I tapped the "Mark Location" function on my

GPS and noted the eight-digit grid coordinate that appeared on its screen, reflecting for a moment on the unusually sequential pattern of the numbers my device registered.

We were always moving while on patrol. This day was no different, and we soon stepped off the bridge to make our way back to the patrol base. On the way, we passed a squad from Charlie Company headed in the direction from which we'd just come. We exchanged a few words, continued our movement, and arrived at Patrol Base Jaker thirty minutes later.

I sat in a corner of the operations center to prepare my report on the patrol, casually noting the background noise of the exchange on the radio from the Charlie Company squad we had passed. They had discovered an IED propped up by sticks and cement blocks in a bridge culvert and were arranging for an explosive ordnance disposal (EOD) team to evaluate and safely remove it. They explained that it had been well concealed, discovered only because a Marine saw the thin, faintly visible detonation wire in the mud and grass of the canal, where it ran for about fifty meters to a thick clump of bushes in which someone could hide and touch its leads to a nine-volt battery to ignite the device. IED finds were daily occurrences, so this conversation didn't particularly interest me—until I heard the squad leader relay the grid coordinate of the IED. They were the same sequential numbers I had marked on my own GPS.

I had been standing on top of that IED barely an hour before. The description I overheard on the radio noted it had been carefully set. It was unlikely that it had been put in place in the time between our crossing the bridge and when the Charlie Company squad arrived. While standing on that bridge, I'd given every sign to anyone who might have been watching us that I was important enough to have detonated the IED: I looked at a map, talked on the radio, led the conversations with the locals we met, directed other Marines, and gave the command to continue the patrol.

I listened to the clipped conversations over the radio as the EOD team arrived at the site, evaluated the IED, and skillfully deactivated it. I heard the description of the bomb's composition and size, large enough to rupture the top of the culvert and send shards of rock, concrete, and metal into and through anybody within twenty meters and certainly to shred anybody standing on top of it. The insurgent, whose job it was to man the post and touch the ends of the control wire to his battery, might not have shown up for work that day, or perhaps he had passed on the opportunity to do his task, hoping for a larger target such as a Humvee or an MRAP rather than a foot patrol. Or maybe when he saw us on the bridge, holding the wire in his hand, contemplating the lethality at his fingertips, he had simply had a change of heart, a moment of compassion that moved him to reconsider carrying out his violent duty.

That night, I laid my thin sleeping bag on top of the ratty cardboard I used as a bed, propped my flak jacket under my head, and stared at the open sky above me, gazing at Orion and the Big Dipper. As I oriented my direction off the North Star, I reflected on the curses I had sent to God, damning him to fuck off, to go to hell. I still thought it inexplicably senseless and arbitrarily cruel that my teammate had been killed or that an Afghan family in a war zone had the burden of a disabled child thrust upon them. But I also thought about my own smallness in this world, and that perhaps it was not my calling to comprehend, let alone explain, all that unfolded around us. I also thought about the IED I had stood over, separated from death by a few inches of dirt and concrete, oblivious to the ferocious mangling it would have inflicted on me and my fellow Marines.

Perhaps God had heard my curses but had given me a free pass. As I closed my eyes and drifted toward sleep, I spoke to God once again, apologizing for my words earlier that day. Thanking him for the gift of another sunrise ahead.

CHAPTER 16

PID

Man is the only animal that deals in that atrocity of atrocities, War.
He is the only one that gathers his brethren about him and goes
forth in cold blood and calm pulse to exterminate his kind.
—MARK TWAIN, *What Is Man?*

AUGUST 26, 2009

IT WAS EARLY, AND THE SUN HADN'T YET CLIMBED OVER THE ochre-colored hills to our east. As the black night began to evolve into lighter shades of blue, a few wispy clouds floated through the sky, chasing away the stars for the clear day ahead. Despite the early hour, the rising heat and humidity we had fought every day for the past several months reminded us that they would once again be our constant companions. A sheen of sweat already covered the squad of Marines who had just finished a patrol brief and were queued up to step outside the wire even before the sun made its presence fully known.

Pushing aside a heavy plastic curtain, I walked into the COC—the battalion's Combat Operations Center—to tell the Marines on watch that I would be joining the patrol with the assembled squad. A gust of cool air greeted me as I entered, a welcome respite from the ovenlike temperature outside.

The COC was a cramped, dark room on the ground floor of the rundown building we had occupied at Patrol Base Jaker. It was not much bigger than a typical New York City studio apartment, and about a dozen Marines usually worked in its tight quarters, huddled around radios, maps, and troop-monitoring computer systems. The equipment and workstations were arranged in clusters along its walls and in the middle of the room. The furniture was purely functional; comfort and appearance had no bearing on its selection. Some of the tables were cobbled together from salvaged lumber strewn around the patrol base, sturdy enough to hold the weight of several computer systems. Marines at work in the COC sat in flimsy foldable aluminum chairs, many reinforced with duct tape and nylon "550 cord" to extend their useful life just a bit.

The computers and other technical equipment in the COC were always at risk of overheating in Helmand's temperatures, routinely exceeding one hundred degrees in summer. Their constant din of beeps, squawks, and hisses was accompanied by the steady whir of an outdoor air-conditioning unit piping cool air through a small window in a corner of the room. A chunk of plywood patched with strips of olive-green duct tape surrounded the AC unit's corrugated plastic ventilation tube that ran from the window to the large machine outside. The makeshift contraption kept the COC—and the people and equipment inside it—reasonably cool, but it was by no means a comfortable or relaxing post. The grinding whir of three diesel-powered generators keeping all these gadgets working added to the dissonance of the busy center.

A dozen Marines working around the clock in a confined space in the middle of a war zone generate a funky aroma. The smells of weeks-old sweat embedded in our uniforms, gun oil liberally applied to the rifles placed in a rack in the corner, and freshly opened MREs hovered over the room. Every MRE comes with a water-activated heating sleeve; its mixture of magnesium, iron, and sodium chloride (a.k.a. "salt") warms up with a small dose of water. That's how the gooey gel in the main meal melts into a creamy layer of sauce. A few MREs being heated early in the morning effused a faintly chemical scent, which added to the other aromas wafting among us. A constantly brewing pot of coffee and the mintlike fragrances of Purell hand sanitizer and Gold Bond powder—which Marines generously sprinkled on their crotches and feet—mixed with the other odors to round out an olfactory experience that even the most hardened senses couldn't ignore.

Stepping into the COC, I saw that all eyes were glued to a forty-inch screen hanging from a pair of hooks screwed into the concrete ceiling. On the screen was a real-time video streaming from the infrared camera of a ScanEagle, an unarmed aerial drone that we used to gain visual intelligence in our district. About the size of a large model airplane, a ScanEagle could be launched by hand. A Marine with a running start simply tossed it into the air like a javelin. It could fly for several hours high enough to avoid being seen or heard from the ground, but its zoomable camera could discern key details of the people and terrain it watched from more than two thousand meters above. A remote-control system allowed an operator to direct the drone and aim its camera, fixing on a designated point of interest as necessary. When its power began to run low, it could be guided to a short landing, where it would be retrieved, folded up, and packed away until it was recharged and deployed again.

The monitor that the Marines in the COC were watching showed a trio of men whose predawn behavior had raised the suspicions of some Marines manning an observation post earlier in the morning. From about two hundred meters away, they had heard the faint—but distinct—sounds of metal clinking and scraping against dirt. Through their night vision goggles and rifle scopes, they saw some men appearing to hastily dig a hole by the side of a road that was regularly traveled on by foot and in vehicles driven by Marines and locals. When they called in their observations to the COC, the ScanEagle was launched, and we soon had a clear view of what the men were up to.

There were three men, awake and active before sunrise. Two small motorcycles were parked nearby. One of the men was using a shovel and another was using a pickax to chip and dig away at a hole about three feet square. The third man paced around, casting quick looks up and down the road between glances at his hand, which held what appeared to be a mobile phone or small walkie-talkie. A boxlike apparatus, smaller than the hole being dug, sat on the side of the road a few feet away.

Positive Identification—PID—is what we needed to confirm before going lethal. We had spent many pre-deployment hours in class-rooms going through "what if" exercises to gauge our understanding of that concept and to gain an appreciation for the rules of engage-ment (ROE) that governed our actions in Afghanistan.

In the fields and along the canals of Nawa, it came down to seeing "hostile action" or "hostile intent" from an insurgent. A man shooting an AK-47 or an RPG at a squad of Marines was an easy case study. Another man strolling along a canal trail with a rifle slung over his shoulder, vaguely matching the description of a known insurgent, is a tougher call. Two teenaged boys, no visible weapons in hand, sprinting out the back side of a compound from which Marines had been taking fire moments before would not meet the criteria for hostile intent or hostile action. Even if our gut instincts told us they were the ones who had been firing at us we had to refrain. (By the way, it was often the case that our instincts were confirmed when we entered the compound and found hidden or abandoned weapons there.) The need for certainty was clear to us; a wrong choice resulting in two dead *innocent* teenagers could turn an entire tribe against us and nullify months of progress. It was just as common to learn that locals had been held captive inside their compound while insurgents fired from inside, as it was to find abandoned weapons left behind by fleeing gunmen.

We were in a counterinsurgency battle where earning the trust and confidence of the locals was crucial to our success. Every unwarranted civilian death eroded that trust and gave the insurgency propaganda to exploit among an impressionable population. Some felt the ROE were too restrictive and impractical at the tactical level for young Marines and soldiers whose pre-deployment training often emphasized the need for them to be fierce killers. But tactical decisions, particularly whether or not to pull the trigger, have strategic implications. We were fighting the Taliban not just with bullets, but with information. While it was important for us to hold key terrain, a more critical objective was holding the emotions of the locals, particularly their trust.

On the eve of Operation Khanjar, General McChrystal issued revised guidance for COIN operations to the forces under his command. Included in that guidance was an emphasis on decreasing civilian casualties. Some felt this guidance was a shift toward a too-restrictive ROE that would put NATO forces at increased risk and mocked the praise given to Marines and soldiers who exercised "courageous restraint" when they weren't certain of the actions or intent of a potential target.

Those criticisms ignored several crucial factors. First, General McChrystal was by no means a weak or conservative leader hesitant to use force in a war. Before taking command in Afghanistan, he was the leader of the Joint Special Operations Command at the peak of Operation Iraqi Freedom. During that command, his mission was killing or capturing the leaders of the terrorist networks fighting coalition forces, and those willingly fighting alongside them. Killing the enemy was not an abstract concept to him. Second, the criticisms ignored the overarching mission of any war: to win. In a COIN battle, winning isn't about seizing terrain or amassing high enemy body counts; it's about earning—and keeping—the trust and confidence of the population. That trust can't be won or maintained with an incautious attitude about who gets killed and why. Finally, there is the fundamental tenet that taking another human life is a heavy, morally wrenching act, even when the malignancy of the enemy is certain. Marines will never hesitate to go lethal when necessary, but they'd just as soon live up to General James Mattis's tribute: "No better friend, no worse enemy."

Given what we were witnessing via ScanEagle, there would be no restraint from us that morning. Three men digging a hole by the side of a heavily trafficked road, trying to get their work done before the sun rose, meant one thing to the Marines watching them in action from the COC. They were planting an IED—the boxlike apparatus on the ground beside them—and wanted to have it in place before the farmers and Marines in Nawa started their day. We weren't going to let them finish the job.

"We can't get a clean shot from here," came the hoarsely whispered message from the Marines watching the men through their NVGs and rifle scopes. "Too many tree branches in our line of sight."

"We have Cobras on station," said the battalion's senior FAC, who had been on the radio to check for available close air support. A pair of Cobras, the Marine Corps' primary attack helicopter, was in the air several miles away. With a speed of nearly two hundred miles per hour, the Cobras could be on the targets within minutes of an order.

"What do you think, Gus?" Lieutenant Colonel McCollough had probably made up his mind before he turned to me for my opinion. As the battalion commander, the responsibility for what to do was ultimately his. But he had a methodical and professional decision-making approach and was receptive to hearing different reasoned views.

In the several months I'd been on the ground in Nawa, I had learned enough about the indiscriminate tactics of the insurgents trying to disrupt our efforts to be certain about what I was watching. Wartime decisions rarely achieve the certainty of legal conclusions like "beyond a reasonable doubt" or even "preponderance of evidence." The fog of war and the consequences of delaying while waiting for more and more data force decision makers to act on the information at hand and to fill in the gaps with the knowledge that comes with experience and instinct. Eisenhower faced this dilemma on the eve of D-Day, and countless other commanders before and after him faced a similar quandary. I'm no Eisenhower, but I had seen the horrible carnage an IED could inflict on another human being and knew the one about to be concealed by the men we were watching would do the same to others.

"It's PID, sir. No doubt in my mind. Hostile action, hostile intent," I replied without hesitation.

Turning to the FAC, the battalion commander coolly ordered, "Go ahead, escalate it." The FAC keyed his radio handset and gave the coordinates and description of the target to the pilots. He described some of the key terrain features in the area, noted the location of the Marines who were hunkered in a concealed position a few hundred meters away, and confirmed there were no other friendly forces nearby. Knowing the rising sun might create a glare that could distract the pilots, he suggested a north-to-south flight path directly along the dirt road where the men were hurriedly digging, oblivious of what was about to happen to them.

The pilots acknowledged the message with a terse, "Roger, copy all."

In the COC, we watched the silent video streaming from the ScanEagle. Enough daylight had crested over the eastern hills to allow the camera to switch from infrared imagery to a crisp black-and-white video. The incoming Cobras would fly just over the tops of the thirty-foot trees lining the dirt road that was guiding them to their target. The ScanEagle was flying in tight circles high enough to avoid the flight path of the Cobras and give us an uninterrupted view of our targets.

The usual noises in the COC seemed to be drowned out by the silence of tense anticipation. The men digging the IED hole were close to finishing their work when they stopped abruptly and turned in unison to face the rapid thumping noise of the helicopters bearing down on them. Panicked, they began to run, but the lead Cobra's M134 Minigun fired several rapid bursts, chewing up the ground around the fleeing men before finding its mark. The M134 fires 7.62 mm rounds through a rotating six-barrel Gatling-style assembly at thousands of rounds per minute. The fleeing insurgents stood little chance of escaping their fate. Two fell almost immediately, one unquestionably dead. The other sprawled in the middle of the road, writhing in pain from the twisted and broken limbs we could see in the video feed. The lightning-fast rate of fire from the M134 can tear apart a human being like a chain saw, and it was clear to us that he would bleed out quickly. The third man had been hit but had escaped a mortal wound. He dragged an injured leg along the ground, frantically limping toward one of the motorcycles parked on the road.

"Take him?" came the query from the pilot in the second Cobra that had trailed its partner along the same flight path. The first pilot had banked off the target after firing its lethal machine-gun bursts.

"Roger, take him," the FAC answered immediately.

The injured man had just straddled the seat of his motorcycle when explosions of dirt erupted around him. He went into a stiffening spasm and slumped over before the motorcycle rolled on top of his lifeless body.

Tufts of dust were still floating around the three motionless bodies when the lead Cobra pilot keyed his radio and confirmed, "Need us for anything else?"

"Negative, we're all good," responded the FAC. "Thanks for your help."

There was no cheering, gloating, or high-fiving in the COC. But there was no remorse or pity either. We all shared the same scorn for the dead insurgents who cared little for the random havoc their IED would wreak. Killing them was a necessary, almost routine part of our mission, so it was done professionally, swiftly, and unemotionally. A sense of normalcy settled in, and everybody resumed their tasks with a sanguine, calm focus.

As I turned to head outside and join my patrol, one of the Marines in the COC took his MRE out of its heating sleeve, having ignored it while fixated on the striking drama in the ScanEagle's images. The aroma of cheese tortellini drifted gently across the room.

A whiff of cool air followed me as I stepped out of the air-conditioned room to join the squad waiting for me in the rising heat. We had a patrol to do, after all; this was just another day in the war.[†]

---

† A squad of Marines went to check the site and confirmed that the boxlike object we could see from the ScanEagle was an IED. One of the motorcycles had a saddlebag strapped across its seat. Inside was an AK-47 with a collapsible stock, several magazines of ammunition, spools of copper wire, and detonating devices. A team of engineers dismantled the IED, and the three dead men were buried near where they were killed.

CHAPTER 17

TINY LITTLE GRAVES

*He was quick and alert in the things of life, but only
in the things, and not in the significances.*
—JACK LONDON, "To Build a Fire"

EVERY CULTURE HAS ITS DEATH RITUALS. IN PASHTUN-DOMINATED
Helmand Province, these include centuries-old tribal customs
combined with practices from sacred Islamic tenets. When an Afghan
dies, a mullah or other distinguished male from the deceased's
village will methodically cleanse the body before tightly wrapping it
in a white linen shroud, called a *kafan*. The village women form a
circle around the shrouded body and emit wailing lamentations that
also include beating their faces and chests. While the women engage
in these emotive displays, young children and teenagers, usually all
boys, dig a grave.

Burials must occur on the day of death or the next day at the latest,
a tradition that likely arose centuries ago from practical hygienic
considerations as much as religious ones. The dead are placed in
their grave with their head pointing in the direction of the Muslim
holy city of Mecca, about 2,400 miles to the southwest of Nawa. A
white linen cloth is placed over the face before the work of filling in

the grave begins. Since much of the ground in Helmand Province is rugged and hard, graves are shallow, and once the body is buried, fist-sized rocks and small pebbles are placed on top of the freshly piled dirt. Tradition calls for wreaths of flowers to be placed on the graves as well, but in hardscrabble Helmand, ornamental flowers are rare, so sticks with colored strips of fabric tied to their ends are pushed through the rocks covering the graves like tiny flagpoles, flitting with the wind.

Adult men are rarely openly involved in the burial and mourning process. They leave those tasks to the women as they return to labor in their fields, drink tea, or smoke a hookah pipe. The female villagers will visit a freshly buried Afghan several times a day for a week or more, wailing on their knees if it is a family member and replenishing the fabric strips that have faded or fallen off the sticks they've placed atop of the grave earlier. Other than those adornments, the graves are unmarked, a nod to the Muslim tradition of avoiding lavish displays as well as the practical reality that much of Helmand's population is illiterate. Because people have to be pragmatic in Helmand, the mourning rituals eventually end with villagers getting back to their daily existence. The sadness of the loss, however, certainly lingers.

The British soldiers who were in Nawa before the Marines arrived called the mysterious spot on the map the "Rugby Ball." As viewed in a satellite photo, it is a tan oval shape set off by surrounding greenery. The imagery we examined revealed dozens of cigar-shaped discolorations of various sizes marking the ground in orderly rows. Early intelligence reports suggested that the Rugby Ball was an insurgent staging area because drone surveillance often showed large groups of Afghans gathered there, usually at dusk. But one analyst proposed that the Rugby Ball was actually a burial ground, and that the frequent gatherings appearing in drone images were services for the continuous cycle of death Nawa experienced. Perhaps these were not the nefarious conclaves of scheming insurgents after all.

The Marines who first patrolled near the Rugby Ball after arriving in the district weren't surprised to see a cluster of women surrounding a fresh pile of rocks. The colored streamers on the sticks that were wedged into the rock mounds sometimes made a snapping sound as they danced in the wind. Other times when there was no breeze to lift them, the streamers dangled lifelessly. The women's rhythmic chanting penetrated the air. It was interrupted occasionally by a long, sad wail. We strode by, keeping a respectful distance, realizing that the cigar-shaped discolorations we'd seen on our satellite images were indeed burial plots.

As I glanced at the mourners kneeling beside a fresh grave, I saw that the pile of rocks where they were keening was not much longer than one of my strides. I slowly began noticing how many other piles in the graveyard were that small—how many were the same size as my son, whom I hadn't seen in months.

I thought of the young boys and girls under those rocks and pitied them, knowing they would never see a sunrise, feel the sting of rain on their face, scribble a picture, read a book, or fall in love. Instead, they would just decay in their unmarked graves and ultimately be forgotten. Then I thought to myself that those who say death doesn't discriminate have probably never been in a place like Helmand, where death too often chooses the young.

CHAPTER 18
TIME AND TOIL

The credit belongs to the man who is actually in the arena, whose face is marred by dust and sweat and blood; who strives valiantly; who errs, who comes short again and again, because there is no effort without error and shortcoming; but who does actually strive to do the deeds; who knows great enthusiasms, the great devotions; who spends himself in a worthy cause; who at the best knows in the end the triumph of high achievement, and who at the worst, if he fails, at least fails while daring greatly, so that his place shall never be with those cold and timid souls who neither know victory nor defeat.
—PRESIDENT THEODORE ROOSEVELT,
"The Man in the Arena," from *Citizenship in a Republic*

WITHIN A MONTH OF THE START OF OPERATION KHANJAR IN EARLY July 2009, the battalion had platoons operating out of more than twenty outposts around Nawa. Each forty-man platoon was divided into squads of about a dozen Marines, and a squad from each platoon was on patrol almost around the clock. The constant patrolling gave the Marines an intimate familiarity with the terrain and people in their AO. It was a decentralized approach in which captains, lieutenants, and sergeants had a tremendous amount of autonomy and the trust and confidence of the battalion leadership. The Marines of 1/5 continually emphasized to the Afghans they met on patrols that we were there to make their district safer for them and for their appointed and elected officials to govern properly. The reticence shown by some residents during our early days in Nawa began to wane as Marines on patrol approached them with their helmets and sunglasses removed and their hands extended, using the fundamental Pashto language training they had received before deployment.

"*Taso senge yast? Zma num zih . . .*" ("How are you? My name is . . ."), patrolling Marines said to every Afghan they encountered. The Pashtun hospitality we had been told about was evident as groups of residents began inviting patrolling Marines to sit under the shade of a canal-side tree and have a cup of tea. No invitation was declined, and the prediction General Nicholson made before Operation Khanjar began, about the amount of tea we would drink, proved to be spot-on and maybe even an underestimate.

Conversations ranged from agricultural techniques and crop cycles to politics and children's education. The Afghans had a raw sense of humor that Marines could relate to. Some of the older Afghans gave marital advice, warning their younger counterparts and Marines about the challenges of keeping multiple wives happy. One spouse was challenging enough, they advised. We began to see our common likenesses. Our fundamental needs and wants, including happy and healthy children, stable work, as well as decent food and shelter, transcended our cultural and geographic differences. We even spoke about the recent death of Michael Jackson, who died on June 25, barely a week before Operation Khanjar began.[†] The King of Pop proved he had a global reign. Many Afghans were familiar with him and his music, even though the Taliban had banned Western music—in fact, all music—in the country. After mid-July, some

---

† Farrah Fawcett, the childhood heartthrob and favorite of *Charlie's Angels* for many Marines my age, died the same day.

Afghans asked about and pondered the fate of an American soldier named Bowe Bergdahl. Through their mobile texting network and word of mouth, they had heard about Bergdahl's disappearance from his unit's patrol base in the eastern province of Paktika, about four hundred kilometers to the east of Nawa. We later learned that Bergdahl had snuck off his base and ended up in the hands of the Taliban. He remained their captive for nearly five years, when he was released in exchange for five Taliban members who were being held at Guantanamo Bay.[43]

After a few weeks on the ground, Marines found that Nawa's residents were not just inviting them to sit for tea when they passed by on patrols but would also stop by the austere patrol bases to say hello and deliver gifts of watermelons, grapes, or pomegranates.

Marines were able to trade some of their MREs for a few chickens and locally grown vegetables, giving them a chance to make a "home-cooked" meal, which they shared with their Afghan neighbors. Like people everywhere, the Afghans liked to talk, and they regaled Marines with stories of how Nawa had thrived before the Taliban arrived. We sat on the ground during our meetings and, if we were inside a patrol base, took off our boots when the Afghans removed their sandals. If you closed your eyes and thought really hard, you could mistake the pungent odor of fermentation that hovered over these conversations as coming from a fancy French cheese shop rather than the weathered and caked feet that were its real source.

The security situation in Nawa improved dramatically after Marines arrived in the summer of 2009. The Afghans were happy with the change but skeptical about its longevity, certain we would leave soon after the presidential elections scheduled for August 20. When that day came and went, we pointed out to the skeptics that we were still there and that they were able to travel about freely on the dirt roads of Nawa because of the security that we, along with our Afghan police and army counterparts, were providing.

Before Marines came to Nawa, its district center had been a desolate place. Just a month after our arrival, fifty shops were active with some sort of business, ranging from small electronics stores to motorcycle repair centers to hardware shops. There was even a bit of competition going on—four of the newly opened shops sold veterinary supplies, seeking to serve the owners of Nawa's thousands of sheep, goats, and cattle, along with a handful of horses, donkeys, and an occasional camel. By the time 1/5 passed its baton to the next Marine battalion deployed to Nawa, over eighty shops were open along the district center's main drag, and a bustling Friday market was as active as any major flea market in the U.S. Afghans came from all corners of Nawa to buy, sell, and trade their wares on that day each week, confident in the newly reestablished security that made it possible for them to travel to the district center from their homes in its outer villages.

The renewed sense of security that led to improved commerce made it inevitable that other aspects of normalcy would arrive. By late August, Marines were handing out notebooks, pens, and backpacks donated by a school in the U.S. to twenty-five Afghan teachers, led by a Gandalf look-alike elder who said he was their superintendent. For nearly two years, the teachers had been absent from Nawa because they were threatened and robbed by the Taliban for accepting a government salary. Half a dozen schools opened their doors in early September, and hundreds of young boys were back in classrooms, grateful for the much-needed supplies given to them by their American peers from thousands of miles away.[†] Health care came next, and one of the projects we were able to support, with the help of our NATO civilian counterparts, was the renovation of a basic services clinic that opened in the heart of the district in late

---

† Despite the progress in Nawa, some Afghan customs were hard to break, including forbidding education to girls, and the local schools opened only to boys.

November, complete with a staff of two Afghan doctors and several nurses and administrators.

As these events occurred, a district governor and his deputy had begun working out of a small, refurbished building they used as their office. A district council composed of about forty-five tribal and village leaders was elected in an openly democratic process, and government-sponsored programs designed to discourage local farmers from growing and selling poppy were implemented. The corrupt and unscrupulous police chief who, before Marines arrived, had been the only representative of the Afghan government in the district was unceremoniously "reassigned" to a staff job at police headquarters in Helmand's capital and replaced by a Nawa-born police officer known and respected throughout the district.

Several NGOs began sending governance and agricultural advisors to Nawa, confident that their staff would be safe in the secure environment we had established. One NGO convinced several farmers to plant grapes in the fields where they had previously grown highly profitable poppies (from which the sap was extracted to make opium) each spring. A grape seedling needs five or more years to grow into a viable fruit-producing plant, so the fact that these farmers were willing to forego an income from their fields over several years and multiple crop cycles was an oft-noted success in Nawa.[†] The long growing cycle for grape vines became an agriculture metaphor for the steady patience needed for a successful COIN vision.

When we first arrived, locals complained about security, violence, and their general safety. They still found things to complain about when we were coordinating our handover to a new battalion seven months later, but the topics of their complaints had changed to

† The farmers agreeing to diversify and plant grapes instead of wheat and corn were given a yearly stipend to compensate them for their lost income. They were *not* compensated for the lost income that ceasing to grow poppy in those fields caused.

manageable and predictable things like the quality of the furniture in the schools, speed limits on the busy street in the district center, the quality of water irrigating their crops, and the price of corn and wheat in the markets.

We were winning.

CHAPTER 19
AN HONEST MAN IN THE 'STAN

The Afghans are wild, ragged, fierce mountain tribesmen, hardly out of the Middle Ages. They're said to be elaborately polite, brave as lions and pitilessly cruel. Their country is harsh, and arid and barren.

—KEN FOLLETT, *Lie Down with Lions*

SEPTEMBER 2009

PASHTUNWALI, MEANING "THE WAY OF THE PASHTUNS," IS THE unwritten code of conduct of the Pashtun tribes of Afghanistan and northern Pakistan.[44] Before Afghanistan was an Islamic state, it was a tribal one (and still is), and the Pashtuns have always been its largest tribe. Their code often takes precedence over any religious obligations, emphasizing self-reliance and community. The code has specific components relating to mercy (*nanawatai*), hospitality (*melmastia*), loyalty (*sabat*), and bravery (*tureh*). Its concept of revenge (*badal*) would compel an entire village to seek reprisal for a wrong committed against one of its own, so Afghans nodded with understanding when Marines compared the rationale for the United States' swift and violent entry into the country in late 2001 to their own code's precepts.

Pashtunwali's core principal is honor (*nang*). Marines emphasized this when asking Nawa's residents to work with them and their
Afghan colleagues to bring stability to the previously ungoverned
district. "*Wuuh, wuuh*"—"Yes, yes"—they would say, nodding and
thumping their right hands over their hearts when we reminded
them of their obligation to their community and stressed that we were
there to help secure the environment in which they could succeed
on their own. Their code set the Afghans above the latest twists of
modern society and politics, and it helped us forge an understanding
with them. After all, except that they had a few centuries on us, the
Marines' commitment to honor, courage, and integrity took power
from a similar endurance through changing times.

Despite the insurgents in Nawa who sniped at Marines on patrol,
planted IEDs, or tried to sway the local population's support in their
favor, most of the residents lived up to the principles of their code,
particularly with respect to hospitality. Marines on patrols along the
wooded canals of the district often found themselves shedding their
combat gear and sitting down to enjoy tea and nuts with farmers
who, while taking a break from working their fields, had invited
them to rest for a while. In the face of hardship and depravity, the
Afghans were generous and friendly. Even those who scowled at us
and shooed their children away when they saw us approaching would
invite us to sit and drink tea if a patrol leader extended his hand to
them in greeting.

A few months after securing our presence in Nawa, however,
I saw some cracks in this supposedly inviolable code that defined
the Pashtuns. I reflected on a late nineteenth-century observation attributed to a young war reporter named Winston Churchill,
in which he shrugged off the romantic mystique of Pashtunwali,
dismissing it as "a system of ethics which regards treachery and
violence as virtues rather than vices."[45]

One of the jobs of my Civil Affairs team was to dole out money for damage to property caused during firefights, compensate locals who had been injured in fighting between Marines and insurgents, and pay for small projects that would get locals to work and improve their economy. When word spread through the district that a Marine called "Jagran Gus"—"Captain Gus" in Pashto—had money to dispense, the tent I had set up just inside the walls of Patrol Base Jaker to conduct meetings with Nawa's locals became a common destination. Most of the battle-damage claims I was asked to pay were legitimate, and I either knew about their details because I had been involved in the firefight myself or had received a note from the claimant given to him by a Marine who was there. Paying these claims showed that Marines were as magnanimous as they were lethal and helped us gain the trust of a wary population. But some claimants were outright swindlers and cheats who saw me as a gullible dupe who would dole out money for every sympathetic, but far-fetched, story told to me. For instance, firefights usually didn't result in dead cows, but one local farmer tried to wrest a healthy sum from me for the death of a cow he claimed had gotten caught in the middle of a gunfight between Marines and a group of insurgents.

"Do you have any pictures of the dead cow on your phone?" I asked when we sat in my tent to discuss his claim.

"No. All that was left is this," he replied, holding up a withered black-and-white tail.

"What happened to the rest of the cow? You don't even have a foot or a bone?" I countered, starting to suspect this was a scam.

"The wolves ate it."

"The *wolves*?" I asked.

"Yes, the wolves. The wolves of Helmand," he replied with an unflinching poker face.

"I've never heard of any wolves in Helmand," I said, peering over my glasses as a bead of sweat rolled to the tip of my nose in the stifling tent.

"Oh yes, there are many wolves here. Helmand is famous for its wolves. They are very dangerous and eat anything, even bones," he explained.

"But not tails, huh?" I responded, with a tone that made clear this wasn't really a question. He knew there would be no money exchanged today. He smiled, shrugged, and handed the tail to his young son, who had been watching our interaction. As we said our goodbyes, I was sort of amused by the conversation but wondered what tenet of Pashtunwali sanctioned the blatant lies I had just been told.

The projects we paid for were usually minor infrastructure improvements, like constructing bridge crossings or dredging and widening irrigation channels. Like any contractor, locals typically asked for a portion of the project cost up front to buy supplies and equipment to complete their work. These were fairly low-cost efforts, and the down payments we made were rarely more than $500, so they were low-risk ventures. Even if someone took the down payment and was never seen again, we weren't out very much. Despite numerous attempts to deceive me, I hadn't been burned on a small project yet, so I had no trepidation when, one night in early September, I was told someone wanted to speak with me in the *shura* tent about getting money to build a bridge across a canal south of the district center.

Inside the tent was a man fidgeting with a string of prayer beads, introduced to me as Mohamed Wotak. He looked to be about sixty but could have been younger. The harsh Afghan environment and rugged life there seemed to age people's appearance by years, if not decades. His beard was mostly white but with some darker gray spots on his chin. He had a stocky build, which along with the firm grip from his calloused hands suggested a lifetime of tough physical work. He seemed impatient and nervous, rushing through the requisite polite formalities that began all conversations with an Afghan and shifting his gaze constantly, rarely keeping eye contact with me or my interpreter for more than a few seconds at a time.

He said he was a farmer from a village about five kilometers south of the district center and wanted money to rebuild a cement bridge across a five-meter-wide canal near it. Showing me pictures of the site on the small screen of his Nokia mobile phone, he explained that building a bridge strong enough to withstand the weight of a pickup truck or tractor hauling a load of grain to the market in the district center would cut travel by thirty kilometers. Residents of Shoshurak, his village, had to go far out of their way to visit the market now because there were too few bridges between it and the district center.

"If you start tomorrow, how long will it take you to finish?" I asked. It was obviously a worthwhile project. I knew the location he spoke of and had frequently heard about the problems Shoshurak's residents had getting to the district center.

"I think three weeks. I have six people ready to help," he replied, and listed the supplies and equipment he needed to complete the task.

"How much?" I asked, expecting a high-ball figure and a lengthy negotiation to haggle the price down to an amount in line with the $5,000 limit I was authorized to spend.

Pulling a piece of paper from a folded crease in his turban, he showed me a rough sketch of the bridge he proposed to build. In the margins was what looked like a shopping list, with numbers next to each item. He told me "125,000 Afghanis" (about $2,500), fixing his gaze firmly on me for the first time.

"Deal," I said, reaching out to Mohamed to formalize our agreement with a handshake. I filled out the forms required for me to disburse money to a foreign national and gave Mr. Wotak fifty thousand Afghanis as a down payment to buy the equipment and supplies he needed. I explained that when he was done in three weeks, he should come to the patrol base to let me know so that I could take a patrol to inspect the bridge and pay him the balance owed once I had confirmed the work was done as we had agreed. He unfurled the long green-and-brown plaid cloth that formed his turban, tucked the cash I had given him into one of its folds, and rewrapped it around his head.

As we rose to walk out of the tent, he resumed the nervous demeanor he had first shown. Shifting his gaze cautiously toward the gate of our patrol base, he implored me to not walk outside with him, explaining that he was worried that, if insurgents knew he took money from Marines for a project, he would get an unwelcome night visit and be robbed, at the least. I understood, wished him well, and told him I looked forward to seeing him in about three weeks.

Two weeks later, a Marine on watch shook me by the shoulder at 4:00 a.m. "Sir, that guy from Shoshurak is here to see you."

I grumbled myself awake, put on my trousers and boots, holstered my pistol to my belt, and shuffled my way toward my meeting tent. The sun had not yet begun peeking over the hills across the Helmand River, and the sky was a crisp navy blue, but even this early in the morning the heat wafted across the ground, almost visibly.

Mohamed Wotak was inside the tent, sitting on his haunches, fingering his prayer beads with the same nervousness he'd shown when we first met. One of our interpreters had already joined him, and they were making small talk.

"*Salam alekum*," I greeted him, patting my chest and taking a seat on the ground across from him.

"*Wa-alekum salam*," he replied, and pulled out his phone to scroll through some photos. He explained that he had finished the bridge and had come to collect the balance owed to him. He emphasized that he had arrived so early to avoid being seen by any insurgents or their supporters, fearing a robbery or a "tax assessment" if they found out he received money from the Marines.

I was still groggy from being unexpectedly awakened but scrolling through the photos on Mohamed's phone piqued the frustration brewing in me after several months of efforts by other Afghans to swindle money from me for nonexistent battle-damage claims and grossly inflated bids for projects. The photos I saw were of a bridge that was carefully designed and thoroughly constructed. It had three large culverts to allow canal water to flow through and was framed by concrete, neatly leveled on all sides. The tips of some half-inch rebar poking out of a few spots suggested it was steel-reinforced. The top was smooth and even, formed with a bit of a slope to allow water to run off its sides rather than accumulate in puddles on top of it. It was a professional job, and I couldn't believe this was the bridge I had expected to take at least three weeks to complete. I assumed that Mohamed had taken pictures of a different bridge across a canal elsewhere in Afghanistan and was trying to pass it off as his own work.

"Can I have the rest of my money?" he asked timidly as I continued scrolling through the pictures.

"I still need to see the bridge myself to make sure it's done properly and take pictures for my paperwork. I'm going on a patrol in a few hours, so why don't you meet me there," I replied, trying to hide my skepticism.

"No, it's too dangerous. If the *dushman* see me with you, they'll rob me later in the day," he implored. [†]

[†] *Dushman* roughly translates to "insurgent" in Pashto.

My patience had worn out. Raising my voice and chopping my hand toward him, I blurted, "You think I'm an idiot? You didn't build that bridge. That's why you don't want to go there with me because *you know* that *I know YOU are full of shit!* You all talk about honor and your Pashtunwali and now you look me in the eye and lie to me about this bridge and think I'm dumb enough to give you *more* money?"

Mohamed looked at the ground with a furrowed brow, clutching his prayer beads as he listened to the translation.

I calmed down during the time it took to translate my rant, but my mood was still sour as I said, "I'm going to the bridge site on my patrol in a few hours. I'm betting there's no bridge there. But if there is, come back here tonight and I'll give you the rest of the money. If there's not a bridge there, I don't ever want to see you again. Got it?"

As my interpreter translated, Mohamed nodded in understanding. He stood up and turned to leave and then glanced back to murmur the typical Pashtun goodbye, "*Hodai paman.*" It means, "Go with God."

Ninety minutes later, I stepped off with a squad of Marines to look for a crossing I was certain didn't exist. An hour later, soaked in sweat under our combat load, we arrived at our destination and I stared in awe at the perfectly constructed bridge I had seen before daybreak on Mohamed's phone. It was beautiful and looked impregnable. Just then, a convoy of Marines in armored Humvees drove up. I stopped the lead vehicle and asked the driver if he knew how long the bridge had been here. "They just finished it two days ago, sir. A couple of guys were working on it 24/7 last week. Then some guys were camping on both sides of the canal for a few days telling people to not drive over it until the concrete dried. We drove over it a few times yesterday and it's solid."

I felt small and pathetic, and the invective I'd hurled at Mohamed earlier in the day dripped shame inside my head.

I knew I would see him later in the day and I had to eat some crow. I owed him an apology as much as I owed him the rest of his money. Returning to the patrol base, I implored the Marines to give me anything they could spare from care packages to lay out a spread for Mohamed when he showed up. It didn't take long for me to put together a platter of Oreos, Ritz crackers, and sunflower seeds. I added a bottle of orange-flavored Gatorade and had a scorched aluminum kettle ready to boil some water for tea when he arrived.

Later that afternoon, when the sun was starting to set, Mohamed and I made our way to the tent, where I gestured toward the gourmet spread (at least by remote patrol base standards) laid out before us and motioned for him to have a seat. As I began counting out some paper bills, I explained I had indeed seen the bridge and was amazed. I made a point of laying out the bills so that he could see how much was there. I also noted that because he had done such a tremendous job ahead of schedule, I was going to pay him an additional twenty-five thousand Afghanis.

Once the money was laid out, I asked him to sign the forms I needed to submit to the cashier's office at Camp Leatherneck, scooped up the bills, and ceremoniously held them in both hands before him. He took them with a grin, his nervousness now gone, popped an Oreo in his mouth, and patiently chewed as he started counting the bills. I stammered out how sorry I was for the way I had spoken to him earlier, explaining that so many of his countrymen had blatantly tried to cheat me. I was nervous and embarrassed, and I rambled as my interpreter patiently waited for a pause to interject a translation of what I'd said.

When I stopped, and my bumbling apology was being repeated in Pashto, Mohamed calmly began rewrapping his head in the turban he had removed to stash his money just as he had done with the down payment I'd given him a little more than a week ago.

When the message was finally conveyed, Mohamed took another Oreo, twisted its two chocolate wafers apart, and smiled at the cream center. He looked at me, nodded understandingly, shrugged, and replied with a smile, "Oh, *Saheb*," (a Pashto honorific), "I don't blame you. I wouldn't trust an Afghan either."

CHAPTER 20
THE MULLAHS

The business of politics is the conciliation of differing interests.
—BERNARD CRICK, *In Defense of Politics*

SEPTEMBER 28, 2009

THE NAWA DISTRICT GOVERNOR, HAJI ABDUL MANAF, UNDERSTOOD the precept that "all politics is local." When representatives from Kabul and the provincial capital came to Nawa to hold a government *shura*, he joined his counterparts from the national government in front of a crowd of several hundred men from the district. They assembled themselves in the main auditorium at the school in the district center, a large, open room about the size of a grade school basketball court. Its walls were once painted white but had absorbed years of dust and sand and had turned pale brown in the spots where the paint hadn't yet chipped off. A dozen large pillars supported the low roof and provided a place for many of the men to lean against as they sat on the uneven concrete floor. The glassless windows allowed a comfortable breeze to glide through the room, cooling the air a tad for the men in the crowd whose emotions would soon run hot.

The visiting dignitaries sat on chairs behind a row of tables at the front of the room and began the meeting, as all official events did, with a prayer. But soon after the typical polite and deferential greetings and blessings were exchanged, the mood became agitated and tense. The locals attending the meeting fiddled with their prayer beads and often pulled on their beards, many of which were orange-tinged from liberally applied henna dye, which also stained their fingernails and hands. Listening to the visitors from Lashkar Gah and Kabul, the others steadily took on a sterner look, often shaking their heads in contempt and turning to their friends to mutter among themselves. Eventually, several local men, who had been patiently and studiously sitting on the floor with legs crossed, rose to shout at the government leaders, gesticulating wildly, hurling accusations of corruption, ineptitude, and indifference to the day-to-day struggles in Nawa. This was an Afghan-led meeting, so only a few Marines were present. We sat on the floor or stood in a corner of the room mainly to observe but also to take note of the concerns raised and be on the alert for any threats like a suicide bomber or enraged gunman. As the tension in the conversations rose, the translators who stood at our side feverishly tried to capture the words of several of the speakers, but the tone was crystal clear, and eventually the translations consisted simply of, "He's very angry."

Amid all this invective, Manaf deftly slid out of his seat at the front of the room and positioned himself on the floor among his constituents. The leader of the Barakzai tribe (the most prominent in Nawa) was seated on the floor close to him. He was a charismatic white-bearded man who looked like the common image of a sorcerer. He, like the others, had been finger wagging and shouting. When he paused, Manaf suddenly sprang to his feet and blurted that he, too, was tired of the bureaucracy and graft and that he would not rest until it was eradicated. He faced the seated masses as he spoke, his back now to the Afghan government officials who had traveled to Nawa from the provincial and national capitals. The crowd loved it, rising to cheer.

The *shura* adjourned a few minutes later, and soon after, the visitors joined Manaf in a quieter setting, slouching on secondhand couches in his newly renovated office. Manaf hastily apologized for his outburst, and his guests laughed and nodded, recognizing the balancing act he needed to perform. He had to appeal to the immediate emotional needs of his constituents while also handling the practical aspects of getting things done in Afghanistan.

While always quick to smile and joke, the heavy burden of his job took a visible toll on Manaf. His eyelids and jowls seemed weighed down from gravity, fatigue, and frustration. Afghani politics isn't just local—it's tribal. He needed to accommodate the interests of tribes such as the Alakozai, Barakzai, Kuchi, Noorzai, and Popolzai, as well as the many villages in the district, from Aynak and Khalach to Shoshorab and everywhere in between. But one "tribe" in particular was a constant agitator for Manaf: the mullahs.

There were scores of mosques throughout Nawa, and each one had a mullah. The mosques themselves were simple mud structures, often only ten by ten meters square, with little to distinguish them as holy sites other than a *mihrab*—a semicircular niche in the outer wall indicating the direction of Mecca. This niche was also where the resident copy of the Quran rested on a pedestal in most mosques. In some cases, there was also a long pole with an attached loudspeaker, through which the resident mullah's call to prayer was broadcast five times per day. The credentialing process for mullahs was questionable. Often, simply declaring oneself a mullah was enough. The mullahs came together as an informal but influential network of

political operatives, capable of shaping the mood of those who gathered with them to pray and gossip.

Manaf continually fretted about the mullahs threatening the
tenuous support he had raised in the district and was devising a plan
to gather them for a dedicated mullahs' *shura* in the district center.

Wondering about the logistics of such a gathering, I asked him,
"How many mullahs are there in Nawa?"

He looked at me with a profound, heavy-lidded exhaustion,
clapped his hands to his cheeks, and pulled them down through his
beard, tugging on it with both his fists. I often saw this gesture when
he was particularly tired or frustrated. Letting out a long, guttural
sigh, he looked me in the eye, and in slow, distinct English said,
"Too . . . fucking . . . many!"

We accomplished a lot together in Nawa, but we never got around
to having the *shura* with the mullahs.

CHAPTER 21
ON THE HOME FRONT

How lucky I am to have something that makes saying goodbye so hard.
—A.A. MILNE, *Winnie the Pooh*

OCTOBER 2009

HUMANITY HAS ALWAYS LOOKED TO THE SKY FOR SOLACE AND GUID-
ance, and sometimes, answers to questions we might never even
know we are asking. Thousands of years before the Magi followed
a star to Bethlehem, sailors and traveling caravans relied on the
tiny dots of light above them to find their way. And sometimes they
just stared pensively at the images they imagined were staring back
at them as they nodded off to sleep. Like those distant ancestors,
I spent many nights in Afghanistan staring in wonderment at the
night sky, searching for and finding the menagerie of creatures in
the constellations revolving above me before I drifted into slumber.

The vastness of the night sky could be literally and figura-
tively illuminating, yet simultaneously oppressive and heavy. Some
nights while I gazed at the cosmos, I felt a profound loneliness I'd
never known. It was a paradoxical emotion, because in a combat
zone, you're never really alone. You are always surrounded by other

Marines, whether on a patrol, in a guard post, sleeping in a barracks or under the stars. Yet often, I was so damned lonely.

When the weight of that emotion felt like an anvil on my soul, I thought of my wife back home. While I had a battalion of Marines to share my solitude, she was truly alone, with just our young son for company—and another child on the way. We both had daily routines and rituals to perform, but I had the Marines to my left and right to inspect my gear, check my radio, and cover my back while we were on patrol. My wife just had her wits and patience—both certainly pushed to their limits—to help her manage the demands of a toddler, the stresses of work, and the discomfort of a pregnancy in a sultry East Coast summer all by herself.

In Afghanistan, the day's skies were usually clear and blue. Though much of the time it was uncomfortably hot, we sometimes had a respite from the heat when puffy cumulus clouds lent some cover from the sun's direct rays. But for our families back home, the clouds that hung over them much of the time were metaphorical and dark. There is an anxiety that comes with having a loved one in harm's way. It accompanies our loved ones throughout their daily routines. For those family members, the war on the other side of the world—and a dread of the death and horror it might bring into their lives—is the reality they wake up to each day. It is not some abstract concept they can choose to ignore.

Our families serve, just as much as the armor-clad, rifle-bearing Marines who marched with me in Afghanistan's dirt. Indeed, some of the greatest sacrifices made during a war are by the ones we leave behind on the home front. They perform their service with no thought of a medal, a promotion, or the pageantry of a change-of-command ceremony when it ends.

The parents, siblings, children, and spouses of those who go off to fight in America's conflicts often put careers on hold, celebrate anniversaries and birthdays alone, run a household, or pack their bags and move every two years when a new duty assignment comes along. Spouses can only dream about a date night. Kids bounce a ball against a wall, imagining the day when their dad will be there to play catch with them. They can find spots on a map named Khe Sanh, Hue City, Mogadishu, Fallujah, Ramadi, or Sangin, not because they're geography buffs but because they have a loved one who fought there, and they've been glued to the news coming from those places. Some have held the hand of a friend whose family member returned in a casket; others have answered a knock on the door to be greeted by a chaplain and two others in uniform, there to give them the most grim news imaginable. Indeed, they've served too.

One night in early October, I found myself staring again at the sky, breathing in the autumn air, which was starting to chill. I was watching a thin trail of clouds drift past a nearly full moon. As their luminescence shifted in the moonlight, I imagined those clouds as big sheets of gauze, undulating in the wind. It was as if an invisible giant were blowing them through the ether. I had just finished a satellite phone call with my wife, in which she told me that our new son had been born that morning. She described him as beautiful, with almond-shaped eyes and skinny little fingers. She added that he gets perky dimples in his cheek when she tickles his chin, and that his big brother is amazed at his tiny little feet.

We finished our call, and again I felt the weight of that pervasive loneliness as I smiled at the moon. After a few moments, I went into the canvas tent that served as our operations center and shared my news with the Marines working the midnight shift, monitoring the radios. We toasted my good fortune with a swill of orange-flavored Gatorade, and I thought there was no one else on earth I was prouder to share my loneliness with than those Marines.

CHAPTER 22

IZZY

Coauthored with Nick Martz

The average dog is a nicer person than the average person.

—ANDY ROONEY, former *60 Minutes* commentator

SHE HAD THE MISFORTUNE OF BEING BORN IN AFGHANISTAN, WHERE kindness to dogs is not considered a virtue. Weeks after being ejected from the womb, lost, or abandoned by her mother and littermates, she was found, then teased and tormented by some bored Afghan boys. She had endured pokes from sticks and was pelted with rocks. She would have died but for some patrolling British soldiers who came across those boys punishing her simply because she was a dog and they had nothing better to do. The soldiers brought her back to Patrol Base Jaker where they watered and fed her and sheltered her from those who would do her harm.

The Brits named her Esmerelda, shortened to "Ezzy." Later, when U.S. Marines arrived at the patrol base, her name was Americanized to "Izzy," and, as she lay in the shade to escape the radiating Afghan summer heat, some even suggested that her name should have been "Lazy." She responded to them all.

Izzy was mostly white, with a brown head that was striped with black fur along her muzzle. Her eyes were a queer yellow, always with a playful glint, and she hoped for little more than a scratch behind the ears, a belly rub, or a spot on the next patrol roster. Her long, ratty tail stretched behind her like an empty fishhook, and would sashay breezily as she sauntered about. Her ears were broad, brown, and when she felt playful or spotted something that piqued her interest, they perked up. Although small as a pup, she was growing quickly. Her already massive paws suggested that she would one day grow quite large.

She was prissy. Though clearly starving at first, she refused much of the food she was offered from British rations and, later, from the Marines' MREs. We said that despite being a mutt, a social outcast of sorts, she at least had good taste. When Marines noticed the MRE enchilada or omelet Izzy had left to rot in her food dish, they began to wonder what they were eating if even a scruffy, malnourished dog refused it.

Izzy got by, though, as Marines fed her morsels of fresh bread or lamb bought from local bakers and farmers. She often made out like a bandit, accepting scraps from all who offered them—sometimes so much that she vomited up the fare she'd come across that day.

The kindness shown her by the British soldiers and later the Marines caused her to love them. In her mind, she was a member of their pack. She joined the Marines on patrols, sloshing through irrigation canals and trudging through muddy fields with her fellow Devil Dogs, the nickname given to Marines by German soldiers during World War I. She did her part as a member of the pack, barking at local Afghans she perceived to be threats, or sometimes freezing in place and staring into a distant field or tree line that, upon closer inspection, yielded an Afghan trying not to be seen.

Her company was not always certain, nor was it always welcome. The Marines often remarked, as Izzy sat awkwardly on her haunches waiting for the next patrol to step outside the wire, that one day she might simply disappear. They thought it was likely that at some point Izzy's mangled body would be found lying alongside an irrigation canal somewhere after she'd tripped an IED intended for Marines. Or perhaps a local Afghan would entice her into his compound, tether her neck, and turn her into a menacing guard dog, making her mean, and chopping off her ears and tail so she'd look like the other dogs in the villages nearby.

And then there was the issue of the mullah at the local mosque, whom the Marines frequently visited and who clearly did not appreciate Izzy's loud bark. Her gentle nuzzle at the back of a trouser leg, her playful nip at the pants cuff, or her general filthiness didn't appeal to him either. Izzy was, after all, a dog, and a wild one at that. She enjoyed chewing on a piece of rancid meat or rolling in the foul-smelling wastewater pits that contained the runoff from the Marines' and British soldiers' ablutions. In the early morning, she moseyed about, covered in this foulness, infested with ticks and other exotic parasites, lapping a bit of water from the small tin pan the British soldiers had provided her, as happy as a dog in Afghanistan could be. The Marines recognized that Izzy's presence, although welcome in some circumstances, could also hinder their mission.

They made occasional half-hearted attempts to keep Izzy from patrolling with them or to lock her away somewhere out of sight when generals and diplomats visited the patrol base. These attempts rarely succeeded. When Stanley McChrystal, the four-star general in charge of all NATO forces in Afghanistan, visited Patrol Base Jaker, the Marines locked Izzy inside the adjacent Afghan National Army compound. Thinking she was safely tucked away, they prepared for the general's visit by arranging a long row of tables, at which General McChrystal could sit while the battalion commander gave a brief on operations in the area. As the general took his seat, the Marines glanced beneath the table and saw Izzy lying there, panting contentedly, having escaped her temporary pen to join her pack at what was, in her mind, her rightful place. Clearly, she was undeterred by the four stars on the general's uniform. General McChrystal smirked as he pulled his long runner's legs under his bench to accommodate her. Izzy did not appear to notice, or mind.

Shortly after General McChrystal's visit, Izzy got her fifteen minutes of fame. She was a dog, true, and a mangy, wild, nocturnal Afghan one at that, but her name was immortalized one day in a *Washington Post* article, in which the reporter, describing our patrol base, wrote: "A mangy dog named Izzy scampers about."[46] Some Marines grumbled that Izzy had achieved fame before they had, but this one sentence endeared her to them all the more and made her as permanent a fixture on the base as was possible under the circumstances.

As unfortunate as she was to have been born a dog in Afghanistan, Izzy had also been born in a time of war. She had survived the blows and cruelty of idle children and the almost nightly attacks on the patrol base by insurgents with AK-47s and RPGs. But she did not know that the blows of cruel children and insurgent attacks were the least of her worries.

The Marines knew that one day the American order prohibiting pets and mascots would have to be enforced. Another problem was that Izzy was a female dog and, by canine standards, probably a hot little number. She began to attract a few local strays and distract the Marines' highly and expensively trained military bomb-sniffing dogs. She also showed some signs of sickness, likely from a tick-borne disease that the military medical professionals warned would be especially dreadful if transmitted to humans. In late August, a few nights after the last of the Brits left the patrol base for good, a few senior Marines discussed what to do about Izzy, knowing what the answer would be. No one wanted to give her to a local Afghan—in the short time they had known Izzy they had come to love her, and they knew the hard life of an Afghan dog. That left one option.

And so, one morning before the sun's feeble rays shone over the dirt-filled barriers and concertina wire that surrounded Patrol Base Jaker, a Marine awoke, dressed, and holstered his pistol after checking that a round was in the chamber. A quick whistle brought Izzy from her slumber nearby, and she greeted her friend after a quick detour through the weeds and wastewater pits. She was always playful in the mornings and obediently followed the Marine outside the gate where she bounded through a recently harvested field, then stopped to stare to the east where something had caught her attention in the first light of the rising sun beginning to creep over the mountains across the river. The Marine came behind her, stroked her back, and scratched her behind the ears one last time. "I'm sorry, Izzy," he whispered. He held his breath, his eyes welling with tears. Placing the muzzle of his pistol against the back of her head, exhaling slowly, he asked God for forgiveness. Then he pulled the trigger.

It is unfortunate sometimes, the circumstances in which God's creatures find themselves. Izzy had not asked to be born a dog. She had not asked to be born in Afghanistan or despised by the humans she initially found herself surrounded by. She had not asked to be beaten and clubbed by unkind children. She had borne all these burdens as a creature of instinct and limited intellect. And when she finally discovered a pack of her own, she was loyal to the end, never failing to accompany the Marines on a patrol, rub against a leg, or playfully nip a hand or trouser cuff. Even on her last morning as she greeted the sad Marine who awoke before dawn to end Izzy's life.

There was a favorite story about Izzy, told by a young Marine, that warrants sharing here. He had been suffering from diarrhea and stomach cramps caused by an illness sarcastically named the "Jakers," after our patrol base. He arose late at night to make a head call and then sought some water to wash his face. In his discomfort, he thought about his elderly father who had recently received his first chemotherapy treatment back home, and he turned his head toward the sky in a silent prayer for guidance and comfort. Moments later, on his way back to the crumbling brick building where he slept, he felt a cold, wet nose gently nudge his hand. It was Izzy, trying to play with, or just offer some reassuring sympathy to, one of her pack.

The Marines have long since left Patrol Base Jaker, first to an adjacent field where temporary plywood structures were erected for their use, and then from Nawa altogether. Before vacating, they had hired a contractor from the provincial capital to patch up the bullet holes and renovate the decrepit old building where they'd lived, and then ceded the building back to the Afghan government for the use of officials working to make their country a better place. Izzy remains there, too, buried at the edge of a field that once grew poppies but has since grown several cycles of wheat, watermelon, and corn. The wooden sign the Marines placed over her is certainly gone now, probably pulled up and used by a local farmer for firewood.

It simply read, "Devil Dog."

CHAPTER 23
HOLY COW!

Cows are my passion. What I have ever sighed for has been to retreat
to a Swiss farm, and live entirely surrounded by cows.
—Mrs. Skewton, in Charles Dickens, *Dombey and Son*

NOVEMBER 6, 2009

As NOTED BEFORE, RAW NUMBERS ARE OFTEN THE MEASURES RELIED
upon to assess success (or failure) in war. Body counts, bombs
dropped, ships and planes destroyed or deployed, and "boots on
the ground" are all means by which a war's progress is typically
judged. In COIN operations, however, metrics such as reconstruction dollars spent, schools opened, clinics made operational,
government functions resuming, and commercial growth are also
used to gauge success. The number of cups of tea shared with the
locals would also have been illustrative of our progress after several
months on the ground in Nawa.

In early November, though, a new metric came to symbolize
success in Nawa: cow breeding. Animals responding to their repro-
ductive instincts isn't itself remarkable. But *how* and *why* two of them
in Nawa were brought together is.

Before Marines arrived in the district, the Taliban was well entrenched as the de facto government there. Schools were closed because teachers knew they wouldn't be paid by the Ministry of Education, or if they were, they might be robbed of their salaries or even killed for being Afghan government employees. The three clinics in the district were empty, as doctors and staff had the same disincentives as did the teachers. About fifty Afghan police officers were the only face of the national government in the district. They were as corrupt as the Taliban, smoking marijuana during the day and lazily driving around in their green pickup trucks, extorting cash and property from the locals whom they were supposed to be protecting. Residents who still lived in Nawa stayed close to their homes as much as they could. Many of the district's roads and bridges had been destroyed by years of war and neglect, so even routine trips were logistically cumbersome. On the rare occasions anyone did have to venture away from their compounds and fields, they were always at risk of being shaken down by the Taliban.

Communicating from one end of the district to another was difficult, if not impossible. The Taliban warned the employees of Roshan Telecom (Afghanistan's main telecom provider) that their heads would rest atop their cellular towers if they turned on the power. Not surprisingly, the towers were dormant, and cell phone reception in Nawa was spotty and unreliable.

But a few months after our Marines came to the district in July 2009, things changed for the better. Teachers went back to work, the district center clinic was renovated and staffed, new and better-trained police officers replaced the lackadaisical and crooked members of the force, competent government officials began working in functioning offices, and sturdy bridges were rebuilt or installed across canals at key travel junctions. Several of the Roshan Telecom towers were turned on and manned around the clock, providing the reception that allowed Nawa's residents to call and text one another on secondhand Nokia or Samsung phones they bought in one of the district center's shops that had been boarded up for months. And the large, barren field in the district center that had been a dusty patch when we first arrived began regularly hosting a bustling Friday market. Hundreds of residents from all corners of Nawa converged there every week to hock their wares, barter and trade livestock, buy needed supplies, and socialize with friends.

The confluence of all these successes paid off for two farmers at one Friday market in early November. One was from the district's north-ernmost village, called Aynak. He owned a bull that had a reputation as one of the most virile studs in all of Helmand. The other was from a southern village called Pinjadoo, and he owned a cow that was ready to be bred. The two men spoke and texted on their cell phones, arranged to meet at the Friday market, loaded their animals into trailers towed behind tractors, and traveled safely from their homes to the bustling commercial hub in the center of the district.

The coupling would occur just outside the main market center, a carnal encounter freely on display for any interested passersby. Indeed, a small crowd, including a few Marines, had already begun to gather as the two bovine owners pulled their tractors up to the dusty arena-like expanse of dirt and trampled grass. The men quickly greeted each other, exchanged a few words while gesturing to the space where the mating would take place, and then returned to their respective tractors to retrieve their animals. The bull's owner had a confident, almost arrogant demeanor. He knew that he had a needed commodity—a virile stud to impregnate the fertile cow—and he seemed to revel in the attention and respect shown toward him. In some sense, he may have felt he was living vicariously through the bull, pampered and respected for exerting its most masculine tendencies on a hapless, servile female.

Four teenaged Afghan boys, probably sons or younger siblings of the bull's owner, began to push the black-skinned, dust-covered bull down a plywood ramp reinforced with two-by-fours propped against the back of the trailer in which it had arrived. They were backing it out as the space in the trailer was too narrow for the thousand-pound beast to turn around and walk out headfirst. One of the boys grasped the bull's tail and pulled snugly while another pushed it from its head and shoulders. The two other boys tugged the bull by ropes tied around its horns and neck. The bull stubbornly resisted, grunting and bellowing against the boys' efforts.

The owner watched from a few feet away, occasionally giving unsolicited advice to his crew and smacking the bull on its haunches with a thin stick he carried. The plywood ramp bowed precariously as the bull warily put its full weight onto it. After a few minutes of tugging and pushing, the bull was on solid ground. It pulled against its tethers a few times, then pawed the ground and loudly snorted, sending a long stream of snot out its nostrils that dangled in the air. Taking in his surroundings, the bull twitched its head suddenly to one side, sending the tendril of mucous slapping against the shirt of one of the teenaged cowhands, leaving a thick horizontal streak of slime across the boy's *shalwar kamiz*. The other boys erupted in laughter, no doubt thankful they were outside the line of fire. The bull was not savage or menacing looking, like the huge beasts slaughtered in Spanish bullfights. But it was large and densely muscled, and it certainly had the heft to overpower its handlers had it not been for a nose ring attached to a lead rope that kept it in line.

The owner of the cow had, in the meantime, led it to a midpoint between the two trailers, where he waited for the bull to be brought over. Like the bull's owner, he had an entourage of assistants—two preteens who I later learned were his twin sons. The boys were lean and tall, without much excess weight on them. They each stood with a lead rope in hand on either side of the cow. One held a shaft of hay, which the cow munched on with a bored comportment. The cow was by no means tiny, but she was several inches shorter and a few hundred pounds lighter than the bull. She stood in place, calmly chewing on the hay being fed to her, as the bull was led around her a half-dozen times. The cow's rear legs were tied at each ankle to prevent her making a quick getaway and from kicking either one of the handlers or the bull when it prepared to mount her. A well-placed kick from the cow would leave a mark on the unfortunate recipient; a kick in the bull's scrotum might render him worthless for future stud servicing. Her owner had splashed several buckets of water drawn from a nearby well on the cow's backside and had wiped her nether regions with a dingy cloth that at one time had probably been white.

After several laps around the cow, the bull had become agitated and visibly aroused. A group of young boys who stood among the Marines watching the breeding spectacle pointed and joked about the size of the penis hanging underneath the bull—just like their peers in the U.S. would have done. The two owners nodded to each other and then barked orders at the animal handlers, who obediently readied themselves for the animals to congress. The bull was aggressive and simultaneously had to be led and restrained from forcefully mounting the cow, lest the sudden weight on top of her would collapse her legs. The cow's two handlers pushed their shoulders into her chest to keep her from moving forward as the bull's team moved closer to their mark. When they were inches away, the cow seemed to sense what was occurring and twitched her tail, moving it to the side, just as the bull rose up on its hind legs and oafishly pounced on top of her. Its owner used the small stick he had been holding to steer the bull into the cow, then stepped back and let his team manage their reins. The cow remained stoically in place, almost oblivious to what was occurring, tranquilly chewing on her cud.

The bovine coupling itself was efficient and earnest, aided by the farmers and others who held reins and leashes, pushed against loins to balance the cow underneath, and deftly peeked between legs to make sure all parts were properly aligning. A few vigorous but passionless minutes after the union began, the bull's half-ton of heaving flesh quivered for a moment before he pounced off his mount. He had drooled a line of snot onto the cow's back, which her owner wiped off with the grayish rag he had used to wipe her loins a few minutes earlier. The transaction was complete. With his muscular aggression depleted, the bull let himself be led back to his trailer, head bowed with fatigue from his few moments of exertion.

The small crowd that had watched the episode dispersed. As the animals were being hitched and secured back in the trailers that brought them both to Nawa's district center, the bull's owner was making arrangements with another cattleman for a tryst the following week. The farmer from Pinjadoo walked past me, muttering something to the interpreter standing by my side. The interpreter whispered to me, "He hopes to get twins."

"*Inshallah*," I yelled after him—"God willing."

He turned and smiled, nodded his head, pointed to the sky, and repeated my hopes: "*Inshallah*."

CHAPTER 24
TEA WITH THE TALIBAN

Afghans are treacherous and generally inclined towards double-dealing.
—From a British Army Field Manual, 1915 Field Notes: Afghanistan [47]

November 2009

The Taliban pictured in Hollywood movies are fearsome looking and possess a certain mystique about them. Their dark eyes glare piercingly from under sinister, arched brows; their angular features lend them a rugged handsomeness almost like the Marlboro Man; and their bronzed, weathered skin suggests a lifetime of toil, an air of confidence, and even wisdom. They're portrayed as hardy, industrious, and cunning and savage warriors, intimately familiar with the terrain they haunt and the myriad ways of killing enemies who dare tread there. Exactly what you'd expect a terrorist to look like.

In early November 2009, the eight Taliban-inspired insurgents who shuffled into a room before a group of Marines, Afghan government officials, and tribal elders, looked nothing like their silver screen "doppelgängers." They were a frightened, confused group of mostly young men not many years beyond their teens—if they weren't, in fact, still teenagers. Their gaunt bodies showed their sinewy muscles, but the tightness of their skin, their long, thin fingers, and bony features made them look more fragile than athletic. The youngest among them sported irregular patches of soft fur from their cheeks and chins rather than the robust beards their Taliban role models displayed in their propaganda images.

They were a ragtag group, unkempt and disorganized. Their baggy pants were torn, frayed, and muddied. In place of their *shalwar kamiz*, most wore a hospital gown we'd given them, loosely tied at the back. Several had large gauze patches taped to their skin, courtesy of our battalion's corpsmen, who attended to the bullet holes and abrasions they'd acquired after they fired at a squad of Marines from the back of a pickup truck and were thrown from its bed when the driver was killed by a well-aimed shot to the head and their vehicle crashed into a ditch.

They weren't real soldiers. They lacked military bearing and had never had any legitimate training in tactics or weapons employment. Instead, they had probably only been given a few minutes of instruction on how to point the AK-47 handed to them in the direction of the Marines they shot at. A few might have known how to reload the weapon after it ran out of ammunition, but the swift response of the Marines they engaged never gave them a chance to test that skill. Perhaps fearing the mockery of their peers, or wanting to live up to the fabled exploits of their uncles and fathers who claimed to have fought the Russians years before, they feigned bravery and commitment to a cause that might never have been clearly explained to them—or they never really believed in—when they loaded themselves into a truck to go shoot at Marines. They were unsophisticated and simple, not the guileful and mysterious villains imagined in fiction. With one or two exceptions, they were probably all virgins.

It wasn't clear which of them was actually in charge. By default, they deferred to the oldest, a haggard, balding, white-bearded man of about sixty who seemed to be more confused than any of the youngsters who trailed behind him. As they tottered into the Nawa district governor's office, we greeted them with a freshly brewed pot of tea and a no-nonsense tone that made it clear there was some serious business to discuss.

There is a beast in many of us. For some, it lies just below the surface, and even in a lifetime of antagonism, it may never reveal itself. But the Marine Corps' primary function—killing its country's enemies on the battlefield—demands that the beast be uncaged. A warrior ethic, however, requires that despite the savage exhilaration that can sometimes come from fighting and killing, that beast must be managed, even when the fighting is fierce, and *especially* when the fighting stops.

The moral demands on soldiers and Marines—most of whom are the same age as the befuddled Taliban gunmen described here—are immense. They are asked to do things that would be unthinkable in civil society, but which in wartime, are considered necessary and just—and even "legal" in the context of the law of war. Some may find a perplexing irony in that term, "law of war," but the goal of any war is its end. And when the war is finally over, enemies may become allies and their warriors will eventually return to their communities as citizens who served when called.

The military has a duty not only to prepare its warriors for combat and for coping with the destruction and carnage that comes with it, but they also have a duty to prepare them for the day when they fold up their uniforms for the last time. Although the demands placed on warriors are often extreme, no one should be exempt from adhering to the requirements of a civil society.

From the earliest days of our republic, our leaders have recognized a common humanity, even among our enemies. In 1775,

George Washington agreed with his British foe that the Revolutionary War would be "carried on agreeable to the rules which humanity formed."[48] Mindful of the risks that frenzied acts by his soldiers could pose to the cause of independence, General Washington required the members of his Continental Army to sign a copy of rules intended to limit harm to civilians. The rules further ensured that the soldiers' conduct respected what he called "the rights of humanity," so that their restraint "justly secured to us the attachment of all good men."[49]

Armed adversaries have often found their common humanity in the midst of their mutual suffering. The Christmas Truce of 1914, when German and British troops called a cease fire, sang carols to one another in their respective languages, and reportedly even had a soccer match in the deadly no-man's land between their trench lines, is one of the most common tales of mutual respect among enemies, even if some elements of this event have been embellished over time.[50]

Germans and Brits again frequently demonstrated an unusual fellowship during World War II.[†] Of particular note was the engagement between German Major Hans von Luck and his British counterparts from the Royal Dragoons as they fought one another in the deserts of Africa. In the midst of combat operations, the belligerents shared information about prisoners on both sides who had gotten lost and had been captured in the desert. They exchanged life-saving medicines at times, even though such exchanges surely made otherwise incapacitated men combat-ready. The Germans even suspended offensive operations against the Brits during "tea time," observing from afar as their foes set up portable stoves to engage in

---

† This may be, in part at least, because their respective royal families were kin. During WWI the blood connection was more obvious as King George V of Great Britain and Kaiser Wilhelm II were first cousins (as was Russia's Tsar Nicholas II); their grandmother was Queen Victoria.

their daily ritual. When the war ended, the commanding officer of the Royal Dragoons wrote a letter to Major von Luck, delivered to him by a Bedouin shepherd, which read:

Dear Major von Luck,

. . . The war in Africa has been decided, I'm glad to say, not in your favor.

I should like, therefore, to thank you and all your people, in the name of my officers and men, for the fair play with which we have fought against each other on both sides.

I and my Battalion hope that all of you will come out of the war safe and sound and that we may find the opportunity to meet again sometime, in more favorable circumstances.

With greatest respect.[51]

Admittedly, Americans at war haven't always regarded their enemies in the same respectful manner as Major von Luck and his British antagonists. We've dehumanized some of our enemies, with names such as "krauts," "nips," "chinks," "gooks," "skinnies," "ragheads," or "camel fuckers." I'm not saying it's right, but in war, it can make killing—war's business—easier. Even with those slurs, however, America's service members have largely comported themselves with honor and dignity on battlefields around the world and treated our enemies with respect. We did the same in Afghanistan.

So here we were, dedicated adversaries, sharing tea on a crisp November afternoon. Forty-eight hours earlier, we had been shooting at one another, determined to kill. Only the Marines succeeded in that endeavor. When the gun smoke settled after the brazen attack by the inexperienced teenagers, the truck from which they were firing was disabled, its driver and another assailant were dead, and the remaining few were sprawled on the ground with guns pointed at their heads while their hands were secured with flex-cuffs. The ones who had been wounded in the firefight or injured when the truck crashed were treated by the Navy corpsmen patrolling with the Marines.

Two days after that shootout, the former combatants were in the Nawa district governor's office with hangdog countenances. They were accompanied by three elders from their village. They were given a choice: go on trial or sign a "reintegration agreement" pledging not to rejoin or help the Taliban in any way, and to cooperate with the Afghan government's efforts to build its capacity in the district. The village elders served as their sponsors, signing similar agreements attesting to the young men's character and commitment to their pledge. The young men gazed at the floor with sullen frowns as they were being harangued by their elders, the district governor, and his deputy. In other moments, they sipped their tea and nodded meekly as they were encouraged to do good for their community. There was no self-righteousness about their cause, or ours. Just a clear understanding that they were on the losing side of an argument, and probably wouldn't fare well the next time they made such a foolhardy decision. We Marines stayed out of the discussion most of the time. This was, after all, an Afghan issue, to be resolved by Afghans. There was, however, a bit of empathetic respect between the young gunmen and the Marines. Not quite camaraderie, but an understanding of sorts.

The lectures concluded and the sheepish youngsters and their ancient comrade signed the documents in front of them. Then they took a last swig of tea and walked out of the room in a daze. They were probably dumbfounded by the opportunity for a second chance, something the Taliban would never have offered. As they filed out of the district governor's office, we shook their hands and told them, "*Hodai pamam*" ("Go with God").[52]

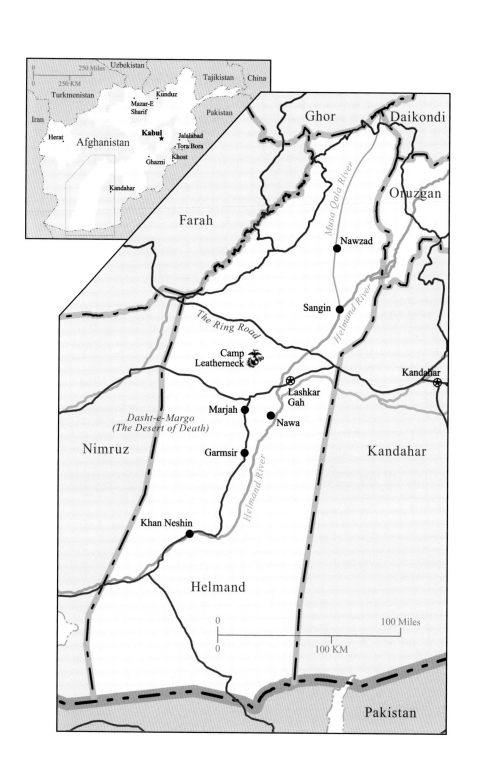

Inset map

250 Miles

250 KM

Uzbekistan

Tajikistan   China

Turkmenistan   Kunduz

Mazar-E
Sharif

Iran

Pakistan

Herat

Kabul   Jalalabad
★   Tora Bora

Afghanistan

Ghazni   Khost

Kandahar

Main map

Ghor   Daikondi

Oruzgan

Musa Qala River

Farah

Nawzad

Helmand River

Sangin

The Ring Road

Camp
Leatherneck

Kandahar

Lashkar
Gah

Marjah

Dasht-e-Margo
(The Desert of Death)

Nawa

Nimruz

Garmsir

Kandahar

Helmand River

Khan Neshin

Helmand

0   100 Miles

0   100 KM

Pakistan

Patrol Base Jaker a few days before the start of Operation Khanjar.

One way or another, we got across the many canals in Nawa.

Our Navy doctors
and corpsmen
treated everything
from combat
injuries to
household
mishaps.

Lt. Col McCollough (with Sergeant Major Sowers) in the Combat Operations Center at the start of Operation Khanjar...

...and at an impromptu shura with the leader of the Barakzai tribe.

USMC (Shvartsberg)

America's
finest.

USMC (Greeson)

USMC (Greeson)

USMC (Elgie)

Shuras were an effective way to get the community together, but sometimes tempers flared.

Curious kids watched
us on every patrol.

John Wendle

John Wendle

John Wendle

USMC (Harris)

Some of the locals we worked with who made Nawa a better place,
including Ishmael (bottom right trying on a Marine's helmet).

USMC (Greeson)

USMC (Purschwitz)

John Wendle

Haji Abdul Manaf

USMC (Shvartsberg)

A family returning to Nawa with all their
belongings after learning it was safe again.

USMC (Purschwitz)

A grain merchant weighs his
goods at the Friday market.

USMC (Shvartsberg)

USMC (Greeson)

A local farmer taking his flock of
sheep across a newly built bridge.

Boys on a break during
the first week of school.

Izzy on patrol
with Marines.

A new grave near
the Rugby Ball.

This Polaroid was the first photo this man ever had with his sons.

USMC (Purschwitz)

USMC (Elgie)

The Afghans always had a pot of tea on hand, and
Marines often joined them for a cup.

There is no better friend, and no worse
enemy, than a United States Marine.

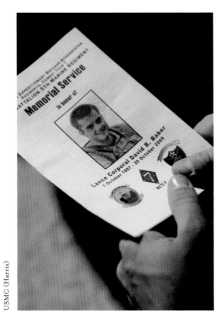

Always remembered, always honored. Clockwise from top left: Bill Cahir, Donald Hogan, Justin Swanson, David Baker

CHAPTER 25
INDECENT PROPOSAL

Loving goes by haps; Some Cupid kills with arrows, some with traps.
—WILLIAM SHAKESPEARE, *Much Ado About Nothing*

NOVEMBER 26, 2009

IT WAS THANKSGIVING DAY, AND ACROSS AMERICA, PEOPLE WERE gathering to watch football and gorge themselves on turkey, stuffing, cranberry sauce, yams, and traditional family desserts made from secret recipes passed down over generations. Later in the day, belts would be loosened and couches settled into after second and third helpings. Following one too many beers, opinions would also be loosened, and crazy uncles and nutty grandparents would enliven conversations with their cantankerous views on race, religion, and war, among other topics.

As some people indulged themselves in heated conversations, others planned tactics for their Black Friday shopping sprees, to start just after the stroke of midnight. A few emergency crews around the country would respond to fires caused when overzealous but under-cautious chefs ignored the instructions on how to deep-fry a whole turkey and ignited a garage or shed in a brilliant burst of flaming oil and exploding poultry.

While Americans were enjoying the holiday, I was twelve-and-a-half time zones[†] away from my family, wearing my least filthy uniform, sitting with about fifteen other Marines and a dozen Afghans on the dusty floor of a dilapidated building, about to enjoy a feast of our own. The floor of the room where we were seated was covered by a large rug, which gave off a subtle odor of wet wool. Splayed across the rug was a clear plastic tarp, and in front of each person seated around the room was a metal plate. Just outside the room, several Afghans, a few of whom were members of the local police force, stirred a brothy mixture of meat, oil, and spices in a large cauldron. A few others chopped up tomatoes and cucumbers or boiled rice in a separate large cauldron.

The air was heavy with the aromas of meat and spices mingled with the wood-and- charcoal burning fires heating up these concoctions. A faint whiff of musty feet also lingered; we had taken our boots off, and the Afghans who served us walked across the plastic carpet covering with their hairy bare feet, slapping a piece of fresh-cooked flatbread in our laps, pieces of which we would use to scoop up the stew being ladled onto our plates. Another Afghan walked among the assembled diners plucking small, deep-fried whole fish off a platter and laying them beside the other food being heaped in front of us, each time saying in broken English, "Is from Helmand River."

I hadn't thought of the Helmand River, a shallow, muddy body of water that meandered south toward Pakistan, as much of a fishing hot spot, but staring through a heavily battered eyeball on my plate was proof that there were indeed some fish in there. In the center of

† Among the many oddities of Afghanistan is its decision to skew its time zone by a half hour, a distinction shared by only a few other countries in the world, such as Iran, North Korea, Myanmar, and French Polynesia.

the room was a large plastic bowl of grapes, watermelon slices, and pomegranates broken into quarters—the pomegranates' ruby-hued seeds sparkling enticingly.

Although there was no beer, fancy dessert, or football game on a large-screen TV, there was plenty to be thankful for. We had begun the turnover to the battalion that would be replacing 1/5, nicknamed the "Lava Dogs." I was proud of what we had accomplished and felt confident that we were handing our work off to well-qualified successors. This Thanksgiving meal provided an opportunity to celebrate not just the holiday, but, our recent and future achievements with some of the Afghan leaders with whom we'd worked over the past seven months. They knew I would be leaving in a few days, so this was my going-away dinner as well, and I took the honored seat next to District Governor Haji Abdul Manaf. Even without beer and a football game to elevate our mood, it was a high-spirited gathering.

Manaf slapped my back and asked if I really wanted to leave Afghanistan.

"Yes," I replied. I explained that I was eager to see my wife, the son who was sixteen months old when I left and whose second birthday I was about to miss, and my other son, whose birth I missed and who would be nearly three months old before I met him for the first time.

"You could have a family here, Jagran Gus. I can arrange something with a woman I know who could use a husband," Manaf said with a smirk.

He continued, "She's a widow, and you get forty *jeribs* of land with her. She hasn't had any kids, so she's not, you know, stretched out," gesturing toward his crotch.

I paused for a moment, absorbing the translation.

"Is she pretty?" I eventually asked, humoring Manaf and our audience, reflecting that even though we were thousands of miles away from a traditional Thanksgiving dinner, we were having our own creepy uncle conversation.

"She was a cute child, but I haven't seen her face in years. Her nose is a bit crooked, though, because she got kicked in the face by a cow when she was a little kid. But that shouldn't matter. No one else will see her anyway. This is Afghanistan, after all," he answered.

It was a well-intentioned—albeit strange—offer, and the value of the land would place me firmly in the ranks of the upper middle class of Nawa residents. But I wasn't interested; I had much to look forward to in America, as I had explained. I placed my hand across my chest, a typical sign of gratitude in Afghanistan, and thanked Manaf for the generous offer, which I politely declined. I doubt he ever expected me to consider it seriously.

I took a scrap of bread and scooped up a handful of rice and bits of meat from my dinner tray, looked across the assembled group of Marines and Afghans I was sharing the meal with, raised the greasy mixture in the air, and announced, *"Noshe jan!"*—roughly "Cheers!" in Pashto.

They all responded in kind. It was a happy Thanksgiving.

CHAPTER 26
THE HIDDEN HALF

There are two powers in the world; one is the sword and the other is the pen. There is a third power stronger than both, that of women.

—MALALA YOUSAFZAI, *I Am Malala*

NOVEMBER 29, 2009

LIKE A SPECTRAL PRESENCE, THE WOMEN OF NAWA WERE ALWAYS— yet never—*there*. They loitered in small clusters on the outskirts of the Friday market or the fringes of a *shura,* but they never mingled with or browsed among the merchants (all of whom were men). Instead, they just waited until given an abrupt order to leave after being handed a heavy sack of produce or a leash tethered to a goat to lug (or tug) back home. From the back of a motorcycle or while walking a few steps behind their husbands, they would often turn their heads and watch us with wordless sideways glances through the mesh eye openings of the *burkhas* that otherwise obscured them. On patrol along Nawa's dirt roads and trails, we silently watched them back.

When Taliban insurgents were ousted from Nawa in the summer of 2009, many archaic views and practices went with them. But other cultural, religious, and tribal customs remained. Although women were gaining some independence in Afghanistan's major cities, and were even being elected or appointed to prominent positions in Afghanistan's post-9/11 government,[53] in rural areas like Nawa they were still relegated to the role of quiet, subservient functionary. They remained largely forbidden from interacting with adult males who were not in their immediate family, especially American Marines.[54] So we accepted the fact that a thousand U.S. Marines from an infantry battalion dispersed throughout a 350-square-mile district would have little or no contact with half of the population we were tasked to protect. (The infantry was an all-male force in 2009.)

Women get married young in Afghanistan. "Married off" is probably a better term, as the women have little choice in the matter. Like weddings throughout the world, Afghan nuptials include rituals dating back centuries. Prewedding dowry negotiations, wedding-day henna painting, and color-themed dresses (Afghan brides typically wear green on their wedding day) are all part of the festive ceremonies. But ultimately, it's a transactional matter, as the bride's father barters with a new family over the price they must pay for his offspring. Many of these weddings take place when the bride is barely a teen, at an age that would be shocking—or illegal—in most countries. The husbands are often several decades older.

It was a strange, and almost discomfiting, aspect of life in the Afghan hinterlands. But our job was to make the district secure for self-governance, not impose a women's liberation agenda. So we worked with the men, saw schools open for the boys, and kept a wary distance from the adult women we passed on our patrols.

"Jagran Gus, can you help us out in the medical tent?"

It was late November. I was a short-timer, with just a few more days left in Nawa before my journey back home would begin. The battalion replacing 1/5 was on deck, and I had handed over my duties to its Civil Affairs team leader. But I didn't like being idle and was happy to oblige when one of the battalion's Navy corpsmen asked for my help late in the morning.

The medical tent at our austere patrol base was not a particularly sterile facility—fighting the dirt dragged in on boots and the dust floating through the air with every gust of wind was a constant battle—but it worked well as a first-response triage center. The battalion's Navy doctors and corpsmen were well trained and level-headed. During our time in Nawa, they had treated injuries from gunshots, shrapnel, burning phosphorous, and vehicle rollovers. Their patients weren't just Marines wounded in combat. As in any small town, Nawa's residents had their share of injuries, whether from household mishaps, farming accidents, or domestic brawls. It was a reassuring sign of the trust and confidence the locals had in us that they frequently came (or were brought) to our patrol base asking for our assistance. The local clinic that we had helped rehabilitate was not yet open for business, so our docs were still seeing local patients almost daily.

I ducked through the sturdy nylon flaps of the tent and took a moment to adjust my eyes from the bright sunlight to the vivid glow of fluorescent lights strung along its roof seams. It was chilly inside, as a portable air-conditioning unit ran around the clock to keep critical supplies cold. The buzz of the fluorescent lights and the growl of the generator keeping the tent's electrical appliances running were being drowned out by a busy conversation around one of the aluminum and canvas cots set up in the tent's "operating room."

On the cot was an Afghan woman. She was actually more of a teenager, probably not much older than twenty years of age. She had removed her *burkha* inside the tent to reveal a large gash on her scalp that had bled heavily down her face and neck. The blood had become dry and crusty, matting her hair into a tangled mess. Her husband was with her, explaining that she had tumbled off his motorcycle the evening before when he unexpectedly hit a rut in the road. Her left shoulder to her elbow was covered with abrasions that were embedded with dirt and small bits of gravel. Her left wrist was bruised and swollen, likely fractured when she made an effort to break her fall. Despite her injuries, she was alert and poised, focused on the conversation taking place between her husband and the docs, who were explaining how they were going to treat her injuries.

Even with her tattered appearance, she was stunningly attractive. Her hair was straight, thick, and raven black, almost like velvet. She had an angular, lean face, with olive-tan skin and golden brown eyes that exuded a confidence she was probably never able to exert. She nodded silently but with an intelligent, understanding air as the docs spoke with her husband. She was also showing the obvious signs of a baby that was probably due in a month or two. That's why the docs had asked for my help—they were worried about the baby after the motorcycle tumble, and I had a pool of funds I could give to locals to help them travel to and receive treatment at a larger hospital in Kandahar.

The corpsmen began rinsing the woman's hair into a stainless steel bowl, gingerly scraping out a poultice-like compound that had been packed onto the gash in her head to stanch the bleeding. She would need stitches, one of the docs explained to the husband, and they would need to shave away some of the hair around the wound. Another one of the corpsmen worked on splinting her injured wrist and dabbing the scabs that had formed on her abrasions with an antiseptic before wrapping her arm in gauze.

When their prep work was done, the corpsmen began stitching the wound together with quick, practiced ease. I was standing by the woman's side when the first needle stroke went into her scalp. Even with a topical anesthetic, she suddenly tensed up and instinctively grasped my hand in a viselike grip as she stoically gritted her teeth.

As her calloused fingers dug into my hand, I explained to her husband that we wanted him to take his wife to Kandahar to get a checkup. He was stubbornly reluctant to heed our advice, even after my offer of 12,250 Afghanis (about $250) to help him with the three-hundred-kilometer round trip.

"The stitches should be fine, and her hair will grow back," he argued.

"Yes, but she might have a concussion and maybe a broken arm," we explained, making sure our interpreters understood and conveyed our concerns.

Holding up a bottle of generic ibuprofen that a corpsman had given him, he asked, "But these pills will stop her pain, right?" not grasping that we had other concerns for the woman than just her immediate discomfort.

Realizing that I had never mentioned the baby on the way, I told him, "The doctors in Kandahar will also be able to make sure your son is okay," subtly gesturing to our patient's stomach.

My reference to a son was inadvertent, but it changed the man's perspective immediately.

"*Inshallah, Inshallah*" ("God willing"), he beamed, proud of the prospect of a son, "the boy will be fine. But I will take her to Kandahar to be sure."

As the corpsmen finished their work, I pried my hand from the woman's grasp and finished my transaction with the husband, handing over a small bundle of cash in exchange for his signature on a receipt and a promise that he would go to Kandahar the same day.

Our patient stood up from the cot and picked up her *burkha* to once again obscure herself from the men around her when she put it back on. I noticed a single tear-streak on her otherwise expression-less, slightly dusty face. I would never know if it was from the pain she had endured, her relief when her husband agreed to take her to Kandahar, or sadness at the realization of the hard life that awaited her as a young mother in Afghanistan. When I caught her eye for a moment, she muttered in a hoarse whisper, *"Deh-deh, mahnana"* ("Thank you very much"). It was the only sound she had made in the presence of half a dozen men over the course of nearly an hour, even as she was the center of our attention.

We escorted the couple out the main gate of the patrol base, the now *burkha*-covered woman silently trailing a few feet behind us. I shook hands with the husband, reminding him to head east toward Kandahar. As he pumped the kick start on his small motorcycle, his wife bundled up the heavy fabric of her *burkha* and waited for the engine to rumble, then took her perch on the back. As the motorcycle sputtered away, she cast a sideward glance at me.

I silently watched her drive away.

CHAPTER 27
CALL ME ISHMAEL

War may sometimes be a necessary evil. But no matter how
necessary, it is always an evil, never a good. We will not learn how
to live together in peace by killing each other's children.
—President Jimmy Carter, Nobel Peace Prize
acceptance speech, December 10, 2002

The first time Ishmael came to Patrol Base Jaker, he struggled behind the weight of a wheelbarrow he was pushing through
the dusty, gravelly path that led to its gates. In the wheelbarrow were
some of the bloody, broken remains of his parents and other family
members, killed when a five-hundred-pound bomb was dropped on
their compound from an F-18 jet thousands of feet above them. He
was ten years old, and his younger brother tried to help him navigate the wheelbarrow full of carnage through the ruts in the dirty
trail they lumbered along. Some villagers accompanied the boys and
their grandmother, pushing additional wheelbarrows holding more
mangled remains of the boys' family members.

It was early March of 2009, before the battalion of 1,000 Marines
had arrived in Nawa. A group of British soldiers on patrol had been
shot at from the compound where Ishmael's family lived and decided

to put a swift end to the harassing fire by calling in an air strike from an F-18 circling thirty thousand feet above. Holding families hostage in their compound while they used it as a fortress from which to shoot at patrolling NATO forces was a common Taliban tactic. Typically, they engaged the patrol for a few minutes, then swiftly ran out a back passageway and blended into the scenery, unburdened by the cumbersome combat load NATO forces wore. Just as common was the response the Brits chose to take: call in air power and send a decisive (and indiscriminate) message that they were not to be trifled with.

Ishmael, his brother, and his grandmother survived because they had been tending the family's small plot of land a few hundred meters from their mud-walled compound when the bomb strike arrived. They had brought the remains of their family members to the patrol base to show the Brits the results of their actions, and ask for some help to properly bury them.

So, barely a decade old, Ishmael became the man of the family, responsible for its surviving members. He had every reason to hate the foreign troops who had settled in his district. But he became pragmatic and resourceful instead, lingering at the patrol base gates asking to do menial tasks in exchange for a bag of rice, cooking oil, or unopened packets from an MRE. His grandmother was often with him, but in keeping with the male-female hierarchy in Afghanistan, she lingered a few feet behind him, squatting on her haunches while Ishmael bartered with the foreigners at the patrol base. She was the elder, but Ishmael was the man.

For all their macho toughness, Marines have a soft spot for kids, and Ishmael's cool demeanor and quick smile endeared him to us. He became a regular presence at the patrol base, taking on odd jobs, asking for rudimentary English lessons, and eventually leading a small squad of Nawa kids drawn to the patrol base gates out of bored curiosity or looking for trinkets the Marines might give away. When generals, ambassadors, members of Congress, or journalists came to Nawa, Ishmael and his brother were like mascots and served as examples for our vision of success. We told the visiting dignitaries that we needed to get the schools open so boys like Ishmael could get an education; we needed to drive out the Taliban so he wouldn't get conscripted into their service when he became a teenager; we needed to get the local government running so kids like Ishmael could trust their leaders. It would be fair to say that Ishmael was a local VIP himself.

On the morning of my last day in Nawa, word spread among some of the locals who knew me that Jagran Gus was leaving, and Ishmael led an entourage of kids we had come to know over several months to Patrol Base Jaker to bid me farewell. The local kids were always rambunctious and friendly, but Ishmael took a moment to extend his hand: "You've been very kind to us, Jagran Gus. How can I thank you?"

I was humbled by his sincerity, but I didn't want to burden him with deep sentiments that might get lost in translation, so I said, "Stay in school, study hard, don't join the Taliban. And always remember that we came here to help you."

He responded with his characteristic bright smile, emphatic nodding, and "*Wuuh, wuuh.*" Then he held up his hands to his face and mimed taking a picture, pointing back and forth between us, and asked "*Akus?*" ("Picture?") Glad to oblige, I took out the dust-covered Polaroid camera I always carried with me and asked another Marine to snap our photo. As the image began to emerge, I wrote in the large white space at the bottom of the print, "To Ishmael, A true hero of Nawa. Your friend, Jagran Gus."

As the distant thump of helicopter rotors drew close, signaling my ride out of Nawa was on the way, I assembled my gear to walk to the landing zone. A raspy voice behind me called out "Jagran Gus." Turning, I saw Ishmael's grandmother, stoop shouldered and beaming with a partly toothless smile, extending her hand. She said, "*Deh-deh mahnana*" ("Thank you very much"), repeatedly. I had never expected to speak with, let alone shake the hand of, an adult Afghan woman, but I caught my composure, grasped her hand in mine, and stumbled through my limited Pashto farewells.

A few minutes later, the helicopter landed. After some farewells with fellow Marines and some of our Afghan friends who came to see me off, I hustled up its lowered ramp, strapped down my gear, and put on my seat belt. Before the helo lifted off to turn and bank into the sky, I looked out its open back and glimpsed three figures walking contentedly away from Patrol Base Jaker. It was my friend Ishmael, his brother, and his grandmother, each carrying a yellow container of cooking oil and a white bag of rice.

CHAPTER 28

WINNING

Operation Claret proceeded with the sort of smoothness that
suggested no one in authority was paying adequate attention.
—BEN MACINTYRE, *A Spy Among Friends*

IN THE EARLY DAYS OF OPERATION KHANJAR, SKEPTICS COMPARED
the increased troop levels, changing mission, and seemingly endless
presence in Afghanistan to the Vietnam War, with similar consequences[55] and public frustration.[56] While these skeptics were right
to demand forthright answers to hard questions, there could be no
doubt that in at least one district in the country, there was undeniable progress. At one time, Nawa seemed like a ghost town and a lost
cause. But a few months after their arrival, Marines patrolling the
district frequently encountered tractors pulling large trailers loaded
with beds, furniture, and cooking utensils. Sitting atop these masses
of household goods were family members ranging from matriarchs
to toddlers. When we stopped these convoys to chat with the driver,
we learned that this family had been hunkered down in Lashkar Gah
(Helmand's capital city) or Kandahar for the past several years but
had decided to return to Nawa because they had heard about the
improved security situation. We'd send them on their way with a

cheery smile, place our hands across our hearts, wish them *"Deh-deh mahnana! Hodai paman,"* and invite them to visit the nearest Marine patrol base after resettling in their homes.

It was by no means easy going, and the Marines never let down their guard. Even with the positive changes in Nawa, it was still a dangerous place, and the battalion's Marines engaged in firefights or found or hit an IED several times a week. The twentysome-thing-year-old Marines patrolling Nawa had the delicate task of being poised to kill any legitimate threat at a moment's notice or to host an impromptu tea party. They performed spectacularly as they battled not just lethal threats and brutal heat, but also rumors spread by the Taliban and its sympathizers to discredit the Marines and Afghan leaders spearheading Nawa's revival. The rumors ranged from ridiculous to religiously charged: in one instance it was said that the Nestlé water the Marines offered was bottled in Pakistan and poisoned with hallucinogens; in another it was that the Marines were burning Qurans and trying to convert Afghans to Christianity. The high illiteracy rate in Helmand likely contributed to the spread of the rumors, but the constant presence of patrolling, socially active Marines quashed many of these falsehoods and misperceptions in their early stages. With the help of a U.S.-based nonprofit organization called Spirit of America, Marines were able to provide hundreds of Afghans with prayer rugs and Pashto-language Qurans, given to the district governor to distribute during his meetings with tribal elders. Spirit of America, a nonprofit group based in Virginia, also supplied thousands of small hand-cranked radios, which Marines handed out on patrols. We urged the recipients to tune in to Radio Nawa, an FM station the battalion operated, which regularly broadcast messages from Helmand's and Nawa's leaders. The radio station also delivered daily summaries of global news through one of our interpreters.

We began to see events, which would have likely been benignly ignored or taken for granted in the U.S., become routine occurrences in Nawa. Children were flying kites to pass the time. The warm winds pushing off the Helmand River had kept the paper crafts with their long trailing tails aloft for hours. A traveling band of minstrels played their traditional instruments at Eid al-Fitr celebrations following the holy month of Ramadan while their audience danced and hopped around in circles, rhythmically banging sticks together in time to the beat set by the musicians. Voters in Nawa were able to peacefully submit a ballot at one of a dozen polling places throughout the district during the August presidential elections; the vague threats of violence whispered by the Taliban never materialized.[57] Children and old men began to integrate themselves within the patrols of Marines trekking along Nawa's roads and canals, a sign they welcomed and trusted the Marines and the security they brought.[†] Ordinary Afghans started to tell Marines they sensed that the issues most important to them were being addressed by the local Afghan government representatives, the Marines, our civilian advisors, and some of the NGOs that now felt safe spending time in the district. They could see the far-fetched and often whimsical priorities set by faraway policy makers subsiding.

We still fought the Taliban on an almost daily basis, a task made difficult by the fact that identifying *who* actually constituted the Taliban was not always certain. For one thing, they had no clear uniform. That was a typical tactic of an insurgent who sought to blend in with the local population. Additionally, we wrestled with telling the die-hard

† Even when locals integrated themselves in and among our foot patrols, they were watched with a wary eye for signs of trouble, including a hidden suicide vest or weapon.

zealots apart from those who were likely driven by economic neces-sity or youthful folly to join the insurgency. We called the former "Capital T" Taliban (like their leader Mullah Omar) and the latter, "Little t" fighters. Of course, we didn't worry too much about the distinction when they were shooting at us. But eventually *turning* the Taliban, and not just *killing* them (especially those "Little t" fighters), was another pivotal strategy that led to success in Nawa. The idea had been discussed by some senior commanders[58] but had just as often been dismissed by others (usually policy makers or pundits operating from the comfort of a TV studio in the US rather than on the ground in Taliban country).

Marines have been sent to fight America's wars for almost two-and-a-half centuries. When they've been deployed, they've gone to win. As I've mentioned, sometimes winning is defined by body counts, bullets fired, or terrain seized and held. But in the type of war we were fighting in Afghanistan in 2009, progress could be measured by the number of schools, clinics, and government offices opened, and the innumerable cups of tea we drank with the people we met. And while the tally of kids flying kites or the frequency of traveling minstrels performing at local celebrations had never before been a measure that a country's military used to assess success in war, in late 2009, this is what winning looked like in Nawa.

CHAPTER 29
COMING HOME (PART 2)

When this sad war is over, we will all return to our homes, and feel that we can ask no higher honor than the proud consciousness that we belonged to the Army of the Potomac.
—General George McClellan

December 1, 2009

By late fall, the Afghan days were cool enough that the hefty weight of our body armor provided a welcome layer of warmth while we trekked along the dirt roads and canals of Nawa. Mornings were brisk by now. If we were patrolling before the sun rose, we could follow the steps that the Marine in front of us left in the frost that had settled on the ground during the subfreezing night. We could watch our breath float through the frigid air. It was a vivid contrast to the stifling heat and humidity that we labored under during the summer months, when we fought the elements as much as we fought the Taliban. Nawa's cornfields had recently been harvested and were littered with dried stalks and husks that would be plowed into the soil when the next crop of wheat was planted (or when some risk-taking farmers sowed poppy). The leaves on the trees lining the district's vast network of canals had turned various hues of red, yellow, orange, and brown, exuding the familiar colors and smells of fall.

Most of the battalion's Marines had one preferred uniform they wore nearly every day of our seven months on the ground. As we neared our final days in country, those uniforms were sufficiently sweat bleached, frayed, torn, and stained. Our boots were weathered and scuffed, their soles worn from miles of patrols across the sand, dirt, and rocks of our district.

For the past two weeks, sorties of helicopters had been regularly landing in the open field outside Patrol Base Jaker. They were delivering the battalion of Marines that would assume responsibility for the district as part of the regular rotation of units through the Afghan war. The helicopters hovered above the field before easing onto the ground, then let their engines idle while their passengers sauntered out the exit ramps, lugging the gear they would need to get through the next six or seven months. It was different in every way from my frantically rushed night insertion into Patrol Base Jaker months earlier.

On my final morning in Nawa, I stood outside, sipping too-strong coffee from an aluminum canteen cup. My gear was packed, and I had transferred my duties to the Civil Affairs team that had arrived a week earlier. My team members had flown to Camp Leatherneck the day before, so there was little for me to do other than enjoy the relative calm and temporary reprieve from the responsibilities I'd shouldered over the past months. Even in the late morning, the air was cool, and the warm java was comforting. There was a buoyancy to my mood as I chatted with the Marines with whom I had lived for the past seven months and reflected on the changes we had helped bring about. I had much to be proud of, but I also had much to look forward to.

I was going home.

At about 11:00 a.m., Captain Jason Condon, one of the battalion's FACs, finished a conversation on his handheld radio and told me, "Your bird's inbound in ten minutes, Jagran Gus."

I wrestled with competing emotions. I was eager to go home to my family, but at the same time I was already feeling nostalgic for the friends I was about to leave and the hardships we had shared. They were like a family to me, too, and I was reluctant to part ways.

The thump of a helicopter's rotors echoing in the distance told me it was time to go. An entourage of well-wishers joined me at the gate of Patrol Base Jaker. I have already mentioned the moving presence of Ishmael, his brother, his grandmother, and some of their friends. I have also mentioned that Governor Haji Abdul Manaf was there to bid me well. He held my hand as I made my way to the helicopter. And I mean that literally; handholding among men in Afghanistan is a sign of friendship and respect. Our civilian advisors Scott Dempsey and Sir Ian Purvis, a recently knighted British citizen, joined the crowd to see me off too. Lieutenant Colonel Bill McCollough and Sergeant Major Tom Sowers helped me lug my heavy bags into the waiting helicopter.

I was the only passenger boarding the aircraft. After I strapped down my bags and clipped my seat belt, we took off and climbed steadily into the sky. I suspected Lieutenant Colonel McCollough had asked the pilots to give me an aerial tour of Nawa before heading to Camp Leatherneck, and I was grateful for the extra time in the air. I stared out the helicopter's open back ramp, seeing the sights of the district from above for the first time in the daylight, feeling hopeful for the country below and the people living there. As I watched Nawa pass below me, my right hand rested instinctively on the grip of my rifle. My left hand made its way into the pouch on my flak jacket where I took out the small child's shoe I had carried with me since leaving the U.S. in the spring. It belonged to my oldest son, and in a few weeks I would put it on his two-month-old brother after finally meeting him.

An hour after I was picked up at Patrol Base Jaker, I was dropped off at Camp Leatherneck's airfield, where I was greeted by my fellow CAG team leaders. We hadn't been together since mid-May and we enjoyed a laugh at each other's expense about our thinner, sunburned appearances and ragged uniforms. Camp Leatherneck had grown exponentially since I'd been there months before, so large now that some called it "Marine-istan." Despite its massive growth, the base still throbbed and growled with the sounds of round-the-clock construction to make it even larger and more permanent.

The literal buzz of construction echoing around Camp Leatherneck was matched with the buzz of anticipation about the speech President Obama was scheduled to give in front of West Point's corps of cadets that same night. I was interested in what our commander in chief had to say but I was more interested in decompressing for a few days while waiting for our flight out of Afghanistan.

Even after months on the ground, routine patrols were marked by an underlying anxious tension. Despite the incredible gains we saw while there, we could never forget for a moment that the place remained dangerous and the welfare of fellow Marines depended on us doing our job right *every* time. Given that ongoing stress, the few days of outright boredom I anticipated before my flight home would be just fine. The other CAG team leaders and I spent our final days in Afghanistan wandering around Camp Leatherneck. We occasionally attended an operations brief, but we usually just sat in one of its air-conditioned chow halls watching people load up on gushy soft-serve ice cream or pick at rubbery steaks and overboiled lobster tails served on "surf-n-turf" night. I couldn't help but marvel at the journey those saltwater crustaceans had to make to be at a military chow hall in the middle of a landlocked country in Asia.

After a few days at Camp Leatherneck, during which the junior Marines were constantly speculating and trading rumors about our impending departure, we finally received credible news of a flight scheduled for the following day. The Marine Corps has mastered the art of fighting its country's wars and effectively moving its people from one continent to another, but military travel sometimes has its shortcomings. The process mostly involves assembling before dawn to stand in line, then following the person in front of you when the line starts moving several hours later, while being yelled at, regardless of your rank.

Leaving Afghanistan was no different. At 4:00 a.m., we boarded an ancient, Soviet-era bus that coughed out bursts of black smoke from its exhaust pipe, driven by a politely smiling Nepalese man with a grandfatherly demeanor. At the base airfield, our unit's three dozen tan backpacks and olive-green seabags were arranged on a large pallet, covered with a tarp, strapped down with a canvas cargo net, and then set by forklift alongside nine or ten identical pallets. The only identifying features of the hulky pallets were small colored tags noting their respective units fastened to the cargo nets by thin metal wires. Some Marines placed friendly wagers on the odds of our unit's pallet ever meeting us again.

We were then herded into a C-17 transport plane whose seating layout was designed for efficiency rather than comfort. Twenty-five rows of five nonreclining seats were bolted onto the plane's metal deck. Another twenty fold-down canvas seats were arrayed along each side of the plane. Every Marine had to wear their flak jacket and helmet and hold their rifle between their knees. The added bulk made the uncomfortable squeeze into our seats even tighter.

Many of the Marines getting on board carried empty quart-sized Gatorade bottles in anticipation of making a head call on the three-hour flight to Manas Air Base in Kyrgyzstan, the first stop on our journey home. The C-17 only had one small stand-up urinal that required patience and a steady hand to use as the heavy plane shuddered and quaked through turbulent skies. Once every seat on the plane was filled, an incomprehensible brief blatted over its speaker system, its back ramp shut with a hydraulic whine, and conversation became impossible as four mega-engines cranked to their full capacity. The nose of the aircraft turned into the wind and sped down the runway for an agonizingly long takeoff run. Finally, we felt the sensation of "wheels off the deck," and the sound of 165 Marines shouting "Hoo-rah!" briefly drowned out the clamor of the airplane's engines. We were going home.

Manas Air Base was the transit hub for the thousands of U.S. and NATO troops headed to and from the war in Afghanistan. Situated in the northern part of a former Soviet Socialist Republic, the base had been a diplomatic headache for the United States since its initial operational use in the GWOT in late 2001.[59] The U.S. eventually paid the government of Kyrgyzstan over $200 million per year for its use before Kyrgyzstan's president let the lease expire in 2014, making good on his campaign promise to turn the base into a civilian airport.[60]

However, in late 2009, the politics and strategic role of Manas didn't concern us. We were still being herded en masse—for the sake of efficiency and accountability—when our plane landed at Manas and we were crammed, standing up, into seatless buses called "cattle cars." The cattle cars took us to a large aircraft hangar that had been transformed into a barracks, with hundreds of rusty bunk beds lined up on cold concrete floors. Each of us claimed one of the musty, sagging mattresses that countless fellow service members had used before us. We took it as a matter of faith that they had made some efforts at personal hygiene.

It was winter in Kyrgyzstan, and snow being pushed off the nearby Tian Shan mountain range—sometimes referred to as the "Asian Alps"—found its way into our aircraft hangar barracks through one of the many gaps in its walls or was kicked off our boots as we entered from outside. Inside the hanger a cloud of funk hovered above us, the combined odor of hundreds of pairs of feet released from the confines of well-worn combat boots and the phlegmy spittle coughed up from lungs unaccustomed to the cold, moist air.

In Afghanistan, things were always urgent and tense, even in relatively quiet moments. In Kyrgyzstan, we just had to wait. And patiently think. The constant stress that came from living in a combat zone no longer consumed our thoughts. The amenities at Manas, such as hot showers and Wi-Fi, were welcome signs that we were coming back to the twenty-first century. They helped us bide the time while we traded rumors of our departure date the same way as we had at Camp Leatherneck.

After three days, our return flight was confirmed. We woke before dawn and rode the cattle cars to the base's airfield terminal. This time, our plane was a commercial airliner, operated by a carrier that no one had ever heard of. It had reclining seats, a comfortable temperature, small TV screens on the seat backs in front of us with a decent choice of movie options, and preheated meals served by a cheery crew. The empty Gatorade bottles that were an essential carry-on item on our flight from Camp Leatherneck to Manas were tossed into a trash bin. The relative comfort was unfamiliar, almost disconcerting, but we adapted quickly. We put our rifles in the over-head storage bins and settled in for our multileg thirty-six-hour journey, lightly sleeping through a blur of refueling stops somewhere in Eastern Europe and in the U.K. before finally touching down in America.

It's a strange paradox that, for all the potential trauma in going to war, leaving it behind for "normal" life can be as frightening as war itself. When Americans go to war, they come back changed. For some, the changes may be temporary and fleeting, barely perceptible, often positive and character building. For others, things can be a bit tougher. The Marine Corps helps its Marines with this transition in many ways, all of which are well intentioned and most of which are useful. But the best assets we have to help us with coming home are our families.

When my CAG detachment finally made its way to our home base on the southern bank of the Anacostia River, in sight of the U.S. Capitol building's dome and the peak of the Washington Monument, a small mob of parents, spouses, siblings, children, aunts, and uncles, along with some good friends, was there to meet us. The Marines hustled off our bus and moved into formation, their faces lighting up as they spotted someone special in the crowd. They stood at attention for one last roll call and set of instructions. Then, to the order of "Dismissed!" they bolted out of the formation and into the arms of their gleeful relatives. It's a moment when even the most battle-hardened warrior struggles to fight back tears of joy and relief.

My reunion was several days away, since my wife and our two sons were spending her maternity leave with her family in California. So I milled about our headquarters building, helping our unit leadership with some of the administrative aspects of returning from war. I cleaned my rifle and pistol and turned them in to the armory, suddenly realizing that I had been literally connected to those weapons for nearly nine months. Now that they were no longer tethered to me, I was confused about where my hands should go. I found myself seeking out a cup of coffee, not so much for the caffeine but because holding a cup made me cock my arm at a comfortably familiar angle.

After a few days of tedium, I was able to take leave and begin my journey west to finally see my family. The least expensive flight I could find on short notice was a multileg trip that zigzagged across the country from Baltimore to Chicago to Phoenix to Las Vegas to San Francisco over the course of about twelve hours.

During my first layover, I watched a team of college-age boys strut through the airport jostling one another while plugged into their iPods. Their matching athletic suits identified them as the wrestling squad from a prestigious East Coast school. *Tough kids in their own right*, I thought. But they had nothing on the Marines I had the honor of serving with in Afghanistan, many of whom were the same age as those wrestlers—Marines whose toughness could be measured not only by their strength or physical and mental endurance, but by such intangible traits as honor, courage, and commitment.

On another layover, I stood behind an angry customer at a Starbucks counter who had ordered something like a "grande soy double latte decaf with a spritz of hazelnut mocha and a half spritz of vanilla." He was ranting to the hapless barista about his drink being a few degrees cooler than he expected. I ordered a small black coffee and reflected on how some people took trivial things more seriously than I felt they needed to. The receptionists at the airport USO lounges I visited along the way welcomed me like a VIP when I showed them my military ID. Every time I made my way into the comfort of those wonderful establishments, they made me feel like a distinguished first-class traveler.

It was late in the afternoon when I finally touched down in San Francisco, sleep deprived and over-caffeinated, but also giddy knowing that I would soon be eating dinner with my wife and kids. I would probably be changing a few diapers too. I boarded a bus that took me across the Golden Gate Bridge to a depot north of Sausalito, where my father-in-law met me. I had been deliberately coy with my wife about my exact arrival plans in California, and she was expecting me in another day or two. My father-in-law had played along with my plan.

The sun had set by the time we pulled into my in-laws' driveway, and the lights inside their house were aglow. I stood outside, looking through the picture window into the living room to watch the ruckus involving my oldest son and his similarly aged cousins. I had missed his second birthday by only a few days. My wife sat on a beanbag, rocking a little bundle in her arms that was my two-month-old son, whom I had yet to meet. After taking in this wonderful scene for a moment, I strolled through the door to everyone's surprise.

My older son, just learning to talk, looked at me and said, "Hello, Daddy Gus," before standing up, waddling over to me, and hugging me around my legs. I embraced my wife as she handed me the beautiful tiny baby she had been cradling—our newborn son who was now smiling at me while I stroked his cheek. He grasped my finger, as if we were shaking hands.

I was home.

CHAPTER 30
WHAT IT'S LIKE TO GO TO WAR

Soldiering in a war zone, on the front line of the conflict, was a bittersweet profession, best experienced by feeling, smelling, touching and tasting, to truly understand it. Our soldiers had shared in the discomforts, pleasures, fears, pains, and exhilarations of a band of brothers. We had only one another—our lives depended on what the person next to us did. Young men from New York, California, Mississippi, and Minnesota were literally thrown together into a crucible to make the best of it, and we did. Whatever we did together could not be shared with the uninitiated.

—RICHARD TAYLOR, *Prodigals*

DECEMBER 15, 2009

"WHAT WAS IT LIKE?"

I was at a trendy restaurant in San Francisco with two of my closest friends from college when one of them asked this question. Barely two weeks earlier, I had ambled out of my heavily fortified patrol base in Afghanistan's Helmand Province to a waiting helicopter that would take me on the first leg of my journey home. Every day for seven months, I carried a gun or had one within reach, patrolled in heavy body armor in areas infested with IEDs and insurgents, and drank countless cups of tea with the locals along the way. I usually slept for just four or five hours a day, but not always in a row. The dirt that constantly clung to us kept me from ever being truly clean. My feet stunk and itched, my skin was chaffed, and my shoulders ached. I had been shot at, sworn at, even spit at, and had dodged a few rocks for good measure. I had seen the carnage that can be wrought by humanity's most destructive imagination, as well as acts of absolute selflessness and compassion, often within moments of each other.

I furrowed my brow and pursed my lips, staring blankly through the restaurant for a moment as a flood of answers came to mind. I had chosen a booth in the back of the restaurant, taking a seat where I could watch everybody come and go, because unexpected movement in my peripheral vision caused my hackles to rise and my right hand to drop to my side to grasp the pistol that until just recently had always been on my hip. I tried to formulate a way to explain that the hyperalertness every Marine felt in the wilderness of Helmand hadn't wound down in the short time I had been back stateside.

So what was it like?

Thinking about the question while watching the frost on the beer bottle in front of me melt and trickle down into a small pool on the table, I remembered the taste of the water I drank from dusty plastic bottles in Helmand. It was room temperature at best, but the "room" was always at least 90 degrees. Our server had just brought our food to us. It was neatly displayed and garnished on real plates and would be eaten with real metal cutlery. It was a stark contrast to how I had eaten in Afghanistan, which was typically with my bare hands. And it was definitely a stark contrast to *what* I usually ate: an MRE, or if I was dining with some Afghans, lamb boiled in oily vegetable broth served on top of rice. The former almost always guaranteed constipation and the latter, diarrhea.

What was it like?

How could I explain, without seeming like a bloodthirsty freak, that going to war, in my experience, was outright *exciting*, an

opportunity to test one's mettle against the most perverse confluence of events imaginable. How could I explain that the fear I felt
the first time I flew over a hot zone, stepped outside the wire, or
was shot at wasn't really fear of being killed or maimed? It was fear
of fucking up, of letting down my fellow Marines, of looking like
a coward. How could I explain that the drive of going to war isn't
so much about seeking violence, but about gaining the wisdom and
maturity that comes from responding to that violence with unhesi-
tating decisiveness? That it's about fulfilling the proverbial cycle of
leaving home a boy and returning as a man?

What was it like?

How could I describe the constant *guilt* I felt in the war zone?
I saw other Marines wounded and thought they didn't deserve the
pain they were enduring; that it should have been me. Then I felt
relief that it wasn't me, and then guilt *again* because I felt relief. I felt
guilty because I had put my own adventurous desires ahead of family
commitments. I had left my pregnant wife behind. I went off to fight
in a war while she held down the fort at home caring for our sixteen-
month-old son. I felt guilty because I had to ask that pregnant wife
to attend the funeral of my team chief in the stifling humidity of a
Washington, D.C., summer, and extend her condolences to *his* pregnant wife.

I felt guilty when I missed family milestones including my anni-
versary, my oldest son's first words, potty training, and the birth of
my second son. I felt guilty because I did nothing to save a dying
man—a teenaged boy, actually—writhing in agony with three bullets
in his guts, because he wasn't a Marine, a member of *my* tribe. I felt
guilty when I paid that boy's father the equivalent of $2,500 and
told him how sorry I was for his loss, then had him ink his thumb
and press it on my receipt book, as if that bureaucratic act absolved
me of any complicity in the boy's death. I felt guilty because it took
me three months to write a letter to the parents and wife of my team

chief who was killed in action, partly because I couldn't figure out the right words to convey how I felt, but also because sometimes when I had a moment to find the words to express my thoughts, I was just too damn tired to think clearly and chose to sleep instead.

What was it like?

I wanted to describe how feeling the heft of a loaded pistol on my hip relaxed me, how my hands instinctively cradled my rifle to my chest, and how my arms felt naked and awkward, almost useless, without them. I wanted to explain how putting on seventy pounds of battle gear was a soothing act, even though it strained the shoulders, the back, the knees, and thighs, because it made me feel whole and bizarrely comfortable. I wanted to explain how the sounds of Velcro ripping, ammunition being loaded into magazines, and rifles being charged before we stepped out of the relative safety of our patrol base sent waves of energy through me, and how I looked at my fellow Marines with awe and humility, knowing they would have my back when the shit went down.

What was it like?

I wanted to tell my friends that being in a war isn't always about fighting the bad guys and that sometimes it's just so *fucking boring* because things are going *exactly* the way they are supposed to be going, and *fucking boring* is just fine considering that the alternative is *fucking crazy*, but even when it's *fucking boring* you can't sleep because there's always *something* that needs to be done, and you never know when it *might* start going *fucking crazy* again, and so you drink more coffee than you should to stay awake, and that just makes you manic, and you speak in rambling run-on sentences, and you can't stop bouncing your fucking legs when you sit down and every fucking phrase out of your mouth has some variation of *fuck* in it but that doesn't fucking matter because you're with Marines, not in a fancy law firm or a stuffy corporate office, and if some motherfucker doesn't like the way I talk, well, then he can go fuck himself!

What was it like?

I wrestled with how to describe my grisly fascination staring at a pile of flesh and pulp and bones and brains that only minutes before had been two insurgents burying an IED for my patrol to walk over. That mess might have been several of us but for the technical flaw that caused the bomb to blow up in the men's hands as they were trying to bury it under a bridge. I thought about how that fascination had shifted to contempt because the shredded corpses I was looking at had wanted to kill my fellow Marines and me. And then I felt pity for them for believing whatever perverse ideology led them to want to kill us. And then I felt sorry for their mothers because their sons' mangled body parts were being shoveled up and dumped in a shallow hole in the ground and covered with dirt and rocks, and they'd never know what really happened to them. And then I worried that someone might have seen me gag and swallow my vomit after the wind shifted and the revolting stench of those dead mens' shit, guts, and sweat invaded my senses.

What was it like?

I strained to come up with a way to describe how we balanced the extreme opposites that teetered in our psyche every day; how one moment we would clean and polish our rifles, wipe off the dust from the copper-jacketed rounds loaded in our magazines, and check that all our gear was in top form, ready to do what it was designed to do—kill—and how we instinctively assessed the *how* and *why* of killing every person we encountered if we had to. Yet at the same moment, we'd broadly smile and be overcome with a melting heart when an Afghan kid came up to us on a patrol, excitedly asking *"Taso senge yast?"* while extending his hand to give us a pomegranate he had picked from a local tree, or another kid handed us a flower he plucked from some scrub brush, which we would tuck into a fold on our flak jacket next to our deadly armaments.

What was it like?

How do I answer them when there are things about going to war I can't even explain to myself? Things I revisit in my mind again and again. Like being *lonely* even though you are *never* ever by yourself. I mean *heartachingly* lonely. You are surrounded by other Marines day and night; you sleep on the dirt or in a dank room in a primitive base with at least half a dozen squad mates; there's always a watch to stand, a patrol stepping off, or a report to file; you are reliant on one another to be your better half in conditions of imminent and ongoing danger. It's a closeness like no other. And yet you miss your *other* better half, the one who without whom you simply never feel complete. The day my wife gave birth to our second son and shared all the details with me by satellite phone, including my firstborn's proud reaction to being a big brother, I was overcome by simultaneous feelings of profound joy and isolation. Never before had I felt so alone. It was close to midnight, and when I finished that call with my wife, I returned to our operations center to share the news with the Marines working the graveyard shift monitoring the radios. I knew they could understand at least part of what I felt—the *missing* part.

What was it like?

When you go to war, you discover a previously unknown sense of thirst. It's one where your mouth gets so dry that your throat swells and itches and your tongue feels like a wire brush had been scraped along its top. You discover a hunger, too, when your guts tighten and rumble, and you can almost tell time by the intensity of your stomach churning. Then there's the fatigue, where a smooth, dry patch of dirt seems like a perfectly fine place to flop on your back and close your eyes, even if just for ten or twenty minutes. It's the exhaustion that gets you more than the thirst and hunger. It makes you angry and tense, where sometimes the most trivial slight can set you off on a nearly rabid, spittle-spewing tirade. You sleep when you can, but you never wake up on your own. It's always someone or something else that wrenches you out of your slumber; whether it's a shake of the shoulder because it's time to go on a patrol, or the whistle and crack of rockets and machine-gun fire zipping over your head, or the deafening, rhythmic rumble of a helicopter circling in the sky. Whatever it is that wakes you, you bolt upright like you've been sleeping on a spring. Without fail, when you open your heavy lids, it feels like a scab has been ripped off your eyeballs. It only takes a few seconds to realize that whatever pleasant dream you were having was just that, a pleasant dream, and here you are, back in the real world of the Afghanistan war, covered in a fine patina of dirt. So you drop a few curse words, scratch your balls, put on your boots, and go wherever it is you need to go. And somehow, even with that heavy fatigue always weighing you down, you find that the depths of your endurance are almost limitless, and you just keep going.

What was it like?

Going to war means realizing that even though you can push your physical and mental limits beyond whatever you had previously imagined, they are in fact *limits*. Confronting the bounds of those limits forces you to remember that, maybe when you have a moment to do something profound and meaningful, even heroic, something nags at your spirit and reminds you that you aren't invincible, and in the flash of a moment you ponder existential questions about luck and fortune, statistics and physics, and choose that moment *not* to be a hero. And after the dust settles, you come to the dread realization that, while some things like bravery may have limits, other things can feel limitless, like shame.

What was it like?

I struggled to find the words to explain that going to war means abandoning any selfish interests because this singular moment, this distinct *now*, requires *absolute dedication* to a collective effort more significant than anything we would ever confront in our lives. I couldn't form the words to explain that I had been part of a tribe that transcended class, age, geography, religion, or education, and my tribe and I had borne the pride not only of our nation but also of our Corps and its centuries of honor and sacrifice. I grasped to think of a way to explain to my college friends that when the warriors of this magnificent tribe I was part of grow old, we will never have to just read with envy about the brave deeds and accomplishments of other men, because others will read about what *we* had done.

All these thoughts sprinted through my mind as I pondered an answer to my friend's question, "What was it like?"

After a moment, I replied, "It's kind of hard to explain. I guess you just had to be there."

CHAPTER 31
BEING HOME

Warrior energy is fierce and wild. It upsets men who don't have it, and
women who are afraid of it, primarily because the only form of it
they know is the negative one that is a result of repression.
—Karl Marlantes, *What It Is Like to Go to War*

April 2010

I WAS BACK HOME FROM THE WAR AND HAD RETURNED TO THE
humdrum regimen at a law firm. My worth was once again being
determined by hitting my billable-hours quota. It was no longer
gauged by the firepower I could bring to a fight or my understanding
of the mortal consequences of a discussion with a group of tribal
elders. I had reentered a world of comfort, limits, and routines,
where I felt too often that I was just going through the motions,
putting in the time.

But something was simmering inside. My feelings vacillated
between combustion and lethargy. Paying attention, weirdly, no
longer seemed to matter. It was as if the men, women, and children I passed on the sidewalk, or with whom I rode the commuter
train, were just blobs in motion all around me. Absent was the

vivid humanity—inviting or threatening—I had encountered amidst friends and foes in Afghanistan. For all its lethal unpredictability; its precarious foothold at the edge of chaos; and its hot, over-the-shoulder breath of danger, the war zone had a clarity that felt manageable—almost controllable. The smothering routine here, engulfing me like waves of cotton, had no edges. I felt no sense of control in the return to the routine.

Don't get me wrong. I loved being back with my family, but in some ways, I missed Afghanistan. Many nights I stood in a nearly scalding hot shower until my skin turned pink and sore, as if I were trying to wash off the normalcy of it all. I tried to use the heat and steam to pry some of the savagery essential to survival from my pores. It was there just a few months ago but had now gone dormant. Something inside felt as if it might be cracking.

"Thank you for your service."

I had heard those words dozens of times since coming back. I always replied, "It was my pleasure," and I really meant it. But sometimes I sensed a tension in the exchanges, as if what was supposed to be a sincere unifying sentiment was only a reflexive—almost obligatory—expression of gratitude, with no real appreciation for what it means to have served. I often wondered if some of the thankers actually pitied me, and other people like me. Our country hadn't had a draft since 1974, so there was no obvious reason why I—a college graduate, a well-paid lawyer with a growing family, living in a hip neighborhood in the middle of a bustling city—would volunteer to go to a war that didn't really pose an existential threat to our country.

What's wrong with this guy? I imagined some of them thinking, as they followed up their ritual remark with queries like, "So why did you join the Marine Corps?" or "Did you *have* to go?" Those questions suggested sadness at the perception of my circumstances—as if I must have had no option, like a delinquent presented a choice by a judge: prison or the military.

I didn't want a parade. A march down Broadway or Pennsylvania Avenue would have felt ostentatious, putting our service members on display like exotic creatures at a zoo to be ogled from grandstands and sidewalks. The thanks extended to me, even by those who were puzzled about my motives, was certainly a welcome alternative to the jeers and taunts flung at veterans returning from Vietnam. But I started to feel there was too much patriotic veneer in the formulaic expressions of gratitude. The flashy tributes and liberal use of the term "hero" mask a problem our society faces: We glorify the wars our country is engaged in, and deify the men and women doing the fighting in those wars. So we, as a society, raise our cups in toast for the "Budweiser Our Hero Seats" recognition, and cheer during the "Bank of America Salute" at professional sporting events.[61] Yet at the same time, the general public remains disengaged—uninterested in the realities of service and war. What's more, much of our political class has never worn a uniform. This disconnect allows the wars to go on endlessly, with little introspection about why, or to what end, they are being fought.

I've never thought less of anyone for not joining the military. No one needs a uniform to serve the country and our communities. It's undeniable, however, that military service uniquely demands one to be prepared to die for one's country. From the first days of our training, we are told that what we have chosen to do is special, responding to a higher calling, and not something that everyone can or should do.

But I worried that I was developing a disdain for the members of our society who opted not to serve, and I resented myself for this. It's *service*, not glory seeking, after all. Thinking I was better than the society I chose to protect—and in fact, serve—cleaves a bigger wedge of misunderstanding and mistrust between our military members and the rest of our society than any knee-jerk praise.

Was I becoming self-righteous and bitter as I negotiated my new routines? Would I be forever mired in nostalgia, and the hubris of having served, no longer moving forward meaningfully in any other way? The pressure became painful.

"Oh my God! I *have* to know: Have you ever killed anyone?"

It wasn't the first time someone asked me this since returning from Afghanistan. I usually deflected the question with a response like, "We did a lot of good stuff in Afghanistan, and sometimes we shot back at people who shot at us." But this was different. Something about the giddy lip-smacking way it was asked—the slapping together and rubbing of the hands and wide-eyed anticipation—as if I had a fascinating secret, perhaps a bit of risqué gossip to disclose—pierced my guard.

I was at a poker game with about a dozen other dads in my neighborhood, most of whom I had never met. Early in the evening, someone mentioned my having been in Afghanistan, prompting the question and a dead silence. It felt as if all eyes had turned to me. I took a swig of my beer as I took in the asker's dopey grin, and thought it was the type of face that could use a slap.

Of course, people are curious. In a normal society, killing has consequences. Most people know they will never experience it, which further piques their curiosity. Just like people might prod a mountain climber, Super Bowl champion, or bullfighter about their deepest emotions while at the peak of their performance, the questioner may be envious or awestruck about the real-life equivalent of something they're likely to only ever experience in a video game. Perhaps they feel a sense of inadequacy because they don't know—or maybe know all too well—how they'd react. But serving in combat is uniquely serious, not just rare. So it is petty, childish, and profoundly thoughtless to ask a veteran about the experience of killing.

I acted like I had taken no notice of the question, while I took another glimpse at my face-down cards in the hand of Texas Hold 'em we were playing. They were crappy, something like a four and a nine, unsuited, not pairing up with any of the other cards we all could see. The bet was to me, so I raised the pot before the final card—the "river" in poker-speak—was dealt. Still no help to me. So I bet again, keeping a steady face as I glanced at the others around the table. They all folded.

As I began stacking the chips from the pot I had just won, I looked at the guy who had asked the question and said, "You know, there are typically two types of people who ask that question: teenagers and twerps."

An uneasy silence hung in the air for a moment before he mumbled, "Thank you for your service." After all my recent soul-searching, I almost laughed. Instead, as the game continued, I kept getting shitty cards, raising the pot, and winning. The good-nights exchanged at the end of the evening were subdued.

Back home, I found my wife and sons were sound asleep, the only noise in the house was their deep, rhythmic breathing. I took my clothes off, stepped into the shower, and gradually turned up the heat until it reached a temperature that made my skin hurt. As the hot water spilled over me, its steam pushed the cold air I'd inhaled on my short walk home out of my lungs. And with each breath, I wondered when I would crack.

I'd always wrestled with being short-tempered, irritable, and occasionally condescending, but something was different after Afghanistan. Explosions were more frequent and—to my shame—meaner. What was worse was that they were levied at the people around me, including my family. I found myself grumbling aloud when strangers dawdled in front of me on the sidewalk. I spoke sharply to my wife about petty things, and often stormed off in a huff, brooding for hours about an annoyance that should have been brushed off with a mere shrug or a nod to the philosophy of the inevitable: *Shit happens.* At work, I stared out my window, searching for the point of whatever project I was working on. Often, I reflected on the trivial cost of a mistake here versus the mortal consequences of an error made in Afghanistan. Death and injury are a constantly lurking presence in a war zone, so you pay attention all the time. Here, with no consequences worth my fear, I descended into detachment. I was truly aloof and distant much of the time.

Then one day, I decided cracking was not an option.

I was driving on one of Washington, D.C.'s main streets along the National Mall on a weekend morning. I was restless and had left the house while it was still dark. Wanting to give my wife a rare treat of sleeping in, I brought my sons, who were in their car seats behind me. A heavy coat of fog hung in the air after a drizzling rain that lasted throughout the night had finally stopped. The slight morning traffic was moving cautiously. The intermittent brake lights flashing on and off were casting distracting glares in the streaks of water that coursed down my windshield.

My window was slightly open, letting in the cool morning air. The fabled cherry trees that adorn much of the nation's capital were in full bloom, along with the other springtime blossoms like dogwoods, tulips, and wisteria, all of which lent an exotic fragrance and an abundance of lush color to my surroundings. "Jumpin' Jack

Flash" was just beginning to play on the radio. I wondered if there
was any significance to Mick Jagger's crooning:

> *I was drowned, I was washed up and left for dead.*
> *I fell down, to my feet and I saw they bled, yeah yeah . . .*
> *But it's all right now, in fact it's a gas.*
> *But it's all right, I'm Jumpin' Jack Flash, it's a gas, gas, gas.*

Was that me?

I was headed to Arlington National Cemetery. It's a place where
I've always found comfort and solace, even while being surrounded
by the reminders of loss and grief. From a distance, the headstones
there all look the same. The military precision of their symmetry
seems at first to confer near anonymity on the souls of those who rest
beneath them. Walking in their midst, however, reading the names
inscribed in bold black letters on white marble, their individuality
begins to emerge. The inscriptions are uncomplicated: name, dates
of birth and death, a military operation, an award, and at the top
of each stone a cross, a Star of David, a crescent moon and star, or
other symbol of religious affiliation. Simple, orderly, dignified.

As one makes the calculations the pairs of dates encourage, their
ages strike fiercely home. Just short of 21—not yet old enough to buy
a beer, but able to wield a weapon of war on behalf of his country.
Forty—awaiting the birth of twins due soon after returning from
deployment. Thirty-two—a newly promoted major ten years into a
planned life of service in uniform. Twenty-two—nearing the end of
an enlistment, a college acceptance letter in hand. It's the age at
which they will be forever remembered, their *forever age.*

My older son, not yet three, was fascinated by the small tokens
placed at some of the tombstones: a unit coin, letters from a loved
one, a small bottle of whiskey, sometimes a stuffed toy. My youngest
was sound asleep in the baby carrier he was strapped into, his head

resting comfortably on my chest. They were too young to understand the meaning of the place, but it mattered to me that they be a part of my regular visits here, as if they might realize the importance through osmosis.

By the time I had reached Section 60, the area in the cemetery where many of the casualties from Iraq and Afghanistan are buried, the fog was burning off the ground and the sun peering over the Lincoln Memorial. The sky was shifting in color from regal purple hues to red and orange swirls that mixed with the clouds greeting the sunrise. The blurred images that surrounded me for the past several months were replaced here, with vivid clarity. As I watched my son stroll confidently among the gravestones, I was struck by a feeling that had eluded me for months: a sense of purpose.

I reached the headstone I was looking for and stood for a moment, silently. Then I said some words aloud, explained some things, apologized for others, and recollected some events that had always made us both smile. My oldest son held my hand as I spoke.

Looking up at me, he asked, "Who you talk to, Daddy?"

"My friend," I replied.

He nodded, as if this was perfectly clear. As if he understood, surrounded by the real, silent parade, that his father was not better or worse than other men. That what mattered was the deep, abiding value of the service his father and his friend had given in an imperfect world. That there are things in life worth living for, and worth fighting for.

Like being home.

CHAPTER 32
THE GOVERNOR'S FAREWELL

Who is the brave man—he who feels no fear? If so, then bravery is but a
polite term for a mind devoid of rationality and imagination. The brave
man, the real hero, quakes with terror, sweats, feels his very bowels betray
him, and in spite of this moves forward to do the act he dreads.

—GERALDINE BROOKS, *March*

MAY 17, 2015

IT HAD ALWAYS SEEMED TO BE A MATTER OF *WHEN*, NOT *IF* IT WOULD
happen. Five and a half years after my return from Afghanistan, I
had once again folded and tucked away my uniform, this time for
good, and settled back into the staid life of a corporate lawyer.
The taut leanness that came from months of infrequent meals and
constant patrolling morphed into a slight pudginess from days spent
in an office poring over contracts and pecking away at a computer,
augmented by working lunches.

Although I was comfortably ensconced back into civilian life, I
followed the generally sparse news about the war with keen interest
and a wary eye. Successes in Afghanistan ebbed and flowed, but a
few years after I left, the news indicated a downward slide in the

country's fortunes. Knots formed in my stomach when I read headlines like "Key Afghan District Falls to Taliban" or "Afghan District Leader Killed by Taliban." I was always relieved that these stories weren't about Nawa or the Afghan friends I had made who were still struggling to maintain the fragile peace there. But in late 2014 and early 2015, a revived insurgency began to form a noose around Nawa after the Taliban took over neighboring districts such as Garmsir, Marjah, Nawzad, and Sangin. The cautious optimism I'd felt that Nawa would be spared a similar fate began to seem more and more naive.

Five and a half years after I'd left, I answered my telephone for a call I always felt would come. It was Scott Dempsey, a former Marine who served as a civilian advisor to 1/5 in Afghanistan in 2009. He reached out to tell me the inevitable. Our friend, Haji Abdul Manaf, Nawa's district governor since the days when Marines first arrived in the war-ravaged district, had been murdered in an ambush while returning to his district offices from an official trip to Kandahar. It seemed to be the beginning of the end for the district we had worked, and literally fought, so hard to secure.

For nearly six years, Manaf had labored tirelessly to bring about peace and normalcy in Nawa. This was a remarkably long tenure compared to those of his peers, many of whom had quit out of frustration over the lack of resources, been scared off the job by threats of violence, or been murdered because they wanted to make their country a better place. As I've described, Manaf's first residence in Nawa was an old goat pen, hastily swept out and whitewashed, with cracked and crumbling cement walls. It was lit by a string of lights hooked up to a generator and held up with duct tape. His quarters improved somewhat during the time I was there, but they never came close to luxury. Although he was portly in stature and not in great physical condition, he walked through the district almost as much as the Marines, knowing that he had to be seen with and among his constituents to gain their trust and confidence.

Manaf was always mindful of the sacrifices others had made to improve his district. He was especially fond of the Marines and was awed by the fact that they had left *their* homes to come to the other side of the world to make *his* home safe. In fact, he always carried with him a carefully penned piece of paper with the names of the Marines, Afghan soldiers, and police who had died during his time as governor, a document he frequently showed to others to emphasize their devotion to the concept of service above self.

On May 17, 2015, he joined the ranks of the Marines and Afghans who had lost their lives in defense of and service to Nawa. When I received the news, I thought of my last contact with Manaf, the day he walked with me to an idling helicopter that would take me out of Nawa on my way home. I recalled the crisp salute he gave me as he told me that I was like a brother to him. I was happy to have that memory of my friend. He certainly knew the odds were stacked against him, yet he carried on and endured.

And for that, Haji Abdul Manaf—my friend, my brother—I salute you.

CHAPTER 33
THERE AND BACK AGAIN

His eyes were now open to new ways. He found that he could look back upon his earlier ideas of the glory of war and see them differently . . . With this recognition came a new assurance. He felt a quiet manliness, calm but strong and healthy . . . Over the river a golden ray of sun came through the masses of gray rain clouds.
—STEPHEN CRANE, *The Red Badge of Courage*

It's been quite some time since I carried my gear out of Nawa and began my journey home. As I put the last touches on this book and ready myself to submit it to the publisher, I can't help but reflect on the many twists and turns that have occurred in the region where I served, and the world at large, since then. You'll recall on the very day I left Helmand Province (December 1, 2009), President Obama gave a speech at West Point outlining the U.S. strategic vision for Afghanistan. Addressing the service academy's corps of cadets, the president pledged increased troop levels but also set clear time-tables for the withdrawal of those troops when responsibility for Afghanistan's security would be handed over to its own forces. Even as he spoke about an eventual downsizing of the U.S. mission in Afghanistan, Marines at Camp Leatherneck were busy planning to push into one of Nawa's neighboring districts, called Nawzad, as part of Operation Cobra's Anger, which would be the first major operation to commence after the West Point speech.

A few months later, NATO and Afghan forces were planning Operation Moshtarek (meaning "Together" in the Dari language), a surge of fifteen thousand troops into Marjah, a district neighboring Nawa.† The specter of Marjah had always loomed over the operations my unit was engaged in, and now the Marines were poised to stop the "bleeding ulcer"[62] of insurgency fomenting there. A governor with a checkered past was on standby to lead the district once it was secure for a locally led government to take charge.[63]

In June of 2010, as NATO and Afghan forces struggled to gain control of Marjah, NATO's leadership was in flux as well. After *Rolling Stone* published an article in which members of General McChrystal's staff were quoted making disparaging remarks about senior civilian leaders, President Obama ordered the general to the White House, accepted his resignation, and appointed General David Petraeus in charge of the Afghan war effort.[64]

In August of that same year, Operation Iraqi Freedom officially ended as the last U.S. troops still in the country made a nighttime withdrawal into Kuwait. The departure from Iraq made Afghanistan the focus of the U.S. military after seven years of engagement in two distinct theaters. Fighting in Afghanistan, particularly in Helmand, continued to rage throughout the year. Meanwhile, Marjah had turned out to be a more intense fight than expected. The battle there has become an iconic milestone in Marine Corps lore, producing no shortage of heroes, including Kyle Carpenter. In November 2010, Carpenter was severely wounded when he hurled himself on top of a grenade that landed between him and a squad mate. The blast devastated his right arm, face, and torso, but the Marine next to him was

† The contingent that took part in Operation Moshtarek, the largest joint operation of the war in Afghanistan up to that point, was comprised of Afghan, American, British, Canadian, Danish, and Estonian troops.

saved from major injuries because Carpenter's body absorbed the blast. An urgent medevac flight was called in. Although the outlook was bleak for the severely wounded Carpenter,[65] he miraculously survived and was later presented with the Medal of Honor for his actions.[66]

Toward the end of 2010, 1/5 was preparing for their next deployment, this time to Sangin, a district in Helmand Province about fifty kilometers north of Nawa. A friend from my first deployment, who was now the battalion's operations officer, had called a few months earlier to ask if I would be interested in tagging along to lead their Civil Affairs team. The idea was alluring, but I declined, keeping the promise I made to my wife some years earlier, when she acceded to my desire to don a Marine uniform *one* more time. I owed my wife the attention our growing family needed. By this time a baby sister had joined my two sons just under a year after my return, lending credence to the claims by my Afghan friends that eating the pomegranates they brought to our patrol base would increase my libido and virility.

The war in Afghanistan was entering its tenth year in the beginning of 2011 when the world turned its attention to the nascent "Arab Spring," which began in Tunisia and wound its way east across North Africa. Spurred on in part by Facebook and Twitter, images of plainclothes police officers atop lumbering camels while whacking at protesters with clubs, hit front pages around the world. The protests ultimately resulted in toppling long-standing regimes in the region, including those of Egypt's Hosni Mubarak and Libya's Muammar Gaddafi, the latter meeting a grisly death at the hands of rebels who found him hiding in a culvert.

On the morning of May 2, 2011, President Obama walked up to a podium at the White House and announced that the person who was the root cause of our presence in Afghanistan—Osama bin Laden—had been killed by U.S. Navy SEALs in a daring nighttime

raid into Pakistan. The unannounced incursion into the territory of
another sovereign nation—with whom we were not at war—in order
to conduct a military operation raised questions about its legality
under international law. But the deed was done, providing a much-
needed morale boost for the country that had been at war for nearly
a decade.[67]

Later that summer, on August 6, NATO forces suffered the
worst single-day loss of life in the Afghan war when a helicopter
carrying troops on their way to help a pinned-down unit was shot
out of the sky with an RPG, killing all thirty-eight people and a military working dog on board. The ominous news revived concerns as
to whether we would suffer through a grim war of attrition like the
Soviets had endured in Afghanistan during the 1980s.

In the fall of 2011, my friends from 1/5 were finishing their
deployment in Sangin. At the end of their eight months on the
ground, they had succeeded in turning over control of the district
to the Afghan National Army, but it came at a high cost: 17 of the
battalion's Marines were killed and 191 received Purple Hearts for
combat wounds.

By early 2012, as the nation's attention was turning to the
upcoming U.S. presidential election, NATO forces continued to
see gains throughout Afghanistan, patiently drinking tea with the
locals, training Afghan security forces, and working with civilian aid
organizations to improve infrastructure and governance. However,
good news from the war was frequently overshadowed by high-pro-
file mishaps and misdeeds, such as errant air strikes that killed
civilians while failing to kill enough—or, as some have argued, *any*—
insurgents. Also grabbing headlines were accounts of corruption by
U.S. government contractors, some of whom were doing their best
to help themselves to foreign-aid dollars intended for the Afghans
they were supposed to be serving.[68] Then, in March 2012, a U.S.
Army sergeant walked out of the front gate of his patrol base, not

very different from Patrol Base Jaker, and executed sixteen Afghan
civilians as they slept in their compounds. Six months later, fifteen
Taliban insurgents wearing U.S. Army uniforms carried out an
attack inside the barriers of Camp Bastion, killing two Marines and
several civilians and destroying six aircraft. In October, another
brazen attack occurred several hundred miles south of Helmand
Province. Gunmen attempted to kill a teenaged girl named Malala
Yousafzai because she had offended their sensibilities by being an
outspoken advocate for women's education in the region. Malala
survived the attack and gained worldwide attention—and eventually a Nobel Peace Prize—for her unwavering advocacy of women's
education.

The next three years saw the world facing turbulent times as
Marines deployed to and from Afghanistan, seeing their efforts take
on a Sisyphean cycle of wins and losses. But Afghanistan was no
longer center stage in the world's armed conflicts. In February 2014,
Russian troops pushed into the Crimean Peninsula and then into
Ukraine in a nationalist-inspired land grab that threatened NATO's
resolve to deter a threat at its borders. At the same time, U.S. troops
were deploying to Syria, assisting rebels opposed to Bashar al-As-
sad's military, who were supported by Russia's military.

In late 2014, Marines, Brits, and Afghans held an elaborate ceremony formally turning over operational control of Camp Bastion
to Afghan forces. The Union Jack and the Stars and Stripes were
lowered at the base, congratulatory speeches were given, and the
Afghans were put in charge of their own destiny.[69] But a lack of seri-
ousness and commitment to the long-term challenges Afghanistan
faced started to become evident as civilian advisors who were poorly
trained, unqualified, and uncommitted—and who had little firepower to back up their efforts—made only tepid attempts to assess
and respond to the country's needs.[70]

Amid all these events, Helmand started to fall back into the Taliban's hands.

In early 2015, it was Nawzad—the district that Marines were preparing to seize when I left the country in late 2009—that had succumbed. In July Lashkar Gah (Helmand's capital city) and Musa Qala followed. The next year, 2016, it was Garmsir, Khan Neshin, and Sangin. In the summer of 2016, my friend, National Public Radio photojournalist David Gilkey, and his interpreter, Zabihullah Tamanna, were killed near Marjah, which had once again become a hotbed of violence as the local government and security forces fled, leaving its residents to largely fend for themselves against Taliban and insurgent rule. Predictably, Nawa met the fate of its neighbors by late 2016, but this sad event escaped the attention of major newspapers and was reported only in regional papers and websites.[71]

Marines returned to Helmand Province in 2017 to advise and support a better-trained and equipped Afghan National Army, and help them take back some of the districts the Taliban had seized.[72] By the end of the year, Afghan security forces (with the help of U.S. Marines) had retaken some of the province's key districts, including Nawa,[73] giving a glimmer of hope—albeit fleetingly—that an era of normalcy and peace might come about. By that time, the war in Afghanistan was on its third U.S. president.

Through the first half of 2020, as I was writing this final chapter of *The Wolves of Helmand*, events in Afghanistan continued on a course of predictable chaos. The U.S. continued its counterinsurgency efforts, though with significantly reduced troop strength and allied cooperation. Afghan leaders sought ways to strike a grand bargain with the Taliban, often with the well-intentioned involvement of the U.S. At one point, even Russia—perhaps seeing an opportunity to further disrupt America's standing in Afghanistan, to reclaim its own lost honor in the country, or to seek ways in which to capitalize on Afghanistan's mineral wealth—tried to interject itself into the process.[74] But these efforts seemed always to be riven by violence, and progress toward peace and reconciliation was often stalled or even reversed.[75] Eventually, a sense of resignation that *any* deal is better than *no* deal hovered over the prospect of peace talks[76] and the definition of "success" after eighteen years of fighting in the country shifted accordingly.[77]

By early 2020, a peace deal between the U.S. and the Taliban had been signed (but the Afghan government was, amazingly, *not* a party to that deal).[78] I share the optimism of some commentators for what this will mean for Afghanistan, and indeed, the United States.[79] But with a glance backward at history, I do so only with bated breath and fingers crossed.

While confusion abounds around the future of Afghanistan, one thing is certain: it will remain a hub of global friction and a perpetual enigma for years to come. As we begin to read about the first U.S. service members training to deploy to Afghanistan, who weren't even born yet when the events that initially led us there occurred,[80] skeptics might argue that we are on an endless and predictable cycle in the "Graveyard of Empires." Those skeptics are probably right, but I remain hopeful for the country's future, even while wrestling with the notion that it may be well past time for the U.S. to leave Afghanistan and let the Afghans determine their own fate. This is a complex reality to grapple with, especially as I would not want to abandon the Afghan friends I made there who have worked for the betterment of their country.

Not only has much changed for Nawa, and Afghanistan as a whole, in the decade since I flew under the cover of darkness to first set foot in Helmand Province, but much has changed for me personally as well. My brood of children grew to four, I shifted among several jobs in law and finance, and my family had the opportunity to live and work abroad for a few years. My friends who stayed in the Marine Corps are now colonels or senior NCOs, and I am certain a few will attain the Corps' highest ranks over time. Others retired after twenty years of service or left after their initial tour of duty, entering the civilian force as proud ambassadors of what we all humbly (but correctly) feel is our nation's premier military service. I still never miss an opportunity to tell a story that begins with, "One time when I was in the Marine Corps," and many of those stories include events from my time in Afghanistan.

At varying times, the prognosis for success in Afghanistan looked grim. Whenever people learn that I'd spent time there, I am inevitably asked whether it was worth it. It's a simple question that has no simple answer. It will never be for me to say to the families of the Marines whose lives were lost in Afghanistan, in Nawa, or elsewhere, whether it was worth it. But to those families, I can say unequivocally that the service of their loved ones *mattered* and *made a difference*. No policy decision can diminish the achievements of the Marines and our fellow service members who tirelessly walked the ground there.

When I reflect on whether it was worth it, I think of the many Afghans who smiled in amazement as they saw their image emerge from a Polaroid snapshot I'd taken of them with the camera I carried with me everywhere. For many, it was likely the only picture they'd ever had, or will have, of themselves. Those pictures may have disappeared or faded by now, but I like to think the Afghans in those photos still have a positive memory of the armor-clad Marine who told them to smile while looking at the camera. I remember Ishmael, the boy whose parents and other relatives were killed when a five-hundred-pound bomb was dropped on their family compound. He had every reason to hate us, but he did not. Instead, he would come to our patrol base to say hello to the Marines and ask for some basic English lessons. I think about Mohamed Wotak, who quietly endured my insults when I was certain he had tried to pull a fast one on me and get paid for a bridge he never built—when he had in fact built it exceptionally well.

I recall with a smile the man who tried to swindle a payment from me for an imaginary dead cow devoured by a fictitious pack of marauding wolves and who gave me the inspiration for the title of this book. I think of the many Abdul Rahmans I met in Nawa, ranging from infants to ancients, as well as the many Mohameds, Abdullahs, Saeds, and Walis who invited me to sit for tea and chew on a freshly cooked goat. Or a farmer named Wali Jahn, who hadn't had a good job in years but was leading a small construction crew in Nawa's district center by the time I left in late 2009. Or a widow named Sahaba, who cried tears of joy and thanks when Marines gave her enough rice, beans, and cooking oil to last her and her children for a month. Or Haji Mohammed Hajem, who brought his family and all the belongings they could pile into a trailer towed behind a tractor back to Nawa after having fled to the relative safety of Lashkar Gah, eighteen months before Marines made his home district safe enough for their return. Or a giant of a man named Haji Abdul Ghafar, who embraced me in his huge arms when I gave him a Pashto-language Quran and a prayer rug, then looked me in the eye and said in halting, broken English, "You are good men. I will pray for you as long as I live."

Afghanistan wasn't perfect when I arrived there in early 2009 or when I left later that same year. And it's far from perfect today. But we Marines serving with 1/5 did our part when called, and we did a damn good job. I won't speak for those Marines, but for me, it was worth it.

AWARD RECIPIENTS FROM NAWA 2009 DEPLOYMENT

Not only instances of unusual gallantry, but also of extraordinary fidelity and essential service in any way shall meet with a due reward . . . The road to glory in a patriot army and a free country is thus open to all.

—General George Washington on the Badge of Military Merit, the first award designated for U.S. service members

NAVY CROSS

Donald Hogan

LEGION OF MERIT

William McCollough

BRONZE STAR

Christopher Biello ★ Frank Biggio ★ William Cahir ★
Matt Danner ★ Lance Day ★ Matthew Duquette ★ Timothy Eannarino
★ Joseph Giardino ★ Cody Gibson ★ Clinton Hall ★ Lamont Hammond
★ Brian Huysman ★ Thomas Lacroix ★ Jay Lappe ★ Andy Lee ★
James Otto ★ Andrew Schoenmaker ★ Thomas Sowers ★
Simon Trujillo ★ David Wilson

PURPLE HEART

David Baker ★ Robert Behrendt ★ William Cahir ★ Kevin Cameron ★ Chris Conanan ★ Matthew Corson ★ Michael Donoghue ★ Elliott Dunne ★ Aaron Edwards ★ Timothy Evans ★ Mitchell Gentry ★ Cody Gibson ★ Marcus Gill ★ Harry Ho ★ Rocky Hoard ★ Donald Hogan ★ Andy Lee ★ Ryan Lindner ★ Brandon Lux ★ David McCreary ★ Charles McGuire ★ Robert McHugh ★ Michael Medina Sanchez ★ Samuel Meyer ★ Kyle Mirehouse ★ Louis Nagy ★ Antonio Ortega ★ Jose Ortiz Magana ★ Andino Palacio ★ Benjamin Paladino ★ Michael Rivera ★ Aaron Rodgers ★ Eric Santana ★ Scott Santoro ★ Reed Sinks ★ Jeremy Sumrall ★ Justin Swanson ★ Jason Swofford ★ Jordy Vega ★ Cole Wilson

NAVY AND MARINE CORPS COMMENDATION MEDAL

Gerardo Alvarez ★ Marcelino Barajas ★ Jason Black ★ Michael Blejski ★ Adam Boland ★ Kevin Cameron ★ Chester Carter ★ William Childs ★ Shawn Connor ★ Edwin Cruz ★ David Dial ★ Shawn Donovan ★ Jared Doyle ★ Lucas Dyer ★ Kevin Fallon ★ David Garcia ★ Patrick Gascoigne ★ Matthew German ★ William Greeson ★ Bradley Harris ★ Alexander Hawley ★ Justin Hickman ★ Harry Ho ★ Landon Hoeft ★ Shawn Hughes ★ Aiden Katz ★ Robert Kightlinger ★ Stephen Koth ★ Rodney Malone ★ Keith Marine ★ William McLean ★ Sean McNeely ★ Christopher Mullins ★ David O'Connell ★ Patrick O'Shea ★ Travis Onischuk ★ Charles Rinehart ★ Jeremy Sabado ★ John Schippert ★ Christopher Shranko ★ Artur Shvartsberg ★ Paul Silva ★ Eric Stewart ★ Jason Swofford ★ Michael Wilmott ★ Chris Wilson ★ Michael Winchester

NAVY AND MARINE CORPS ACHIEVEMENT MEDAL

Manuel Amial ★ Tomas Armenta ★ David Baker ★ John Barghusen ★ Zachary Bennett ★ Aaron Buczek ★ Thomas Bullifant ★ Sean Cain ★ Carter Calvert ★ Adam Clarke ★ Chris Conanan ★ Matthew Cox ★ Bobby Darhele ★ Joseph Davis ★ Matthew Dean ★ Brett DeMoore ★ Aaron Denning ★ Michael Donoghue ★ Juan Elizondo ★ Cody Elliott ★ John Embry ★ Jose Esquivel ★ Ethan Feuerborn ★ Mark Fields ★ Ryan Fife ★ Nick Gonzales ★ Andres Gonzalez ★ Richard Guerrero ★ Ronald Gunst ★ Shane Hart ★ Josue Hernandez ★ Rocky Hoard ★ Joshua Hume ★ Jonathan Hutson ★ Brian Hylwiak ★ Jason Irons ★ John Jaramillo ★ Kevin Jensen ★ Sean Johnson ★ Jeremiah Jones ★ Steven Kelly ★ Michael Kuiper ★ Adam Kurahashi ★ Shawn Laliberte ★ Rovin Lara ★ David Lombardo ★ Alex Lopezzamora ★ Charles Mahovlic ★ Victor Manon ★ Jose Marquez ★ Seth Martens ★ Chris Martindale ★ Tyrone McCullough ★ Ivan Mejia ★ John Mensch ★ Brice Michalek ★ Cameron Mikael ★ Joseph Misek ★ Brian Monahan ★ David Montiel ★ Vincent Morales ★ Erick Newcomb ★ Colin Newman ★ Joshua Nicholson ★ Robert Orr ★ Benjamin Palacio ★ Claudio Patino ★ Michael Pinedo ★ Adrian Pouchoulen ★ Thomas Prater ★ Brian Pulst ★ Jacob Pustulka ★ Christopher Reyes ★ Scott Riley ★ Joseph Rodriguez ★ Lade Rogers ★ Brendan Runyon ★ Marco Sanchez ★ Christopher Scilingo ★ Justin Scrivner ★ Andrew Shackelford ★ Jonathan Sheets ★ Trevor Simpson ★ Kyle Skeels ★ Scott Spaulding ★ Adam Stanley ★ Hugh Styborski ★ Rex Talcott ★ Jose Tena ★ Mark Tiearney ★ Jorge Valencia ★ Francisco Vanegas ★ Beau Varner ★ Chris Velazquez ★ Gilbert Velez ★ Derrick Villalobos ★ Cole Vollenweider ★ Jerry Weckesser ★ John Woodham

CORPS QUOTES: THINGS PEOPLE SAY IN A WAR ZONE

"Gus, if you fuck this up, I will cleave off the top of your fucking skull and then eat the insides like a grapefruit with one of those serrated-edge spoons."

—A senior Marine encouraging me to do my job well

"Technically he's an adult, but when it comes to doing his job, he literally needs to be led by the ear."

—A senior civilian advisor to the battalion describing a staff officer at the MEB headquarters

"It's times like this that I feel like the only people I can relate to are suicide bombers."

—A battalion staff officer expressing his frustration at some of the conflicting guidance received from higher headquarters elements

"It tastes like chicken."

"Dude, it *is* chicken."

"Yeah, I know. I just thought maybe it would be different since it's an Afghan chicken."

"Did you really just say that?"

—*A conversation between two Marines over dinner with a squad of Afghan Army soldiers, who prepared the meal with locally sourced chicken and vegetables*

"About three hundred years."

—*A senior enlisted Marine's answer to his wife's question, "What's the time difference there?"*

"I don't know much about much."

—*A first lieutenant's candid self-assessment*

"One guy shits the bed, so we all have to wear a diaper."

—*A Marine lamenting the common use of collective punishment*

"It feels like a thousand little snow angels licking your nut sack at the same time."

—*A corporal describing the tingling sensation of Gold Bond powder sprinkled liberally on the crotch*

"He's too smart by half."

—One Marine's roundabout way of saying another Marine isn't too bright

"To save a drowner, you must be a swimmer."

—A platoon sergeant explaining the importance of
continuing education to a group of new NCOs

"All those guys are crooks."

—Nawa district governor Haji Abdul Manaf's opinion of the
Afghan government officials in Lashkar Gah and Kabul

"Keep the window lickers away from the media guys."

—A senior enlisted Marine advising his platoon sergeants to keep some
of the Marines away from reporters on an upcoming press visit

"It's a good idea, but sort of like the scene in *Forrest Gump*
where he reaches the end zone and then keeps on running;
somebody just let it go on and get out of hand."

—A company XO describing an intelligence-gathering
concept adopted by the MEB headquarters

"Yeah, it can be tense at times. Imagine having your dick laid out on an anvil and a blind guy in the same room is swinging around a hammer. It's tense like that."

—*An NCO answering a question from a prominent TV reporter about whether he ever felt tense serving in a combat zone (his interview was not aired)*

"You've got to constantly stir it; otherwise the diesel fuel makes a crusty layer on top and the stuff underneath stays all gooey. Kind of like a crème brûlée, but not one you'd want to eat."

—*A junior Marine who was on latrine-burning detail, explaining to the same TV reporter why it was necessary to constantly stir the noxious mixture (his interview was not aired either)*

"He's not bothered by including petty things like the truth or facts in his writing."

—*A company commander describing a reporter who wrote a poorly researched article about Nawa*

"His men would have followed him anywhere, but more out of curiosity rather than any sense of loyalty or trust in his leadership."

—*A platoon sergeant describing a junior officer he knew earlier in his career*

"Nobody wants to die young, but we're all afraid of getting old."

—*Conversation overheard between two corporals pondering mortality*

"He's like Forrest Gump, but without any of the charm."

—A senior civilian advisor to the battalion describing
a staff officer at the MEB headquarters

"If God is with us on Election Day,
we won't need to worry about a security plan."

—Nawa district governor Haji Abdul Manaf's position on creating a Marine/
Afghan Army and Police security plan for the August 20 elections

Response from a senior Marine: "God will probably
be very busy on Election Day, so let's put a plan
together to help him out just in case."

"Don't be a buddy fucker!"

—A Marine sergeant, on the importance of loyalty and teamwork

"I felt like I was getting relationship advice from Borat."

—A platoon commander recalling a conversation in which an Afghan
police officer gave him some advice on how to keep his wife in line

"I just don't like shit to be *unperfect*."

—A senior Marine explaining his self-diagnosed obsessive-compulsive
disorder and why he likes things to be done a particular way

"The Afghans have mastered the art of telling whoever they
are speaking to whatever it is that person wants to hear."
—*A senior civilian advisor to the MEB describing the duplicity common among Afghans*

"The devil is not wise because he's the devil;
the devil is wise because he's old."
—*A senior Marine explaining the importance of experience*

"Knowledge is knowing that a tomato is a fruit. Wisdom is
knowing that it's not a good idea to put a tomato in a fruit salad."
—*Another senior Marine's perspective on the importance of
practical experience to augment formal education.*

"He's as popular as a porcupine in a bag of popcorn."
—*An engineer's opinion of a colleague with a caustic personality*

"Hold on . . . now usually when someone starts a
sentence with '*with all due respect,*' they're about to say
some disrespectful shit, so slow your roll."
—*A senior enlisted Marine advising a junior NCO to
think twice about what he is going to say*

"If you're going to try to be a smart ass, make sure
you're smart. Otherwise, you're just an ass."
—*That same senior enlisted Marine, in the same
conversation with that same junior NCO*

"If your Marines are sitting on their ass all day,
accomplishing nothing more than converting food
into shit, then you are not doing your job."
—*A senior enlisted Marine on leadership*

"Some of these guys are kind of like Denzel in *Training
Day*, but not in a cool or badass way, just crooked."
—*A platoon commander describing some members of the Afghan National Security Forces*

"I try to not overdo it. When done just right,
profanity can have a certain poetic beauty to it, and
I sometimes like to think of myself as a poet."
—*A senior enlisted Marine explaining his approach to using profanity*

"I never thought I'd have to explain to someone why it's
not a good idea to smoke pot while on patrol."
*—Another platoon commander explaining one of the challenges
of working with the Afghan National Security Forces*

"Why would someone take a perfectly delicious thing like
a cake and stick a dick-shaped carrot in it and fuck it up?
I mean who the hell do these people think they are?"
—A senior Marine's opinion on carrot cake

"If you don't prepare for everything that might
happen, you'll guarantee that some of it will."
*—A senior enlisted Marine explaining the need for intense
and diverse pre-deployment training*

"You'd think there would be plenty of capacity for some
knowledge and a bit of common sense in that huge cranium of
his, but that deer in the headlights look he always has makes me
think that the barriers to entry are just . . . insurmountable."
—A MEB staff officer reflecting on a colleague

"So, I walk around armed to the teeth; a rifle, two
hundred rounds of ammo, a few grenades, a knife,

Kevlar helmet, and a flak jacket. And the first thing I say to every Afghan I see is, 'Peace be upon you!'"

—*A sergeant reflecting on the irony of his appearance as he greets Afghans with the traditional Muslim greeting,* Salam alekum

"We can sleep, we can rest, and we can do what we do, because a Marine is on post."

—*A senior Marine proudly expressing the confidence he has in the Marines standing watch*

"He has a record unblemished by any notable achievement, yet, *there he is.*"

—*A captain's observation after seeing someone's name on a recent promotion list*

"Either you're not listening to me or the 'Meow Mix' song is playing in your head!"

—*A senior enlisted Marine chewing out a junior Marine who didn't seem to be paying attention*

"It's sad, but funny at the same time. You know, like when a clown dies."

—*A Marine captain's perspective on people making bad decisions*

"A small part of me thinks that's a really good idea. But considering that 75% of me is just water, it's only a really, really small part of me that thinks that."

—*Part of a conversation overheard between two NCOs*

"And just so you know, there is such a thing as a stupid question."

—*A senior enlisted Marine forewarning junior Marines before a visit from the Commandant of the Marine Corps and the Sergeant Major of the Marine Corps*

"It would be cool to fly out of here on an Osprey, huh?"

—*A Marine talking about leaving Nawa in one of the Marine Corps' newest fleet of aircraft, the MV-22 Osprey*

Response: "It would be cool just to fly out of here, period. You could put me in a dog kennel."

"It's bad luck to be superstitious."

—*A sergeant explaining to a reporter why he doesn't carry any good luck charms on deployment*

"And make sure you clean up your tent. Don't leave behind a fuck show for someone else to clean up."

—*A senior Marine advising junior Marines to clean up after themselves*

"It's hotter than four foxes fucking in a forest fire!"

—*A Marine describing the weather in Helmand Province*

"If you want to know the future, go find yourself a gypsy."

—*A Marine answering a reporter's question about what he
thought Afghanistan would be like in twenty years*

"The tree falls, and the monkeys scatter."

—*A senior enlisted Marine, sharing a Chinese proverb, describing his frustration with
the lack of commitment by some civilian leaders to military success in Afghanistan*

"This weather could turn Heidi Klum into the
Wicked Witch of the West in no time."

—*An NCO explaining how the heat and humidity in
Helmand can take their toll on a person's skin*

"Why should we give up on these people and this place just
because someone wants to get elected back in America?"

—*A Marine captain's perspective on continuing to help the
Afghans despite political posturing back home*

"You Americans all have watches, but we Afghans have all the time."

—A saying often repeated by older Afghans suggesting that American
patience in the country will eventually wear thin

"We need a strong, charismatic, and effective leader.
Someone like John F. Kennedy, or maybe Joseph Stalin."

—A Kyrgyzstan national working at Manas Air Base, describing
the type of leader he wishes were in charge of his country

"Be the type of Marine who *makes* things
happen, not just *lets* things happen."

—Words of wisdom from a visiting general officer addressing the Marines in Nawa

"If you're gonna be stupid, you better be tough."

—Life advice from an Army Special Forces friend

GLOSSARY OF MILITARY TERMS, ACRONYMS, AND PASHTO WORDS AND PHRASES

Adhan: The Islamic call to worship, announced at five prescribed times each day.

AK-47: The ubiquitous Kalashnikov machine gun used by most non-NATO military forces around the world, terrorists, drug runners, and hooligans. Cheap to produce and easy to maintain.

Akus: "Picture" or "photo."

AO: Area of Operations.

BOLO: Be on the lookout.

Burkha: A long, loose garment covering the whole body from head to feet, worn in public by women in many Muslim countries.

CACO: Casualty Assistance Calls Officer; the Marine who has the unenviable duty to notify next of kin about their loved one's death.

CAG: Civil Affairs Group.

CERP funds: Commander's Emergency Response Program funds; one of the pools of money available to Marines in Helmand to support things like making reparations for combat damage, injuries to non-combatants, rebuilding and reconstruction projects or other community-building initiatives.

CH-53: Also known as the Sea Stallion; A large, heavy-lift helicopter used to transport troops and equipment.

COIN: Counterinsurgency Operations.

Deh-deh mahnana: "Thank you very much."

Dushman: "Insurgent."

EOD: Explosive ordnance disposal; the engineers who have the delicate task of dismantling bombs and IEDs.

FAC: Forward air controller, usually a pilot assigned to a ground unit, responsible for coordinating air support from the ground.

.50 Cal: A heavy, belt-fed machine gun that came into use at the end of World War I that fires a 12.7 mm round at a rate of over 450 rounds per minute at an effective range of approximately 1,800 meters (2,000 yards).

First Civ Div: Slang term meaning First Civilian Division, where Marines go when they leave the service.

FOO funds: Field Ordering Officer funds; one of the pools of money available to Marines in Helmand to purchase certain goods from local sources; similar, but not quite identical to how CERP funds are used.

G-BOSS: Ground-Based Operational Surveillance System; a trailer-mounted surveillance system mounted on a hundred-foot tower.

GIROA: Government of the Islamic Republic of Afghanistan.

GWOT: Global War on Terror.

Hamdullah: "Praise be to God."

HIMARS: High Mobility Artillery Rocket System; a multiple-rocket launching system mounted on a standard M1140 truck frame, capable of launching high-explosive rockets up to three hundred kilometers.

Hodai paman: "Go with God" or "God be with you."

Humvee: Originally HMMWV, meaning High-Mobility Multi-Wheeled Vehicle; a common troop transport vehicle popularized in Operation Desert Storm.

IED: Improvised explosive device; makeshift homemade bomb used by insurgents.

Inshallah: "God willing."

Jagran: "Captain."

Jerib: A traditional measurement of land in many countries in the Middle East and Central Asia. In Afghanistan it is equal to two thousand square meters, just about half an acre.

Kafan: A shroud used to wrap a body before burial, conforming with Islamic tenets; usually made of white linen.

LZ: Landing zone; where helicopters touch down to drop off or pick up their cargo and personnel.

M134: A six-barrel machine gun, often mounted on an attack helicopter, which fires a 7.62 mm round through a rotating Gatling-style assembly at a high, sustained rate (two thousand to six thousand rounds per minute).

M240G: A medium-sized belt-fed machine gun that fires a 7.62 mm round at a rate of over 650 rounds per minute at an effective range of approximately 1,100 meters (1,200 yards).

M4: Standard-issue rifle that fires a 5.56 mm round; roughly the modern-day equivalent of the M16.

MAAWS: Money as a Weapons System, which, along with a hefty manual, described the various funds available to deployed forces to use in support of counterinsurgency operations.

MEB: Marine Expeditionary Brigade; a Marine air-ground task force consisting of ground forces, aviation units, and support elements, numbering between twelve thousand and fifteen thousand Marines; usually commanded by a one-star general.

Mihrab: A niche in the wall of a mosque indicating the direction of Mecca.

MK19: A belt-fed grenade launcher that fires 40 mm grenades at a sustained rate of 40 rounds per minute up to an effective range of about 1,500 meters (1,600 yards).

MRAP: Mine-resistant, ambush-protected vehicle; a large, heavily armored troop transport vehicle.

MRE: Meal ready to eat; a prepackaged meal issued to Marines in the field.

MWR: Morale, welfare, and recreation.

NATO: North Atlantic Treaty Organization; post–World War II military alliance organized to defend against Russian aggression in Europe.

NCO: Noncommissioned officer; an enlisted Marine with the rank of corporal or higher.

Noshe jan: "Cheers" or "Enjoy."

NVGs: Night vision goggles.

OMA funds: Operations and Maintenance, Army funds, one of the pools of money available to Marines in Helmand to support projects or other initiatives.

PFT: Physical fitness test; consisting of a three-mile run, pull-ups, and crunches.

PID: Positive Identification; the rules-of-engagement requirement to fire on a target.

POERF: Post-Operational Emergency Relief Funds, one of the pools of money available to Marines in Helmand to support projects or other initiatives.

REMF: Rear-echelon motherfucker; military service member not on the front lines, popular derogatory term in the Vietnam War era.

ROE: Rules of engagement.

RPG: Rocket-propelled grenade; looks and performs similar to a bazooka.

Saheb: A Pashto honorific used when addressing a distinguished person.

Salam alekum: The typical greeting in Muslim cultures, meaning "peace be upon you," which is answered with *"Wa-alekum salam"* ("And upon you be peace").

Shalwar kamiz: The traditional outfit worn by Afghans, consisting of loose-fitting cotton trousers and a long knee-length shirt.

Shemagh: A traditional Middle Eastern headdress, somewhat like a scarf, also used by Afghan men as a makeshift satchel.

Shura: Literally "consultation" and typically meant to mean a community event focused on making decisions in a collaborative manner, somewhat like a town hall meeting or other public forum in Western culture.

Sta num zih dai?: "What is your name?"

Taso senge yast?: "How are you?"

TCN: Third-country national.

Wah-allah: "Why, God?"

WMD: Weapons of mass destruction.

Wuuh: "Yes."

XO: Executive officer; the second in command of a unit.

Zma num zih . . .: "My name is . . ."

ACKNOWLEDGMENTS

EVERY SUCCESS I'VE ENJOYED IN LIFE CAME ABOUT BECAUSE I WAS part of a team and had the support of others who helped me achieve results I could not have achieved alone. Writing this book was a team effort, too, and I'm grateful to the following people:

My parents, Tony and Minnow, who instilled in me an appreciation for reading and storytelling from an early age and generally raised me right.

Ron Holtman, my Boy Scout troop leader and lifelong family friend, who was an early editor and encouraged me to keep writing.

The teachers and coaches I was privileged to learn from as a kid, including George Bell, Bud Bender, Garth Fowler, Tony Gallagher, Rhoda Green, Frank Hostnick, Tate Hudson, Barb Joliff, Portia Pyle, and Jan Redick, each of whom taught me well while patiently putting up with my youthful antics.

Professor Peter Havholm, from the College of Wooster, whose eye for detail and clever wit resulted in tremendous improvements to my first draft.

Brunella Costagliola and Hope Innelli, whose editing advice made me think a bit harder and write a bit better about my experiences.

Jonathan Merkh and his team at Forefront Books who turned this idea into something real.

General Stanley McChrystal (Ret.) and Ellen Chapin, who graciously lent their experience and talents to the foreword for this book, giving readers an important historical insight into the significance of Nawa in counterinsurgency operations.

My colleagues at Patton Boggs LLP, for their generosity and support during my deployment to Afghanistan.

Members of the media who reported on 1/5's successes in Nawa, including Max Boot (*The Wall Street Journal*), Rajiv Chandrasekaran (*The Washington Post*), Anderson Cooper (CNN), Vanessa Gezari, Eros Hoagland (*The New York Times*), Andrew Lubin (*Leatherneck*), Nick McDonell (*TIME*), Seth Moulton and Lucian Read (CBS's *Dan Rather Reports*), Tony Perry (*Los Angeles Times*), David Scantling, John Wendle, and Bing West.

Civilian advisors Kael Weston, Scott Dempsey, and Sir Ian Purves, and law enforcement professionals Russ Juren and Rex Fullmer, who marched and slept in the same dirt as the Marines in Helmand Province.

The Chindits, past, present, and future, but especially those from IOC 4-94; the Rat Bastards from the 1/1 Heavy Guns Platoon; and Echo Force. You know who you are.

The Marines of the 4th Civil Affairs Group, who welcomed me back into the Marine Corps and helped me learn the art of civil affairs, including George Anikow, Todd Bowers, Jason Brezler, Bill Cahir, Micah Caskey, John Church, Rene Cote, Warren Coughlin, Dale Cutts, Bobby Darhele, Leonard DeFrancisci, Ryan Dexter, Alex Ealley, Gerard Fischer, Jasmin Gagnon, David Garcia, Patrick Gascoigne, Dan Greif, James Hileman, James Keefer, Rovin Lara, Curtis Lee, Nasser Manasterli, Paul Meagher, Pete Neubauer, Alan Parvis, Ryan Pettit, Michelle Shelly, Scott Spaulding, Larry Trimmer, Chris Velazquez, Gilbert Velez, Jerry Weckesser, and James "Butch" Wright.

Bill McCollough and Tom Sowers, whose exemplary leadership and dedication at the helm of 1/5 was contagious; all the staff SNCOs and officers of the battalion who set a similar example; and the junior officers, NCOs, and Marines of 1/5 who know the answer to the question, "Who are we?"

Mike Kuiper, David Wilson, and the other Marines who were part of the "Caggle Squad."

My lovely wife, a consummate professional and wonderful role model to our wolf-dragon kids. Thank you for saying yes.

ENDNOTES

1   This phrase is described in Seth Jones, *In the Graveyard of Empires: America's War in Afghanistan* (New York: W. W. Norton, 2009).

2   See Amy Belasco, "Troop Levels in the Afghan and Iraq Wars," *Congressional Research Service*, July 2, 2009.

3   See, e.g., Bob Herbert, "The Afghan Quagmire," *New York Times*, January 5, 2009.

4   See, e.g., Dexter Filkins, "Taliban Fill NATO's Big Gaps in Afghan South," *New York Times*, January 21, 2009.

5   See John A. Nagl, foreword to the 2006 edition of David Galula, *Counterinsurgency Warfare: Theory and Practice* (Santa Barbara, CA: Praeger Security International, 1964).

6   See, e.g., Helene Cooper et al., "Obama Weighs Adding Troops in Afghanistan," *New York Times*, February 11, 2009.

7   See, e.g., Nicholas Kulish et al., "Holbrooke Says Afghan War 'Tougher Than Iraq,'" *New York Times*, February 8, 2009.

8   See "A General's Marching Orders," *The Economist*, May 14, 2009.

9   See David Ace et al., "Defining Victory to Win a War," *Foreign Policy*, October 6, 2009, which points out that even several months after General McChrystal took charge in Afghanistan, the US strategic objectives were not clearly defined.

10 See Kim Barker, *The Taliban Shuffle: Strange Days in Afghanistan and Pakistan* (New York: Penguin Random House, 2016).

11 For information about Manas Air Base, see Olga Dzyubenko, "U.S. Vacates Base in Central Asia as Russia's Clout Rises," Reuters, June 3, 2014.

12 See Meredith H. Lair, "Easy Living in a Hard War: Behind the Lines in Vietnam," *Military History Quarterly*, May 2, 2012. The contrast between the experiences of front-line soldiers and rear-echelon

support soldiers in Vietnam is further illustrated in Meredith H. Lair, *Armed with Abundance: Consumerism and Soldiering in the Vietnam War* (Chapel Hill: University of North Carolina Press, 2014).

13 For a description of the extent of the amenities at these facilities in Iraq, see Rajiv Chandrasekaran, *Imperial Life in the Emerald City: Inside Iraq's Green Zone* (New York: Alfred A. Knopf, 2006), which served as the basis for the movie *The Green Zone*.

14 See Elizabeth Bumiller, "We Have Met the Enemy and He Is PowerPoint," *The New York Times*, April 27, 2010.

15 See US Forces, Afghanistan, *Money as a Weapon System Afghanistan*, https://info.publicintelligence.net/USFOR-A-MAAWS-2012.pdf, for the 268-page manual.

16 "CERP" means "Commander's Emergency Response Program" and CERP funds can be used to pay for small construction projects and battle-damage claims (including payments for civilian battlefield deaths); "FOO" means "Field Ordering Officer," and FOO funds are used for local purchases of the ambiguously defined "mission-essential" requirements not available from other sources; "OMA" means "Operations and Maintenance, Army," and OMA funds can be used for immediate operational needs of a deployed unit, like fuel or other supplies and material; "POERF" means "Post-Operational Emergency Relief Funds," and these funds (which are provided by NATO and not the US Treasury) can be used for a wide range of humanitarian relief purposes, as field commanders may determine at their own discretion.

17 In modern times, the phrase "crossing the Rubicon" is a metaphor for passing the point of no return, commonly used in the context of embarking on a military campaign or other significant event. Its history dates to a momentous decision by Julius Caesar in 49 BC that led to the Roman Civil War and the expansion of the Roman Empire under Caesar's emperorship. At that time, Caesar was the Roman governor of a region that spanned from southern Gaul (which included parts of France, Switzerland, Luxembourg, and Germany) to Illyricum (which included parts of the Balkans). As the governor,

he had a small army at his command to protect the region, but in accordance with the principle of *imperium*, this army was not permitted in Italy. If Caesar, as their commander, were to lead them into Italy, it would be considered an act of insurrection and treason, punishable by death. When his term ended, the Roman Senate ordered Caesar to return to Rome, and specifically admonished him to disband his army—which had demonstrated loyalty to Caesar the man ahead of loyalty to the empire. The Rubicon River at that time marked the northern boundary of Italy. Dissatisfied with the leadership in Rome, and fancying a new role for himself, Caesar led his army to the Rubicon, pondering his fate and destiny. Legend has it that he uttered the words *"alea iacta est"* (the die is cast), and then marched his army across the river. Although there is no doubt this was a momentous occasion, some facts about the crossing have been exaggerated over time. For instance, the Rubicon was more of a small creek than a large river, and Caesar and his army were able to walk across it without getting wet much higher than their ankles. See Stanley McChrystal, Jeff Eggers and Jason Mangone, *Leaders: Myth and Reality* (Portfolio 2018), for a description about how the myth of the Rubicon crossing has differed from the actual events there.

18 See Yochi J. Dreazen, "U.S. Launches South Afghan Offensive," *The Wall Street Journal*, July 2, 2009; Richard A. Oppel Jr., "U.S. Marines Try to Retake Afghan Valley from Taliban," *The New York Times*, July 1, 2009.

19 See Aaron Pennekamp, "Standards of Engagement: Rethinking Rules of Engagement to More Effectively Fight Counterinsurgency Campaigns," *Georgetown Law Journal*, no. 101 (2013).

20 See Rajiv Chandrasekaran, "Marines Launch Mission in Afghanistan's South Focused on Security and Governance," *The Washington Post*, July 2, 2009.

21 See "Into Taliban Country," *The Economist*, July 9, 2009.

22 Shuja's second reign as Afghanistan's king was short-lived. Never very popular among his own people, whom he often referred to as "dogs" who needed to be taught obedience to their master, he was

assassinated in April 1842. Many Afghans (even to this day) refer to Shuja as the "puppet king" due to his obeisance to the Brits who restored him to power. This moniker would also be applied to Hamid Karzai, put into power with the help of the American and British governments, nearly 160 years after Shuja's death. See James Perry, *Arrogant Armies* (Edison, NJ: Castle Books, 2005).

23 Josiah Harlan's adventurous life in Afghanistan and beyond is recounted in Ben Macintyre, *The Man Who Would Be King: The First American in Afghanistan* (New York: Farrar, Straus and Giroux, 2002).

24 Dr. Brydon's ordeal is recounted in gruesome detail in many books, including William Dalrymple, *Return of a King: The Battle for Afghanistan, 1839–42* (New York: Bloomsbury, 2012).

25 See Steve Coll, *Ghost Wars: The Secret History of the CIA, Afghanistan, and bin Laden, from the Soviet Invasion to September 10, 2001* (New York: Penguin Press, 2004).

26 See Rajiv Chandrasekaran, *Little America: The War within the War for Afghanistan* (New York: Bloomsbury, 2012), for a description of the US efforts in Afghanistan in the 1950s and 1960s.

27 See Seth Jones, *In the Graveyard of Empires: America's War in Afghanistan* (New York: W. W. Norton, 2009).

28 See Amy Chua, *Political Tribes: Group Instinct and the Fate of Nations* (New York: Penguin Press, 2018).

29 See Jerry Caraccioli and Tom Caraccioli, *Boycott: Stolen Dreams of the 1980 Moscow Olympic Games* (New York: New Chapter Press, 2009).

30 See Gregory Feifer, *The Great Gamble: The Soviet War in Afghanistan* (New York: HarperCollins, 2009).

31 See George Crile, *Charlie Wilson's War: The Extraordinary Story of the Largest Covert Operation in History* (New York: Atlantic Monthly Press, 2003).

32 See Milton Bearden and James Risen, *The Main Enemy: The Inside Story of the CIA's Final Showdown with the KGB* (New York: Random House, 2003).

33 See Robert D. Kaplan, *Soldiers of God: With Islamic Warriors in Afghanistan and Pakistan* (New York: Penguin Random House, 2001).

34 Massoud was the inspiration for the hero in Ken Follett's book *Lie Down with Lions* (New York: William Morrow, 1986). He and his

Northern Alliance fighters were largely from the northern Tajik tribes, not the Pashtun tribe that dominates the country. This distinction— and its significance—was lost on many military and political leaders in the early days of Operation Enduring Freedom. In the 1980s, the *mujahideen* (the predecessors of the Northern Alliance) were seen as anticommunist by the U.S. and thus friends worthy of American support, so the nuances of Afghanistan's tribal allegiances were largely ignored. But Afghanistan's largest and strongest tribe is the Pashtuns, who have ruled the country for nearly two consecutive centuries (with the exception of the mid-1990s, when a coalition of Uzbeks and Tajiks was in control after the Soviet withdrawal). In fact, the Taliban was able to regain—and retain—power because of its appeals to Afghan's *Pashtun* as much or more so than their *religious* sentiments. For many Pashtuns, supporting the religious zealotry of the Taliban was largely seen as a reasonable price to pay to reassert Pashtun ethnic influence in the country. Under the Pashtun-dominated Taliban, thousands of Uzbeks, Hazaras, and Tajiks were brutally murdered in late 1998. Those tribes' collective memories are long, and three years later they saw an opportunity to exact revenge. When the first special forces arrived in Afghanistan in the fall of 2001 with the mission to topple the Taliban, they aligned themselves with several prominent Tajik and Uzbek warlords who took advantage of the awesome fire- power of the U.S. military to avenge the killing of their tribesmen a few years earlier. Among Afghanistan's Pashtun population, the patronage and assistance the U.S. gave to the Tajiks and Uzbeks in late 2001 was seen as an endorsement of an anti-Pashtun policy, a belief that exists even today.

35 This line is from the 1974 Mel Brooks movie *Blazing Saddles*. It is para- phrased from the 1927 novel *The Treasure of the Sierra Madre*, which reads: "Badges, to god-damned hell with badges! We have no badges. In fact, we don't need badges. I don't have to show you any stinking badges, you god-damned *cabrón* and *chinga tu madre!*" The line was rephrased in the 1948 film adaptation of the novel, which starred Humphrey Bogart, modified to comply with Hollywood's profanity regulations:

"Badges? We ain't got no badges. We don't need no badges. I don't have to show you any stinkin' badges!"

36 Quoted from Bob Schieffer, *This Just In: What I Couldn't Tell You on TV* (New York: Penguin Putnam, 2003), 65.

37 See Joshua Foust, "Maladies of Interpreters," *The New York Times*, September 21, 2009.

38 See Joseph P. Owens, "Bill Cahir, Journalist, Soldier, Great American, Killed in Afghanistan," *Lehigh Valley Live*, August 13, 2009. See also Alyssa Young, "Bill Cahir Served in 'Particularly Tough Area' as Civil Affairs Officer in Afghanistan," *Lehigh Valley Live*, August 14, 2009.

39 See Jan Norman, "Family, Friends Bid Farewell to Marine," *Orange County Register*, September 7, 2009; Jeff Gottlieb, "Marine Cpl. Donald J. Hogan, 20, San Clemente; Killed by Roadside Bomb," *Los Angeles Times*, September 20, 2009; Chris Carroll, "He'll Grow Up Knowing Hogan's the Reason He's Got a Dad," *Stars and Stripes*, May 31, 2012.

40 See Arlington National Cemetery Website, "David Raymond Baker," http://arlingtoncemetery.net/drbaker.htm.

41 A family friend of the Bakers wrote a book about David. See David Glasier, "Book about Painesville Township Marine Killed in Afghanistan Released," *News Herald*, January 28, 2014, describing Tina Marie Fitzgerald's book, *From Yellow Ribbons to a Gold Star: Biography of a Hero, LCpl. David R. Baker, USMC* (Frederick, MD: America Star, 2014).

42 See Jill Leovy, "Marine Lance Corporal Justin J. Swanson, 21, Anaheim, Killed in Explosion," *Los Angeles Times*, January 10, 2010.

43 See Matt Farwell and Michael Ames, *American Cipher: Bowe Bergdahl and the U.S. Tragedy in Afghanistan* (Penguin Press, 2019).

44 See Yasmeen Aftab Ali, "Understanding Pashtunwali," *The Nation*, August 6, 2013.

45 Referenced in the chapter "A Tale of Two Wars" in Christina Lamb, *Farewell, Kabul: From Afghanistan to a More Dangerous World* (New York: HarperCollins, 2016). This quote is often taken out of context and paraphrased in a way as to make Churchill seem critical of *Islam* rather than Pashtunwali.

46 See Rajiv Chandrasekaran, "A Fight for Ordinary Peace," *The Washington Post*, July 12, 2009.

47 Cited in Christina Lamb, *Farewell Kabul*.

48 Cited in the foreword to *United States Department of Defense Law of War Manual*, June 2015 (Updated December 2016). Noted in Phil Klay, "What We're Fighting For," *The New York Times*, February 10, 2017.

49 Noted in Phil Klay, "What We're Fighting For," *The New York Times*, February 10, 2017.

50 See, e.g., Rob Hughes, "Tale of 1914 Christmas Day Truce Is Inspiring, Though Hard to Believe," *The New York Times*, December 23, 2014.

51 These stories are recounted in Hans von Luck, "The End in North Africa," in *The Quarterly Journal of Military History* (Summer 1989).

52 This meeting is recounted in Nick McDonnell, "Can a Loyalty Oath Ensure the Allegiance of Afghans?" *TIME*, November 25, 2009. Other journalists visiting Nawa also wrote about 1/5's work with local government officials to reintegrate insurgents back into their communities. See, e.g., Vanessa M. Gezari, "Talking to the Enemy," *Slate.com*, October 16, 2009. For another insight on potential discussions with the Taliban, see Aryn Baker, "Talking with the Taliban: Easier Said Than Done," *TIME*, November 30, 2009.

53 One prominent example is Fawzia Koofi, who began her political career soon after the fall of the Taliban by promoting educational programs for girls and was elected to Afghanistan's parliament in 2005. See Fawzia Koofi and Nadene Ghouri, *The Favored Daughter: One Woman's Fight to Lead Afghanistan into the Future* (New York: Palgrave Macmillan, 2012).

54 In late 2018, nearly ten years after 1/5 left Nawa, Afghanistan was still a tough place to be a woman. See Lauren Bohn, "Why Afghanistan Is Still the Worst Place in the World to Be a Woman," *TIME*, December 8, 2018.

55 See John Berry et al., "Afghanistan Is Obama's Vietnam," *Newsweek*, July 15, 2009.

56 See Mark T. Kimmitt, "Losing the War of Exhaustion," *Foreign Policy*, September 21, 2009.

57 Many Afghans were indifferent to the need for a national election, feeling that security, infrastructure improvements, and better commercial opportunities should be higher priorities for the NATO forces and Western advisors to focus their attention. Not surprisingly, eliminating government corruption was also frequently high on the list of things ordinary Afghans wanted. Nonetheless, over forty candidates ran for president in 2009, including the incumbent, Hamid Karzai. Even though there were no major acts of polling place violence in Afghanistan (and none in Nawa), the election was marred by claims of corruption, low turnout, ballot-box stuffing, and incompetence in its management. Karzai won the August election with just under 50 percent of the vote. Because he didn't have a majority, a runoff was set for November against the second-place finisher, Abdullah Abdullah. Abdullah had been the country's foreign minister and an advisor to Northern Alliance commander Ahmad Shah Massoud. He was also an ophthalmologist and had worked as a veterinarian. Abdullah refused to participate in the November runoff election, and Karzai was declared the country's president to serve another five-year term. Abdullah became president in 2014.

58 See Aram Roston, "Talking to the Taliban," *Foreign Policy*, October 8, 2009.

59 See, e.g., Ellen Barry and Michael Schwartz, "Kyrgyzstan Wants to Close U.S. Base Used for Afghan War," *The New York Times*, February 4, 2009; Elizabeth Bumiller and Ellen Barry, "U.S. Searched for Alternative to Central Asia Base," *The New York Times*, February 4, 2009.

60 See Michael Schwartz, "New Leader Says U.S. Base in Kyrgyzstan Will Be Shut," *The New York Times*, November 1, 2011.

61 Adam Kilgore, "Military Tributes at Baseball Games: True Honors or Hollow Gestures? *The Washington Post*, May 23, 2015.

62 See Joe Klein, "A Bleeding Ulcer," *TIME*, May 24, 2010.

63 The story of Marjah's appointed district governor, Abdul Zahir Aryan, would make a great plot for a Coen brothers dark comedy. Before

being appointed as Marjah's district governor, he lived in Germany for fifteen years. Four of those fifteen years were spent in a German prison after he was sentenced for attempted murder for stabbing his stepson when the young man filed a complaint against him for beating the boy's mother, one of Zahir's two wives (Zahir had thirteen children between the two women). After the stabbing, Zahir fled to Holland and the Czech Republic before being arrested near the German-Polish border in January 1998. Zahir was fond of introducing himself as "*Haji Zahir*," the "*Haji*" honorific given to Muslim males who have made the pilgrimage to Mecca and Medina, though there is no evidence he ever actually *did* make the *hajj* pilgrimage. He was replaced as Marjah's governor just about six months into the job in July 2010 (see Karen DeYoung, "Senator Levin Urges State Department to Put Afghan Taliban on List of Terror Groups," *The Washington Post*, July 14, 2010). After his short tenure as Marjah's governor, Zahir joined the Helmand Peace Council, a group of unelected and unappointed Afghans who held occasional gatherings to ostensibly discuss ways to bring peace and prosperity to the province. In April of 2011, Zahir and the head of the council were shot dead while having dinner in Helmand's capital, Lashkar Gah. For other information about Zahir, see Rajiv Chandrasekaran, "Afghan Official Who Will Govern Marja Pays First Visit, Makes Plea to Residents," *The Washington Post*, February 23, 2010; Joshua Partlow and Jabeen Bhatti, "New Top Official in Marjah, Afghanistan, Was Convicted of Stabbing Stepson," *The Washington Post*, March 6, 2010.

64 See Michael Hastings, "The Runaway General," *Rolling Stone*, July 8–22, 2010, issue. A Pentagon inquiry later determined that the seniority of some of the people Hastings's article cited was exaggerated and that General McChrystal and his military and civilian staff had not committed any wrongdoing. See Thom Shanker, "Pentagon Inquiry into Article Clears McChrystal and Aides," *The New York Times*, April 18, 2011.

65 See Dan Lamothe, "'I Had to Fight My Little Inner Demon': The Scramble to Save Wounded Marine Hero Kyle Carpenter," *The Washington Post*, June 18, 2014.

66 See Thomas James Brennan, "Inside the Painstaking Recovery Process of a Medal of Honor Marine," *Vanity Fair*, November 11, 2016. Kyle Carpenter recounts his motivation to join the Marine Corps, his service in Afghanistan and recovery from his injuries, as well as his inspiring message on service and overcoming adversity in his book, *You Are Worth It: Building a Life Worth Fighting For* (William Morrow 2019).

67 For a perspective on why such a military operation is both justified and legal, see Frank Biggio, "Neutralizing the Threat: Reconsidering Existing Doctrines in the Emerging War on Terrorism," *Case Western Reserve Journal of International Law* 34, no. 1 (2002).

68 See Dion Nissenbaum, "Roads to Nowhere: Program to Win Over Afghans Fails," *The Wall Street Journal*, February 10, 2012, describing the financial shenanigans of a USAID contractor called "International Relief & Development" (IRD). Several IRD representatives came to Nawa while 1/5 was there in 2009, and they quickly showed (1) a lack of financial prudence after paying more than $25,000 to have *one* pickup truck load of furniture delivered just twenty kilometers from Lashkar Gah to Nawa along a well-secured route, (2) economic ignorance of the wider-scale impact of increasing the wages of low-skilled workers by over 20 percent, and (3) dismissive contempt for any Marine who questioned the way they spent U.S. taxpayer money: "We know what we're doing. You guys should just stick with the guns and bullets thing," one IRD rep smugly told me in mid-October 2009.

69 The handover ceremony is described in "The Leaving" in Christina Lamb, *Farewell, Kabul: From Afghanistan to a More Dangerous World* (New York: HarperCollins, 2016).

70 See, e.g., Vanessa Gezari, "The Quiet Demise of the Army's Plan to Understand Iraq and Afghanistan," *The New York Times*, August 18, 2015.

71 See, e.g., "Taliban Take Helmand's Nawa District, Kill Its Police Chief," available at http://1tvnews.af/en/news/afghanistan/25186-taliban-take-helmands-nawa-district-kill-its-police-chief.

72 See Dan Lamothe, "Marines Are Back in Afghanistan's Most Violent
   Province, and Their Mission Could Expand," *The Washington Post*, May
   15, 2017.

73 See Shashank Bengali, "The Marines Returned to Helmand Province.
   Is Their Mission a Blueprint for Trump's Afghanistan Strategy?" *Los
   Angeles Times*, November 10, 2017.

74 See, e.g., Kathrin Hille, "Russia offers to host Kabul-Taliban peace
   talks," *Financial Times*, Jan. 18, 2018; Missy Ryan and Amie Ferris-
   Rotman, "The Kremlin's Comeback," *The Washington Post*, October 12,
   2018; Mujib Mashal, "Afghanistan Signs Major Mining Deals Despite
   Legal Concerns," *The New York Times*, October 6, 2018; Amie Ferris-
   Rotman, "Taliban Cofounder Emerges as the Group's New Public
   Face in Moscow Peace Talks," *The Washington Post*, May 28, 2019.

75 See, e.g., "America and the Taliban Are Edging Towards a Deal," *The
   Economist*, February 4, 2019; Mujib Mashal, "As U.S. and Taliban
   Resume Talks, More Deadly Attacks in Afghanistan," *The New York Times*,
   June 29, 2019.

76 See, e.g., Jarrett Blanc, "We Need to Take the Best Deal We Can Get
   in Afghanistan," *The Washington Post*, August 26, 2019.

77 See, e.g., Jim Golby and Peter Feaver, "It Matters If Americans Call
   Afghanistan a Defeat," *The Atlantic*, August 17, 2019.

78 See, e.g., "Peace with Afghan Characteristics," *The Economist*, March
   5, 2020.

79 See, e.g., Andrew Milburn, "At Last an End to the Endless War?"
   Military Times, March 6, 2020.

80 See, e.g., Elliot Ackerman, "Born Into War," *TIME*, October 21, 2019.